The
COWBOY CAVALRY

THE STORY OF THE ROCKY MOUNTAIN RANGERS

Gordon E. Tolton

VICTORIA | VANCOUVER | CALGARY

Heritage House Publishing Company Ltd.
heritagehouse.ca

LIBRARY AND ARCHIVES CANADA CATALOGUING IN PUBLICATION

Tolton, Gordon E. (Gordon Errett), 1963–
   The cowboy cavalry: the story of the Rocky Mountain Rangers / Gordon E. Tolton.

Includes bibliographical references and index.
Also issued in electronic format.

ISBN 978-1-926936-02-4

   1. Canada. Canadian Army. Rocky Mountain Rangers. 2. Riel Rebellion, 1885. 3. Northwest Territories—History—1870-1905. I. Title.

FC3215.T635 2011   971.05'4   C2011-900367-8

Edited by Elizabeth McLachlan and Melva McLean
Proofread by Karla Decker
Cover design by Jacqui Thomas
Interior design by Frances Hunter

Front cover: The Rocky Mountain Rangers on a scouting patrol in the Cypress Hills (Esplanade Archives, PC404.13)
Back cover, left to right: North Axe of the Peigan (GALT PI9770161000), an unidentified Rocky Mountain Ranger (Glenbow Archives NA-670-5) and Louis Riel (Glenbow Archives NA-504-3)

This book was produced using FSC®-certified, acid-free paper, processed chlorine free and printed with vegetable-based inks.

Heritage House acknowledges the financial support for its publishing program from the Government of Canada through the Canada Book Fund (CBF) and the Canada Council for the Arts, and from the Province of British Columbia through the British Columbia Arts Council and the Book Publishing Tax Credit.

Printed in Canada

19 18 17 16 2 3 4 5

CONTENTS

LIST OF ABBREVIATIONS

AFC	American Fur Company
CPR	Canadian Pacific Railway
DLS	Dominion Land Survey
GSC	Geological Survey of Canada
HBC	Hudson's Bay Company
NWC&NC	North Western Coal and Navigation Company
NWC	North West Company
NWMP	North West Mounted Police
RMR	Rocky Mountain Rangers
SWGA	South-Western Stock Growers Association
WSGA	Western Stock Growers Association

FIRST NATION NAMES

I have chosen to refer to First Nations by the names that were in common usage in 1885. These terms are not meant pejoratively or to denigrate. The following list shows those names on the left and their modern-day equivalents on the right.

Assiniboine/Stoney	Nakoda
Blackfoot (*as a Confederacy*)	Niitsitapi
Blackfoot (*as tribe*)	Siksika
Blood	Kainai
Cree	Cree
Gros Ventres	Atsina
Kootenay	Ktunaxa
Peigan (*Canadian spelling*)	North Piikani
Piegan (*American spelling, also known as Blackfeet*)	South Piikani
Sarcee	Tsuu T'ina
Saulteaux	Ojibwa (*prairie*)
Sioux	Lakota

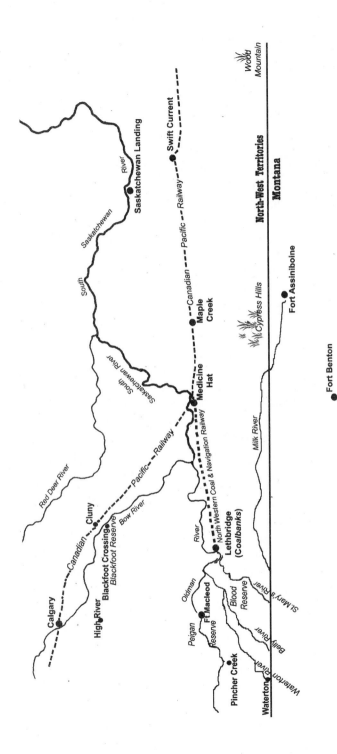

Patrol Area of the Rocky Mountain Rangers, 1885

CHRONOLOGY

1854 • John Stewart is born in Ottawa

1861 • John George "Kootenai" Brown arrives in British Columbia

1864 • Kootenai Brown is wounded at Seven Persons Creek

1868 • Kootenai Brown takes employment as a dispatch rider

1869 • Dominion surveyors begin work in the Red River colony
- Louis Riel seizes Fort Garry

1870 • Canada Firsters attempt to retake Fort Garry
- Thomas Scott is executed
- Canadian Parliament adopts the Manitoba Act

1872-74 • Louis Riel is elected three times as a Member of Parliament
- William Jackson joins Custer's 7th Cavalry as Scout
- Cypress Hills Massacre
- Order-in-council of Parliament creates the North West Mounted Police
- NWMP embarks on the March West from Dufferin, Manitoba
- NWMP establishes Fort Macleod

1875 • Louis Riel is pardoned and leaves Canada
- Fort Walsh in the Cypress Hills is established
- Fort Brisebois, later known as Fort Calgary, is established
- Constable John Herron accompanies Selby-Smythe on inspection tour of the NWMP
- Jackson leaves Fort Abraham Lincoln with the 7th Cavalry

1876 • 268 soldiers are killed in Battle of Little Bighorn in Montana
- Louis Riel is incarcerated in a mental institution in Quebec

1877 • Kootenai Brown is arrested for the murder of pelt dealer Louis Ell
- Treaty 7 is signed

1878 • John Stewart forms the Princess Louise Dragoon Guards
- NWMP Remount Station at Pincher Creek is founded

1879 • Louis Riel moves to Montana and approaches Crowfoot

1881 • Marquis of Lorne tours prairies
- Cochrane Ranche is established at the Big Hill, west of Calgary
- Stewart Ranche is established, and purchases the NWMP Remount Station

1882	• Bull Elk incident occurs on Blackfoot Reserve
1883	• Oxley Ranche is established
	• Crowfoot receives invitation from Big Bear to a Grand Council
1884	• Cochrane Ranche establishes a southern range on the Waterton (Kootenay) River
	• Riel is enticed to Batoche and sends message to Blackfoot leaders
1885	• Mar 25: Stewart files request with the Department of Militia & Defence to form the RMR
	• Mar 26: Battle of Duck Lake
	• Mar 29: RMR accepted into order of battle. Enlistment is opened.
	• April 2: Frog Lake massacre
	• April 15: First roll call of the RMR
	• April 26: Battle of Fish Creek
	• April 29: Two troops of RMR march for Medicine Hat, arriving six days later
	• May 1: Battle of Cut Knife Hill
	• May 9: Wagon-train horses stolen near Medicine Hat; Battle of Batoche begins
	• May 12: After four-day stalemate, Batoche is overrun by the Canadian military
	• May 15: Riel surrenders
	• May 19: Cattle herder near Medicine Hat is fired upon
	• May 23: William Jackson encounters hostile Natives near Peigan Coulee
	• June 2: Battle of Frenchman's Butte
	• June 3: Battle of Loon Lake
	• July 4: Surrender of Big Bear at Fort Carlton
	• July 7: RMR ordered to return to Fort Macleod
	• July 17: RMR is disbanded by government order
	• Nov 16: Louis Riel is executed for treason at Regina NWMP Headquarters
1886	• July 1: RMR reassembles at Pincher Creek to receive the North West Canada 1885 Medal
1893	• John Stewart dies at Calgary

Who Were the Rocky Mountain Rangers?

When someone mentions the Northwest Rebellion (or the Riel Rebellion, as it is more popularly known), we think of people like Louis Riel, Gabriel Dumont, Big Bear, Poundmaker and General Middleton, and battles like Batoche, Duck Lake, Frog Lake and Cut Knife Hill. The Riel Rebellion had a great effect on the entire country, from British Columbia to Nova Scotia, and the conflict can be regarded as Canada's "civil war" for the deep divisions that it caused between Natives and whites, French and English, east and west. It also affected our neighbours to the south; US Army outposts across the Montana and Dakota territories were put on alert out of concern that the rebellion might incite American Indians to rebel.

Historians look at the 1885 series of battles as events associated mainly with the history of the upper regions of the Saskatchewan River. Southern Alberta is not thought to have played a significant part in the rebellion. Historians have tended to focus on General Strange's Alberta Field Force and the Frog Lake massacre, as if they are the only events worthy of mention. It is true that Alberta's involvement in the war came about from a fear by the white populace of the possibility of attack by the Blackfoot, Stoney, Sarcee, Blood and Peigan Indian tribes. As a result, a rancher, a retired British general named Thomas Bland

Strange, was asked by the federal government to organize several local militia units into the Alberta Field Force. It is also true that the force's original mandate was to protect Calgary and southern Alberta, but was later ordered to form a column to go to the scene of the fighting at Frog Lake and the mopping up of the last dissenters at Frenchman's Butte.

The units that made up the Alberta Field Force were the Alberta Mounted Rifles, Steele's Scouts, the 9th Quebec Voltigeurs, the 65th Mount Royal Rifles and the 92nd Winnipeg Light Infantry. Although the Rocky Mountain Rangers did not make Strange's epic march to Fort Edmonton and down the North Saskatchewan River valley, the 114 cowboys, army officers, ex-Mounties, ranchers, settlers, and trappers who made up this militia unit were eager to guard the ranch country and its inhabitants. They were resolutely prepared to fight, as mounted cavalry, should the rebellion spread to involve the discontented Blackfoot tribes or border-jumping American Indian raiding parties. They were to augment patrols of the North West Mounted Police and provide security for railroad construction. This unit was known as the Rocky Mountain Rangers.

These Rangers will not be found at any of the famous rebellion battles that dominate Canadian history texts. Yet their story is worth telling. They provided that "more protection…from the Government" of which William Cochrane wrote on an April day back 1885. Given the explosive nature of the rebellion, and particularly the hysteria and apprehension it caused, neither the white settlers nor the Plains Indians knew what might happen next. Like any time of looming war in any country, faceless, nameless people are always willing to take up arms to protect their homeland. The names of the Rocky Mountain Rangers, volunteers all, are truly a microcosm of southern Alberta of the time. Many would stay in the area and become leading citizens and pioneer ranchers and farmers. Some would become townsmen and build successful business careers. One even became a

British earl. Some of their names, like that of Kootenai Brown, became immortal. Others, like Rattlesnake Jack Robson or William Allen Hamilton, fell through the cracks of history despite their own colourful careers.

The unit's activities lasted only four months in the spring of 1885, and certainly the skirmishes they did see cannot be viewed as ever affecting the course of the rebellion and are scarcely, if at all, reported in history's chronicles. Perhaps troops such as the Rangers, through their patrols and their vigilance, did keep the Northwest Rebellion from being worse than it was. While the Blackfoot-speaking tribes of the southern plains (Blackfoot, Blood and Peigan) eventually rejected Louis Riel's call for uprising, ranch country settlers doubted the Indians' intentions throughout the rebellion's duration. The notion of an armed militia, albeit a "cowboy cavalry," might well have helped cool tempers on both sides and kept the rebellion from spreading. For this reason alone, the tale of the life and times of the Rocky Mountain Rangers is one that has been far too long in coming.

PROLOGUE

———◆———

April 26, 1885

As the late April sun slowly turned the eternal horizon from winter yellow to spring green, William F. Cochrane stood on the stoop of his log ranch house and watched the cowboys of the Cochrane Ranche ply their trade: breaking horses, working on the corrals and buildings, tending to newborn calves and generally keeping watch on their charges. Spring lifted the pall of a bad winter in the foothills of the eastern slopes of the Rockies in 1885. In the hills and on the flat prairie beyond, range cattle were already grazing on new flourishes of native grass. On the few plots of cultivated land, farmers considered the coming growing season. Even though ranching and farming were new things to the hills and plains, stockmen and sodbusters alike had reason to be optimistic about the future.

As Cochrane stood on his stoop, he felt both amazed and troubled. Despite the beauty of the land before him—rolling plains relieved only by the massive sky, the breaks of the rivers and the breathtaking view of the timeless Rocky Mountains—the mood of the people was far from docile. Like most of his fellow cattlemen, Cochrane was a newcomer to this home on the range, and in the age of gunpowder, remote living brought its fears.

When he retired indoors that day, he penned a letter to his father, Senator Matthew Cochrane of Quebec:

There is a great deal of uneasiness about the Indians, who it is expected may break out any day. Riel's runners are in their camps, and it seems doubtful what they will do. Dunlop [the ranch foreman] was at Stand Off Friday and thought it looked a serious threat that he hurried home, and I went immediately into town and got some more rifles and ammunition, as we were not in very good shape here for any trouble...We ought to make every effort to get more protection here from the Government. It has been taken for granted that we will never have any trouble with the Indians, because we have not had any yet. But we are sleeping on a volcano that may break out at any time, and there are enough Indians to clean us all up here before help came if they were minded. The Police have not enough men to give any help outside of Macleod and we will have to look after ourselves. It is not considered safe to be alone on the prairie now and if the half-breeds have any success north we will be pretty sure to have troubles here.[1]

PART ONE
THE FRONTIER

CHAPTER ONE

The Border Frontier: 1885

In the mid-1800s the plains of what is now called southern Alberta were still the realm of the indigenous hunter-and-warrior culture of the Blackfoot nation. From the Red Deer River in the north to the Missouri River in the south and from the Rocky Mountains in the west and far out onto the eastern plains, the Blackfoot, Blood and Peigan tribes held sway for generations. Together with their allies, the Sarcee and Stoney, they comprised the Confederacy that had signed Treaty 7 in 1877 with the government of Canada—a gesture of peace that in implementation often threatened violence.

We know from history that no serious armed conflict occurred in southern Alberta in that tense spring of 1885. The fear in the ranch country was that the Blood, Blackfoot, Stoney, Sarcee and Peigan tribes might ally with the rebellious Metis. Peace in the Calgary, Macleod and Pincher Creek areas hinged on the neutrality of these nations. Hypothetically, had the Rocky Mountain Rangers seen action in 1885, the confrontation would most likely have involved taking up arms against the Blackfoot Confederacy.

In many texts, Crowfoot (*Isapo-Muxika*) is described as the wise leader who chose to remain loyal to the government. The truth is that Crowfoot and his Blood counterpart, Red Crow (*Mekaisto*), had a decision to make that was anything but easy.

The temptation to fight came about over matters that had built up over a number of years. The Canadian prairies had been fortunate in escaping the earlier carnage of the Great Sioux Wars, just across the forty-ninth parallel. Alberta settlers would be just as fortunate to evade direct danger in the Northwest Rebellion, but by 1877, increased hunting competition for disappearing buffalo stocks had forced the Blackfoot-speaking nations to face their future and accept the terms to cede some 35,000 square miles of traditional territory. Though the Dominion of Canada gained title to Rupert's Land by purchasing it from the Hudson's Bay Company, true control—and the avoidance of warfare—depended on the satisfaction of its indigenous inhabitants. The Plains Cree tribes of western Canada had begun to surrender territory, signing several treaties with the government. Now the tribes of the southwestern plains were invited to gather at Blackfoot Crossing on the Bow River on September 27 to sign Treaty 7, one of the most important documents in the history of Canada.

The presence of the NWMP, Constable John Herron among them, at the signing contributed to the aura of trust that Crowfoot, Red Crow, Bull's Head (*Chula*), Sitting on an Eagle Tail Feather (*Zoatze-Tapitapiw*), Crow Eagle (*Maestro Petah*) and others had for the government. The police were called out not just to add their resplendent scarlet to the ceremony but also to preserve the peace. The largest known gathering of original peoples ever in Canada (around 4,800), was taking place, and a simple encampment could easily turn into a battle if measures of control were not in place.

The NWMP's worst fears were nearly realized. Six hundred warriors, stripped and painted, mounted their ponies and rode to the top of the hill above the campsite. Charging down the hill, they circled the treaty tent, shrieking, shouting war cries and firing rifles into the air. The charge was a feint, designed to serve notice to the officials and police that the Blackfoot were a force to be reckoned with. The incident said a lot for the tenacity of the police: one wrong move, false gesture or stray shot could have resulted in bloodshed. The NWMP's restraint was more than a lesson in civility; it was a necessity. The early force was small in numbers and unable to mount an effective defence if a scene were to turn against them. This would continue to be the case when open rebellion did threaten to break the peace.

After Treaty 7 was signed, the Blackfoot and the Bloods, while heavily supervised by the police, were not immediately confined to reserves because the locations and boundaries of their lands were yet to be defined. The bands were permitted to travel in search of game or wood—rights enshrined in the treaty. Freedom of movement, however, was a source of worry to settlers. Inter-tribal fighting was still a problem, as was the habit of raiding horse stock. In the early 1880s, Frederick Ings (a future Ranger) recounted an incident near his Midway Ranche (near modern-day Nanton, Alberta):

> I remember one fight the Bloods and Stoneys had just above the ranch now owned by Frazier Hunt. I was on the range that day, not far from the scene of the hostilities. The Bloods had been stealing Stoney horses; afterwards the Stoneys told me that they killed a Blood and that one of them had been badly wounded in the thigh.[2]

Ings and his fellow Highwood range ranchers often lent rifles to the Stoney, who dutifully returned the weapons when finished their hunt, sometimes offering a trophy head or skin as payment, but friction always existed between the Sarcee and the ranchers. In the face of starvation and ration cutbacks from the government, many Sarcee helped themselves to ranchers' cattle. One could hardly blame them. For hundreds of years they had existed on the meat of the buffalo, but now the buffalo were gone. Treaty 7 was supposed to replace buffalo with beef, but when the Indian agents did not fulfill the agreement, many Sarcee simply took what was promised them. Given the territorial nature of some of the ranchers, it was a miracle that war did not develop sooner than it did.

Chief Sitting on an Eagle Tail Feather signed Treaty 7 for the Peigan and negotiated with the government for a reserve at the foot of the Porcupine Hills along the Oldman River. While their Blood and Blackfoot cousins were in Montana, Eagle Tail Feather's band settled to learn farming. For the next few years the transition was successful: log houses were built, and the river flats produced good crops of potatoes, turnips and oats. Surplus produce was sold to settlers, and seed was supplied to other tribes. The government encouraged them to plant even more acres. Had crops not been successful, the Peigan may have been tempted to join the rebellion, but it wouldn't be until the fall of 1885 that they learned the harsher realities of farming. That fall, a huge surplus of potatoes was produced—more than could be consumed. With a limited market, thousands of pounds went rotten. For the next 15 years, drought and cutworms prevented the Peigan from repeating their 1879–1885 farming successes.

The Blackfoot, namesakes of the Confederacy's common language, took their reserve along the Bow River at Blackfoot Crossing, east of Calgary. The tribe gained a measure of fame from its leader, Crowfoot, who was seen by people unfamiliar with tribal structures and alliances as "spokesman" for the entire Blackfoot Confederacy, although he commanded only one tribe. Crowfoot's fair-minded nature made him a natural choice as the man with whom to negotiate, and his words were often useful tools for the government when publicizing the intent of the Confederacy. Crowfoot did little to dissuade the confusion, much to the annoyance of the Blood leader, Red Crow.

After the treaty signature, the Blackfoot bands spent the late 1870s and early 1880s on the American side of the boundary, following the dwindling buffalo herds that were forced into the regions of the Judith, Musselshell and Milk rivers. While in northern Montana, the Blackfoot began to travel and camp with the Metis, and in 1879 an educated revolutionary walked into Crowfoot's camp: Louis Riel.

CHAPTER TWO

The Revolutionary: Louis Riel

In many ways, Louis Riel had created his own mythology after the events of the Red River Rebellion. In September 1871, the town of St. Boniface, Manitoba, was under threat from the Fenian Brotherhood, the Irish–American movement threatening to attack and hold Canadian territory to force Britain to leave Ireland. The Manitoba invasion was to be led by William B. O'Donoghue, Riel's council member and ally, but the invasion plot was meagre, ill informed and badly executed. O'Donoghue recruited only 35 men to his force, thinking he would receive support from the Metis. Then Riel turned the tables on the Fenians and sided with Canada, informing officials about the plot. He even stood as a volunteer of a citizens' Home Guard, comprised of Metis and Canadian settlers, to defend St. Boniface. After O'Donoghue's laughable attempt to capture and hold the HBC post of Fort Pembina, a post actually on the American side of the line, the Home Guard and the US Army collaborated in the capture and arrest of O'Donoghue's invaders—without a shot fired.

The government, which was grateful to Riel for having revealed the plot, was left with a dilemma: the lobby that wanted his head had political power, but Riel had demonstrated a willingness to defend the country. To solve the dilemma, Sir John A. Macdonald's government quietly sent $1,000 in several small payments as a bribe to entice Riel to leave the country. He did move to Minnesota for a few months, but in June 1872 was back in the province, where he accepted a nomination to become an independent Member of Parliament in the federal riding of Provencher. He stepped aside in order to allow Macdonald's comrade, George Cartier, to parachute into a safe-seat riding so that Cartier could re-enter Parliament after his own defeat in Quebec, but when Cartier died within a few months, Riel challenged the seat and easily won the by-election in October 1873. There was no opportunity for him to travel to Ottawa before the 1874 general election, yet he again won the seat.

While Riel's ally, Ambroise Lepine, was under arrest and headed to trial for his role in the execution of Canadian surveyor Thomas Scott, Riel went to Ottawa to take his seat in Parliament. Warrants for his own arrest in the matter were still valid, and so was a $5,000 bounty on his head. Still, Riel was brazen enough to quietly enter the chambers of the House of Commons, sign the register, swear his oath of office to the clerk and just as quietly slip out. John Schultz, Riel's old foe from the rebellion and the MP for Lisgar, called for a motion to expel Riel from the House. The motion passed, and the people of Manitoba were intransigent. The expulsion triggered another by-election in Provencher in September of 1874, which resulted once again in the election of Riel. Once again, he was expelled in absentia.

Having replaced himself three times in two years, Riel understood he was not wanted in Ottawa and allowed another candidate, Andrew Bannatyne, to stand for the riding. As for Ambroise Lepine, during this time he was found guilty and sentenced to death, although the government did commute the penalty. In 1875 the Liberal government of Alexander Mackenzie pardoned Louis Riel for any of the official charges, on one condition: that Riel leave the country for five years.

In the years following the Red River debacle, many of the Metis in Manitoba had been persuaded to sign over their scrip certificates—the claims giving them title to their land—for a fraction of their real worth. Speculators were flipping the same land to newcomers or immigrants for a tidy profit. Thus swindled, the Metis moved west, many to areas established by kinsmen, such as Lac la Biche, Qu'Appelle, St. Albert, Edmonton, Prince Albert and Batoche. Others founded settlements on former buffalo grounds like Wood Mountain and the Cypress Hills. Several moved into the Dakota and Montana territories, where relatives had worked in the American fur trade. In the summer of 1879, Riel followed them south to join the people he believed he was born to lead. It was in the Blackfoot camps of northern Montana that he met Chief Crowfoot.

By this time Crowfoot's people were under Canadian treaty, and discontent was running high among them because of the loss of their primary subsistence and income. Riel told Crowfoot that the buffalo had left because of the NWMP, and that his treaty would be ignored. He advocated all-out war between the whites and a union of Metis, Cree, Sitting Bull's Sioux and the Blackfoot Confederacy to create a Native-dominated republic. Crowfoot wanted nothing to do with Riel but feared what could happen if younger warriors were stirred up by his tough talk.

Riel knew of a friendly relationship between Sitting Bull and Crowfoot and proposed a three-pronged attack on the NWMP in Wood Mountain, Fort Walsh and Fort Macleod. Both chiefs rejected that plot outright, but in planning his attack, Riel had the Metis attempt to hijack a shipment of guns and ammunition from a wagon train. The assault fizzled when the would-be raiders were unable to bribe the freighters into looking the other way. Without weapons or allies, Riel shelved the scheme.

Stymied in creating a cross-border rebellion, Riel concentrated on improving the conditions of the American Metis. Their close-knit culture, Catholic practices and Native background did not blend with the style of the capitalistic Montanans. Trying to improve their lot by persuading them to settle down, Riel used his influence to obtain land grants for the Montana Metis. He wrote to General Nelson Miles for assistance, but the United States saw the Metis as Canada's problem and refused to get involved in satisfying claims from outsiders.

By the spring of 1881, trouble was brewing between the Canadian tribes camped in the Missouri basin and the American ranchers. The effects of whisky were causing havoc among the Blackfoot and, in June, a party of young warriors raided Crow horses in the Yellowstone River region. Because the Crow were on a reservation and under army protection, the US Cavalry pursued. Crowfoot knew he would lose in any battle, so he admonished the thieves and personally returned the horses to the Rocky Point army post. Yet the biggest issue that spring wasn't violence but starvation. Crowfoot's people were dying. Diseased, malnourished and nearly horseless, the Blackfoot returned to their traditional home at Blackfoot Crossing in the summer of 1881. Crowfoot realized that in order for his people to survive, they were going to have to take rations from the government and learn how to farm.

While some measure of success came from farming, the ration program proved rife with trouble. Each member of the band was allowed a pound of beef and half a pound of flour, per day, per person. Initially the NWMP had been responsible for food distribution, and Crowfoot never had reason to complain, but while the Blackfoot were away, the government instituted a bureaucracy—the Department of Indian Affairs (commonly known as the Indian department)—to administer the terms of the treaty. Storerooms and offices were built on reserves to provide central distribution points, and instructors were hired to teach agricultural practices.

Indian department agents showed little respect for their charges and often withheld rations to obtain compliance or cover up their own ineptness at ordering supplies. With little oversight on the department, corruption was rampant and rations often hoarded to obtain higher prices elsewhere, to sell on a black market for personal gain, or even to force women into prostitution. Complaints were answered with accusations or threats of arrest. When Crowfoot pleaded with the department to administer extra rations, he received only patronizing lectures.

Conditions nearly led to war in December of 1881 when the agents cut the ration allowance and told their charges to hunt if they were hungry. In retaliation, the protective warrior society, the Black Soldiers, took the government men to task. The Soldiers surrounded the ration house and demanded their due or they would shoot the agents. Crowfoot tried to mediate, asking the farm instructor to intervene. But he would not and blocked access to the ration warehouse. In anger, the Soldiers fired shots into an Indian department house.

The shooting was reported to the NWMP and a patrol, commanded by the hapless Inspector Francis Dickens, was sent out. A detachment was established to protect the agents, investigate the corruption charges and bring order to the situation. For a few weeks the scene was subdued, but in January 1882, a small matter got out of control near Blackfoot Crossing. A minor chief, Bull Elk, tried to buy a steer's head from the agency, but a misunderstanding led to accusations of the theft of the head. Incensed, Bull Elk returned to the store with a rifle and fired two shots at the agency warehouse.

Dickens arrested Bull Elk, but before custody could be secured, the Blackfoot closed ranks around the policemen and their prisoner. The Black Soldiers barred the trails out of the settlement, and a scuffle erupted. Bull Elk broke free, and wild shots were fired into the air. Crowfoot arrived on the scene and mediated a solution—he would take Bull Elk into his charge and guarantee his appearance at a hearing. With few options, Dickens relented, but instead of waiting for the magistrate as promised, he sent for help. Superintendent Crozier arrived with 20 men and arrested Bull Elk again on the same charge.

Crowfoot was furious. A deal had been made with the redcoats, and they'd gone back on their word. Again, the Black Soldiers prepared for action, and the police shored up a barricade around their detachment. Still, they were able to take Bull Elk out of the camp for his hearing at Fort Macleod. Crowfoot attended the trial, where James Macleod, former Mounted Police commissioner, was presiding magistrate. While Macleod took into account the conflicting testimonies, he did charge Bull Elk with threatening the agents and sentenced him to 14 days in jail.

The Bull Elk affair, a trivial trade tiff, destroyed the good faith between Crowfoot and the NWMP. Crowfoot had lauded the merits of the redcoats for seven years, carrying the mantle of peacemaker because of the trust extended him by the police. The Indian agents had ruined that faith, and now that the Blackfoot were under treaty, the police appeared to be on the side of the cheaters. Further government contact offered little to prove him wrong. When construction of the Canadian Pacific Railway arrived in 1883, Crowfoot, at the prodding of Father Albert Lacombe, a trusted friend, negotiated a right-of-way to allow the tracks through the reserve. The appearance of the strange iron tracks, the rough-hewn work crews and the fire-breathing steam engine made him skeptical. One drastic change seemed to follow another, and the strong young warriors were not happy. Crowfoot knew that the great changes were being felt in other camps as well. The Blackfoot Confederacy and the Cree had warred with each other for decades, but they'd been at peace since 1871, having made a truce following the Battle of the Belly River near Fort Whoop-Up in 1870.

In the fall of 1883, Crowfoot received a messenger from the Plains Cree chief, Big Bear, with an invitation to a Grand Council being held near Fort Pitt. The messenger told of Big Bear's desire to create a confederation and discuss tactics to stop the CPR from completion. Crowfoot was a man of his word and had allowed the railroad to pass, but he knew there were many in his council who wanted to give Big Bear a hearing. He stalled for time by sending the Cree messenger on to see how the allies in the Peigan and Blood bands might react.

Before contact was made, the messenger was arrested near the Blood reserve and sent home. The NWMP followed up the Cree visit with a directive to the Treaty 7 leaders saying that Big Bear's Grand Council would not be permitted, but a seed had been planted. Over the next few months, others passed through Crowfoot's lodge, bringing word of the conditions to the north and east and of how sympathies among his people were leaning to the Cree cause. Crowfoot also observed that the police and the Indian department tried to shoo these visitors away. Then, in June 1884, a Metis known as Bear's Head appeared to Blackfoot hunters near High River and asked to see Crowfoot. He had a message from Louis Riel.

On June 4, 1884, Riel was finishing the Sunday Mass at St. Peter's Mission when four riders galloped up the hill. Gabriel Dumont, Moise Ouellette, Michael Dumas and James Isbister had ridden over 700 miles from Batoche, the centre of Metis settlement on the South Saskatchewan River, to seek his advice in dealing with the Canadian authority. No one in power would listen; nobody in the Batoche community seemed able to speak the government's language or knew their laws. Dumont's group sought the wisdom of the controversial prophet and needed his education in dealing with their grievances.

The answer was clear. Five days later, the revived leader packed up his family and left with Dumont's party. He would help them out, but he had other goals. The situation provided Riel an opportunity to resurrect his political activism and act upon the complex personal philosophy he had developed. Riel also saw the tribes of the Cree, Blackfoot and Sioux nations as allies to the Metis, similarly oppressed by the cultural clash brought upon them by the Canadian assumption of the prairies. His program was ambitious, but he felt this time Macdonald would deal with him. Riel fully intended to return to St. Peter's by September.

CHAPTER THREE

The Blackfoot Quandary

The timing of Riel's return was significant. After years of abused faith, Crowfoot was in the mood to listen to the revolutionary's message, which was: because the white man had destroyed the buffalo and replaced them with cattle, their livestock belonged to the First Nations; and, furthermore, since the government was not living up to its promises, Crowfoot should join Riel's alliance and send the Dominion of Canada packing.

Inspector Sam Steele of the NWMP was alerted to the meeting between Bear's Head and Crowfoot, and Bear's Head was arrested and put on a track for Calgary, but he got free of his chains, jumped off the train and made his way back into the Blackfoot sun dance camp. Steele personally took charge of the recapture. With two constables, he tracked his quarry to the camp, barged into Crowfoot's teepee during a council and removed Bear's Head physically. Crowfoot was insulted. A Blackfoot chief takes personal responsibility for a guest, even if the guest is arrested. What's more, Steele had violated the sun dance. When Crowfoot approached him, the Mountie prepared to draw his revolver. Given the temperament of his warriors, Crowfoot could have had Steele and his men killed, but he chose discretion and let the Mounties take their prisoner.

Four days later Crowfoot attended the trial in Calgary. Bear's Head was charged with disturbing the peace but acquitted on the condition that he leave the area for good. Crowfoot was satisfied with the verdict but registered his disapproval at his guest's treatment and the police, their laws and the government. The incident tore at Crowfoot's loyalties. He had given his word to the Queen's representatives, the police, the railroad and the missionaries and didn't wish to break it, but the duplicity, the rampant poverty, as well as the mood of his own people, made him wonder how long he could, or should, hold his impetuous young warriors back. For guidance and support, he looked to his allies to the south, the Bloods at the Belly River.

The Bloods were very nearly the holdouts of Treaty 7 and perhaps even more wary and skeptical. While their leader, Red Crow, accepted his friend Crowfoot as the figurehead for the Blackfoot Confederacy, he had made it known to treaty commissioners that each band was distinct. The Bloods had also expected to subsist on traditional buffalo hunting for at least 10 years past the treaty signing, but herds in Canada were devastated in less than two years after the treaty was signed. By 1879 they had travelled into Montana in search of new hunting grounds, but competition from other bands, the Metis and professional hunters, and discouragement from the US Army had led the Bloods to return.

When they arrived back to accept life under the treaty, they found their world had changed. The treaty granted them a communal reserve of five persons per square mile. The land set out for the Bloods was a four-mile wide strip extending east along the Bow and South Saskatchewan rivers, from Blackfoot Crossing to Medicine Hat. At the time, it was nearly a desert: a hot dry climate, little timber and a light soil that supported fewer cattle than the western hill country, but Red Crow was a canny trader. He petitioned the Indian department to move the location. The traditional camping grounds along the Belly and St. Mary's rivers were what Red Crow wanted, and a reserve comprising over 700 square miles was what he received—the largest Aboriginal holding in Canada.

The tribe's leaders encouraged their people to turn from hunting to farming. By 1882, 250 acres of prairie had been broken and 70,000 pounds of potatoes harvested, but the Bloods did not subjugate their spirit and continued to demonstrate fierceness. In 1883 a Cree war party stole 45 horses from the reserve, and White Calf gathered 200 men to pursue the thieves toward Fort Walsh. The Bloods and the NWMP recovered the horses relatively peacefully, but at least one Cree was killed in the melee.

The Bloods were not blameless themselves when it came to horse raiding. Several parties made runs into Montana and used the Medicine Line to escape retribution. On one occasion, two frustrated American cattlemen crossed the border in pursuit, and, with the assistance of the Fort Macleod NWMP, took their recovered mounts home. The NWMP received a letter from Choteau County sheriff John Healy, warning that the people of Montana would no longer tolerate Canadian raiders. Fearing that some of his people might be lynched in Montana, Red Crow announced a ban on all trips south of the border and directed the tribe's warrior societies to make sure his decree was enforced.

In 1882 the government appointed Cecil Denny, a discharged Mountie, as the Indian agent to the Blood reserve. Denny was a refreshing change as an agent; he was incorruptible and respectful of Red Crow. He praised the chief's assistance in making the transition to agriculture and in keeping the ration distribution peaceful and orderly. Still, Denny was first, and foremost, a government man who wanted the upper hand. He gave broad power to the NWMP and even to the Blood warrior societies to compel the Bloods to stay on their reserves, to cease horse-raiding adventures and to stop killing ranchers' cattle. Believing hereditary chiefs retained too much control within the band, he attempted to circumvent Red Crow's leadership by holding elections to replace him. A two-year diplomatic scrap ensued, but Red Crow always came out on top as the traditional leader.

In 1883 the test of wills between Denny and Red Crow came to a head in an incident that could have pushed Red Crow into Louis Riel's faction. In the wake of an economic downturn, cuts to federal government expenditures were ordered. Bureaucrats were ordered to pinch pennies in departments where the people concerned don't vote, like in the Department of Indian Affairs. Under pressure to trim the budget, Deputy Minister Lawrence Vankoughnet declared that too much money was being spent on employees and reserve rations. With no thought to transition, buffalo extinction, promises made, or even humanity, Denny was ordered to economize.

With a fury unknown at other agencies, Cecil Denny took a red pencil to the band rolls. Denny deemed several on the lists to be South Piegan from the American side of the line, and therefore ineligible for Canadian dispensations. There was little documentation to prove one way or another, but still, with the absolute power to do so, Denny arbitrarily decided that more than 1,000 people were not entitled to treaty benefits. What was more, whole families saw daily rations cut by half, or less if Denny decided that a family was claiming too many children.

Denny saved his government masters thousands of dollars, but his actions pushed the proud, fearless people further to the edge of despair. In the absence of promised government-issued beef, all the tribesmen knew was that somebody owed them cattle. The younger warriors saw abundant cattle grazing freely where their former staple, the buffalo, once had—and took what they wanted from the free-ranging herds of the local ranchers. That in turn brought complaints from the ranchers and a situation that could erupt into an ugly scene.

In the spring of 1883, in Pincher Creek, a Cochrane Ranche herder riding along the Kootenay (now the Waterton) River came upon a group of Natives field butchering a fresh cow. He rode back to town with his report and guided a group of volunteers, led by John Herron, in search of the perpetrators. The incident was traced to a hunting party of 14 Stoneys who had drifted south. Herron took them into custody without incident. They were tried and given sentences on the charge of cattle killing.

After witnessing the devastating effects of the cutbacks, Denny was horrified and reconsidered. Further cuts were ordered, and Denny had to lay off much of his staff, which gave him more stress. He complained on the Bloods' behalf to Lieutenant Governor Edgar Dewdney, but to no avail. Dewdney was powerless to overrule a federal government department. Mortified at the despair his actions had caused, Denny declared his position untenable and resigned. He was replaced by another ex-Mountie, William Pocklington.

Dewdney was a shrewd politician, but with no budget to increase the rations he could only replace bread with circuses. Whether or not anybody knew it at the time, the governor may have made a decision that changed history. He invited Crowfoot and Three Bulls of the Blackfoot, Eagle Tail Feather of the Peigan and Red Crow of the Bloods to meet him in Regina and travel with him to Winnipeg, where he hoped their conference could "offset the influences brought to bear upon the Indians of Treaty Seven with a view of prevailing upon them to join in a general stand against the government."[3]

The Native leaders' previous contact with white culture, be it American, British or Canadian, did not prepare any of them for Winnipeg. Crowfoot, Red Crow and Eagle Tail Feather had only seen the newcomers' settlements as rough-hewn log-and-clapboard towns like Fort Macleod, Calgary or Fort Benton. They had no reason to believe the extent of the white man's population and technology was anything more than cabins and shacks, railroads and steamboats.

In just days, locomotive power carried the tribal leaders more that 500 miles across the prairie. What they saw at the forks of the Red and the Assiniboine shocked them. Winnipeg in 1884 boasted 15,000 people in the city alone, more than the chiefs commanded in their combined Confederacy on the eastern slope of the Rockies. Winnipeggers lived in brick row houses and worked in massive sandstone buildings bigger than most of the forts at which they were trading. They were given their first taste of ice cream, attended a stage play and saw a street where electric lights were flicked on with a switch.

In addition to showing them the sights of the city, Dewdney's men also showed the various chiefs what would await any of their people who ran afoul of the Queen's men and indeed what had become of some of their people who'd been taken away by the redcoats. At Stony Mountain Penitentiary, they saw their fellow bandsmen incarcerated behind iron bars, in small, miserable cells. Sam Bedson, warden at the time, also showed them the small buffalo herd he had domesticated—a far cry from the herds that just a few short years ago ran plentiful and wild on Blackfoot territory. The white man had tamed the bison, put them on farms and replaced them with cattle. Crowfoot and Red Crow understood the parallel to their own plight: their people were being domesticated on reserves and could easily be replaced with settlers. The Blackfoot were a highly adaptable people, accepting of new methods, inventions and techniques, but after thousands of years of proud self-reliance, they had difficulty with abrupt changes imposed by a paternalistic bureaucracy. Virtual displacement was a bitter pill to swallow.

The leaders also saw armouries and reviewed a parade of militia. They also visited batteries of artillery and were given an idea of the military arsenal that could be employed. The Blackfoot chiefs were guests of the government, but here before them were the weapons of war that could easily be turned on their people. The lesson was not lost on the leaders, Crowfoot in particular, and he and Red Crow came back with a new assessment on how close they should be aligning with Riel. Crowfoot was shaken, realizing that a prison cell could hold him. Red Crow was less impressed with the show of force and more interested in an audience with Dewdney to air his objections to the cutbacks of rations and the replacement of beef with a cheaper staple.

The issues of fresh beef to families on the Peigan and Blood reserves were replaced by barrels of salted bacon. Pork was alien to the Native diet. Even worse, it was a breach of faith. The Blood had been promised fresh beef, and the new rations were offensive. One chief even slapped a department staff member with a side of bacon. Before he left for Winnipeg, Red Crow ordered his band to reject pork.

In Red Crow's absence, William Pocklington tried to bypass the chief's authority. He fibbed to minor chiefs that Red Crow and Dewdney had agreed to the bacon rations in their meeting. With that understanding, the chiefs agreed to take the bacon, but when Red Crow returned and uncovered the duplicity, he angrily ordered the warrior societies to prevent the bacon from being distributed. Crowfoot and Eagle Tail Feather banned bacon from their reserves outright. Dewdney, worried that his good relations with chiefs were eroding, stepped in and ordered Pocklington and the other agents to suspend the bacon. Eventually, beef was restored.

In the meantime, at the Metis settlement at Batoche's Crossing, Riel had set up a council and laid plans to petition the government. He now began to renew contact with several tribal leaders. Poundmaker, Fine Day and Big Bear would eventually be drawn into the conflict, and other Native leaders across western Canada were contacted, but the leaders of the Blackfoot Confederacy were seen as the force that could make a difference. Before Riel could organize Native alliances, he had to address the white and Metis settlers of Prince Albert, who had a good many grievances against the government. They had settled in the parkland region between the north and south branches of the Saskatchewan River to capitalize on homesteading opportunities and were hopeful that the Canadian Pacific Railway would guarantee an outlet for their grain and cattle. To their horror, the route of the country's first transcontinental railroad was changed; the line would follow the southern prairies, paralleling the US–Canada border. As a result, farm commodity prices deflated, and settlers found the fruits of their tough labours worthless without a transport venue. The settlers of Prince Albert were furious. Their Metis neighbours at Batoche, with their own land problems, were just as provoked. The two communities passed the hat to finance the services of Riel.

Prince Albert was not alone. Many white farmers in the west related to the Metis cause and their fight with the government. The political climate was so bad, the Manitoba & Northwest Farmers Union was formed to advocate for a solution. The leader of the movement, Brandon lawyer Clifford Sifton, threatened the secession of the province of Manitoba to the United States. That proclamation, made in the age of gunpowder diplomacy, was fiery enough to rally Ottawa to organize three militia companies in response. The Union did not literally go to war, but Ottawa dithered until open revolt was threatened again. Western newspaper editors like the inflammatory Frank Oliver of the *Edmonton Bulletin* spoke openly in support of the people of the Northwest—Metis and settler alike—seeking to obtain their rights by the use of force.

As Riel investigated the situation with the Batoche and Prince Albert settlers, Poundmaker and Big Bear met at the Poundmaker reserve near Battleford in August of 1884 to discuss their plight. A council meeting was held at the Thirst Dance ceremony, and demands were made to the Indian agents. The dance itself nearly turned into a battle when a farm instructor claimed he'd been assaulted and called for the NWMP. The police, commanded by the ubiquitous Superintendant Lief Crozier, came out with a force of 90 to arrest the suspect. Crozier took his prisoner, but not without a lot of threats and jostling between the Mounties and the Cree that created a huge setback in diplomacy.

Knowing Riel was in the area, Poundmaker and Big Bear remained in contact with his messengers. Big Bear and Riel met in Prince Albert, but the problems of the Cree had little relation to the Prince Albert and Metis grievances, and the factions were never united. In fact, what would eventually turn the white settlers against Riel was his intention to ally his forces with Natives. Frank Oliver changed his tune as though a switch had been thrown, and his editorials descended from libertarian eloquence to racist rants.

The Blackfoot chiefs were growing ever more disillusioned and were greatly tempted by Riel's offers of an alliance to oppose the discredited Canadian government. In late 1884, Big Bear sent a trusted ally, Little Pine, to the Blackfoot reserve to invite Crowfoot to come north for a council with the Cree and another proposal for a grand alliance on the Red Deer River. Crowfoot began to lose control of his tribe as several warriors threatened to leave with Little Pine. The warriors did not leave, but Little Pine did take with him five Blackfoot horses, a sign of goodwill to Big Bear.

Counter to Crowfoot's indecision, Red Crow wanted nothing to do with the Cree, his traditional enemies. The memory of Big Bear's 1870 attack on the Blood camp near Fort Whoop-Up, and the death of many friends and relatives in that fight, was still vivid. Despite problems with the government, agent Pocklington, treaty disputes and the frequent arrests of tribesmen, Red Crow considered that the Mounted Police had always dealt with him peacefully, and continued to be their ally.

That loyalty was tested in the winter of 1884. Horse theft was a part of the culture and a test of manhood, but with both angry ranchers and trigger-happy insurgents dividing the attention of the law, that practice was a dangerous game threatening the fragile peace. Oral Talker, the son of White Calf, one of Red

Crow's most trusted chiefs, had just returned from the Cypress Hills on a horse-raiding expedition that ended with his arrest. When White Calf protested and interfered with the arrest, both father and son were thrown into the Fort Macleod guardroom. White Calf was kept overnight and released without charge. Red Crow, aghast that the redcoats would throw a leading Blood authority into jail, demanded the release of the son. While White Calf threatened to fight the police, Red Crow bided his time, and soon White Calf lost all support among the Bloods for his war.

On December 16, 1884, Riel addressed the grievances of the Metis and the Prince Albert settlers in his extensive Bill of Rights, requesting free title for Metis land claims, fairer treatment of the Plains tribes, provincial status for the territorial districts, local responsible government, and representation in Parliament. Macdonald ignored the pleas and sought to wait out the crisis. In Regina, the new territorial capital, Lieutenant-Governor Edgar Dewdney also sought to bide through the winter, hoping that enduring the season would tame the Metis' ambitions. His hopes, it would turn out, would be misplaced.

CHAPTER FOUR

The Frontiersmen: Kootenai Brown and William Jackson

In the turmoil that saw Canada and the United States expand across its frontier, the wandering adventurer was more than some Hollywood archetype. For drifters lacking prospects but possessing zest for adventure, the prairies were magnetic. Such men could live on the edge and reinvent themselves in a wild land of opportunity—primitive, anarchic, truly a place for a newcomer to get lost. Two such men were John George Brown and William Jackson. Brown was a newcomer to the land, a slave to wanderlust and curiosity, with unique perspectives on rough justice; Jackson was born to the prairies, a living product of the centuries-old fur trade and survivor of one of the most infamous battles in history. Both were hardened to the environment and no strangers to the dangerous conflicts bred of the times. Their combined experience was invaluable to the mission of the Rocky Mountain Rangers.

It took three continents for John George Brown to make his mark. He was born in Clare, Ireland, in 1839, but it was in the wild west of North America that he became legendary as gold miner, peace officer, whisky trader, express rider, hunter, oil speculator and scout. The son of an English officer, John Brown received a good education from the military college at Sandhurst and a commission in the British Army. As a captain, he was posted to India during the 1857 Sepoy Mutiny but saw no action. After his discharge Brown left Britain for good, sailing for Panama in 1861 and crossing the isthmus to the Pacific Ocean. With a friend, Arthur Vowell, he sailed up the coast to San Francisco. Dead broke upon arrival, Brown worked the docks to raise steamship passage to Victoria, BC, and then travelled up the Fraser River to the interior, the heart of the Cariboo gold rush.

Brown and Vowell spent two years mining and trapping in gold country. They made $3,000 selling furs one winter but lost it in a gold claim the following summer. Brown left Williams Creek in 1864 with little more than the clothes on his back and took a job as a deckhand on the Fraser River freight boats. It was back-breaking work and not at all his life's ambition. With news in 1865 of another gold strike, this time at Wild Horse Creek in the East Kootenay region, John Brown, like all Argonauts, headed toward the latest news of colour.

Brown's luck in the Wild Horse field was no better. Lacking funds, he took a job as a police constable. His biggest arrest was nabbing three con artists selling phony gold dust, but Brown's success as a lawman was short-lived; he quit when his pay was reduced. Returning to the gold pan, Brown took out a placer claim with four other prospectors. That didn't work out either; the claim was sold, and the five prospectors decided to check out rumours of yet another strike. The mythic goldfield lay across the Rockies, near the Hudson's Bay post of Fort Edmonton. None knew what lay beyond the mountains or where Edmonton was. Nonetheless, with a single pack horse, the quintet struck east toward the Continental Divide. Along the way they dealt with the Kootenay band, and left the meeting with four more horses. This deal was the basis for Brown's nickname, a corrupted spelling of the band's tribal name. Nobody ever called him John George again. "Kootenai Brown" was the handle he proudly wore for the rest of his life.

The miners entered the prairie through the North Kootenay Pass. As the eastern slopes of the Rockies broke into a vista of endless prairie, Brown got his first glimpse of Waterton Lake, the area that would one day become his home and his passion. Back then, all he and the party had in mind was gold.

Out of the pines and onto the plains, the gold seekers followed the rivers east, believing the system they travelled, from the Kootenay (Waterton) River to the Belly and onward, would bring them to Edmonton. There were few guidebooks for the use of general travellers of the time. The Kootenai Brown party could not know it was actually following tributaries of the South Saskatchewan River, some 300 miles from Edmonton, which were leading them farther off course.

A few days out of the mountains, they camped in a bluff of cottonwood trees at the mouth of Seven Persons Creek (near the future Medicine Hat). There they were attacked by hostile Assiniboine. During the melee, the warriors let fly a volley of arrows. The miners answered with guns and killed two warriors. That drove off the war party, but not before a horse was lost and Kootenai Brown suffered an arrow shaft in the back. The arrowhead lodged close to the kidneys, and the infection and loss of blood threatened his death. Kootenai's companions removed the offending missile by putting one foot on Kootenai's back and pulling the arrow straight out by the shaft. The resultant screams filled the valley. Frontier medicine became even cruder when the amateur surgeons poured an entire bottle of turpentine into the open wound.

In the wake of that attack came an argument and a split in the party. Three took a horse each and struck out across the prairie, their fates unknown to history. Kootenai Brown and a miner he called Goldtooth took another path, forsaking an overland trip to Edmonton to continue along the South Saskatchewan to see where the river might take them. Goldtooth had lost his horse during the raid, so they constructed a shabby bull boat from a buffalo hide stretched across a wooden frame. Goldtooth took to the water, and a recuperating Kootenai followed on horseback along the bank.

After a few weeks' travel the pair arrived at the settlement of Duck Lake, where they lived among the Metis for the winter. Though this was before the Red River Rebellion, families were already leaving the Red to establish farms along the South Saskatchewan. Kootenai seemed to have forgotten about his lust for gold, and in the early spring of 1865 he and Goldtooth took a sleigh down the Carlton Trail to Fort Garry.

The pair split company in 1866, when Kootenai went to work for Red River whisky merchants trading to the Cree and Salteaux for buffalo hides. When he became embroiled in a shoot-out with a group of Minnesota Sioux attempting to steal whisky from the post, one trader and a Native were killed. Kootenai lost interest in the trade, and in April 1868 headed south to the Dakota Territory.

Kootenai hired himself out to Major Charles A. Ruffee's express company. For $50 a month he carried the US mail from Fort Stevenson to Fort Benton. Express routes included way stations, each with a keeper and a supply of fresh horses. But it was a dangerous time: the army was in conflict with bands of Sioux and Cheyenne in what was called Red Cloud's War. In just a couple of seasons, most of the station keepers were killed and hundreds of company horses stolen. When Ruffee's firm went bankrupt, the United States Army took over the route, and Kootenai was rehired as a military courier.

In May 1868, Kootenai and a Sioux mixed-blood, Joe Martin, assumed the route of two mail carriers killed by the Sioux between Fort Stevenson and Fort Totten. On their first trip, they were captured by a Hunkpapa Sioux war party led by Sitting Bull (*Tatonka Yatonka*). Had they not known the language, both would have been killed instantly, but Martin dropped the name of a Sioux ally, earning some cachet. Kootenai, with his buckskin apparel, leathery tanned face and long flowing hair, was taken to be a Sioux half-blood. Careful not to use English (with an obvious across-the-pond accent), Brown did little to shatter the perception. After deliberation, the sympathetic chief allowed Brown and Martin to live, but as a warning to the Army, they were stripped of everything they had—horses, guns, mail—even clothing. During the night they were allowed to leave the camp and return to Fort Stevenson. Kootenai and Martin appeared at the post the next afternoon, blistered and bitten raw by mosquitoes.

As they walked in, a soldier asked of the naked Kootenai, "What's up?"

"Oh, nothing much," was the reply. "The Sioux have your mail, horses, and our clothes, and came very near to getting us."[4]

Kootenai and Martin then delivered Sitting Bull's message to the post commander, General Phillipe de Trobriand, that he had no intention of meeting with US government peace commissioners. After that experience, Kootenai stayed off the trail for a few months. When in November 1868 he resumed carrying mail, he helped build five way stations between Forts Stevenson and Totten.

Around 1869, Kootenai married young, dark-haired Olivia Lyonnais, a product of the Dakota Metis settlements. In 1871 they moved to Fort Stevenson, where Kootenai took time off from the Army to join the fall buffalo hunt. He rejoined as a scout in 1872 and remained until his pay was reduced two years later, due to a diminishing need for scouts. Refusing to work such a hazardous job for a "pittance," he resigned and joined Olivia's people in the hunting camps.

For the next two to three years, the Browns lived a nomadic existence in the Metis camps. They took part in some of the last Native buffalo hunts to be seen on the high plains. They ranged throughout the border region: the Cypress Hills, Milk River Ridge, Coteau du Missouri, and the Qu'Appelle Valley.

Each hunter had several fast horses capable of outrunning stampeding herds, and men with the best horses, "buffalo runners," made the most kills. Each family was responsible for butchering its own kill. The Metis believed in killing no more than what was needed for subsistence and trade; surplus was distributed to needy families. Competition was heavy, and long-distance travel needed as the beasts' numbers dwindled near extinction. Brown was shocked when he realized the herds were being decimated and the Army was using the creeping extinction to keep their Native charges on reservations, away from the Canadian border.

In 1876 poverty forced Kootenai Brown into the business of wolfing. Wolf hunters—if the practice could be called hunting—captured their prey by poisoning buffalo carcasses with strychnine and letting the wolves' hunger do the work for them. Both Natives and settlers hated wolfers—Natives because their dogs accidentally ate the poisoned meat, settlers and traders because of their rough manners and the trouble they created between white and Native factions—but for wolfers, the profits were great. A $6.00 bottle of poison could net countless wolf skins worth $2.50 each. Kootenai walked in this crude world for a year.

In the spring of 1877, Kootenai Brown came to Fort Benton to sell his winter's take of pelts. His fur merchant, Louis Ell, brought up an old unpaid debt. When Kootenai disputed the note, the argument turned violent. Kootenai plunged a butcher knife into Louis Ell's abdomen, wrenched it sideways and nearly severed the man in half. Ell died in minutes.

Now a murderer, Kootenai galloped out, heading west. Choteau County sheriff William Rowe took pursuit. He arrested Brown about 70 miles up the Marias River and imprisoned him in the Fort Benton jailhouse. During Kootenai's incarceration, Rowe was replaced by John J. Healy, former owner of Fort Whoop-Up. On July 27, 1877, Sheriff Healy arrived with breakfast and was surprised to find that Brown had attempted suicide by thrusting a dirk knife into his chest. Medical attention was administered, and by autumn, Kootenai was fit to stand trial for murder before a grand jury in Helena. Brown entered his plea: not guilty by reason of self-defence. The plea was accepted, and he was acquitted and saved from hanging.

The trial was a turning point for Kootenai Brown. Though he rarely spoke of the incident, he stated in later years that the two sweetest words in the English language were "not guilty." He vowed never again to enter the United States. A free man, Kootenai packed up Olivia and their two daughters and moved to Kootenay (later known as Waterton) Lake, where he'd first entered the prairies 11 years earlier. He built a cabin on the shore of the lake and spent the rest of his life as a professional hunting and tour guide, scout and commercial fisherman. The abundance of trout in the lakes and streams was a steady source of income. In Fort Macleod, a wagonload sold for $75, a fortune in the 1870s. Kootenai enjoyed Macleod, where he could have a drink and chat up the Mounties, bullwhackers and other characters.

Visiting and helping new arrivals in the area—large-scale ranchers and small homesteaders alike—Kootenai endeared himself to the pioneers of Pincher Creek and enjoyed a new audience for his stories. In 1881 he helped Senator Matthew Cochrane of Quebec to locate a range. Cochrane accepted Brown's advice and took out a large lease at the Big Hill, west of Calgary. When the winter of 1882 and 1883 proved disastrous, Kootenai advised the senator to take up a second range near the Kootenay River, where winters were milder. In 1884 the senator's son, William Cochrane, managed the southern operation and appreciated the advice.

Kootenai received plum assignments to help many prominent ranching investors find their home turfs. Alexander Stavely Hill, the Earl of Latham and John Craig hired him to locate the range of the Oxley Ranche in 1883. The genteel British business tourists could not get over the sight of an educated British Army officer adorned like a mountain man, with flowing hair, buckskins and

broad slouch hat. They were even more impressed by his familiarity with the mountains and his expertise as a guide on hunting
and fishing expeditions into British Columbia.

The long trips away from his family brought tragedy in 1883.
Olivia gave birth to their son, Leo, while Kootenai was away on
the Oxley Ranche commission. Complications arose, and Olivia
never fully recovered. She died in the autumn, and Kootenai
buried her along the western shore of Kootenay Lake. Unable
to take care of the children, Brown had Catholic priest Father
Albert Lacombe arrange for their care in mission schools and
convents. Though Leo occasionally returned to visit his father,
the rest of the family was scattered among foster homes and were
never reunited. With his family in tatters, and the love of his
life gone, Kootenai retreated to the mountains and devoted his
broken heart to the wilds near his home.

Kootenai was in Macleod on March 20, 1885, amidst rumours
and rumblings of the threat of a general uprising. He took
note of these rumblings but gave them little attention, leaving
town for his solitary retreat, to be unseen for weeks. Then, one
April morning in 1885, Kootenai's repose was broken when
William Cochrane met him at the ford of the Kootenay River
and informed him that a prairie war had broken out. A call for
volunteers had been issued. Perhaps this excitement was the tonic
Brown needed to purge his grief.

William (Billy) Jackson didn't have to adapt to the prairie way
of life; he was born to it. His lineage alone—with tentacles in
colonial Quebec and Virginia and the world of the Blackfoot—is
the story of the continent and the westward movement as it
evolved in the land later known as Montana and Alberta. His
great-grandparents of European blood were a melding of the
solitudes of Canada: the British Army officer Captain Hugh
Monroe, garrisoned to Quebec in the years after the British loss
of the American colonies, and Québecoise Amélia de la Roche,
"daughter of a noble family of emigres."[5]

The product of their marriage was the younger Hugh Monroe, born in 1798 at Trois-Rivières, where he grew up learning to trap from the Montagnais and selling the pelts in Montreal. When his father was sent to fight in the War of 1812, teenaged Hugh joined the fur trade as an indentured servant of the Hudson's Bay Company. Posted to Rocky Mountain House in 1816, Monroe came to know the prairie bands. Adopted by Lone Walker, chief of the Peigan, Monroe was given the name *Mah-kwi-i-po-ats* (Rising Wolf). Monroe was married three times to women of his adopted band; one of them was *Sinopaki* (Fox Woman). In order to raise their offspring among her people, Monroe switched his allegiance to the American Fur Company.

At Fort Benton, the Monroe family—in particular their daughter, Amelia—came to know other traders and engagés, including Thomas Jackson, a Virginian who brought a little southern gentry into the AFC. The union of Thomas and Amelia furthered the unique bond of trade and indigenous culture. Two boys were conceived of this union: Robert, in 1854, and William, in 1856.

The Jackson boys grew up around the Benton post "taught that, in time to come, we were to take our father's place as bourgeois, clerks, traders, artisans, hunters and laborers."[6] By osmosis, the boys picked up the languages they heard—English, French, Blackfoot and more. Their father made sure they were educated beyond the norms of the territory. "He had patiently taught us to read and write, repeatedly told us that we must live so that we should never shame the good blood that was in us, that of his own Virginia forebears, and that of our great-grandfather, Lone Walker...a Pikuni chief of the highest character."[7]

Their grandfather Hugh made sure they learned from the natural world. He taught them to shoot, hunt and trap—and the ways of the Piegan as well—but as the boys grew, the fur trade changed irrevocably. War, politics, settlement, and the collapse of the AFC made for a new and vastly different world. In time, the unique skills of William Jackson would serve even more newcomers with startling new interests in the prairies beyond that of furs.

The talents of William and Robert Jackson were well known to the US Army. Billy Jackson was but 17 years old when he enrolled, under protest from his father, in the US Scouts at Fort Buford. As Amelia Jackson said, "The wild blood that is in these boys, blood of Hugh Monroe and his fighting Scotch ancestors, blood of generations of Pikuni warriors, that blood is not to be denied."[8] The brothers befriended Bloody Knife, a Sioux–Arikara scout for the Army (known as Custer's favourite Scout) and came to know other legendary guides, like Lonesome Charley Reynolds and Fred Girard. Over the next three years, Billy was attached to the 7th Cavalry and the 6th Infantry and introduced to Colonel George Armstrong Custer.

Jackson was one of 27 scouts accompanying Custer on the Yellowstone Expedition to protect the surveyors of the Northern Pacific Railway in southeastern Montana in 1873. In August, Custer engaged the Hunkpapa Sioux and Oglala Sioux forces of Sitting Bull and Crazy Horse in the Battle of Honsinger Bluff. Casualties were light, but it was a prologue for a looming tragedy.

Billy also rode with the 7th in the 1874 expedition into the Black Hills, when Custer announced to reporters that prospectors had found gold. The published news reports triggered a stampede of interlopers into the area, founding the town of Deadwood, but under the Laramie Treaty of 1868, the hills were Sioux territory, and the gold rush brought conflict. Through 1874 and 1875, more treaty violations and further encroachment on the Great Plains led to escalated conflict between the Sioux and Cheyenne with settlers and soldiers.

Discharged on Christmas Eve 1875, Billy eagerly re-upped in the Scouts the very next day. He didn't wait long for action. In January 1876, Ulysses Grant ordered all bands to report to their agencies and reservations or be considered hostile. With the spring, the Army organized punitive expeditions to enforce the decree, engaging several columns to march on the Sioux position, where Sitting Bull had called for the sun dance alliance on the Little Bighorn River in Montana territory. Closest to the site was Custer's 7th Cavalry. It left Fort Abraham Lincoln in May of 1876. Along the route Billy was reprimanded for shooting a snake in camp. He would soon get unlimited shooting opportunities.

At daybreak on June 25, some 14 miles from the Little Bighorn camp, Custer's Crow scouts reported a large horse herd, which meant a large village of Sioux. Bloody Knife warned that the numbers at the Sioux camp were massive and aware of Custer's movements. Custer rebuffed the scout. Even though his counterparts, Generals Gibbon, Crook and Terry were en route with reinforcements, Custer decided to attack. That caused Bloody Knife to predict to Jackson: "Tomorrow we are going to have a big fight, a losing fight. Myself, I know what is going to happen to me; my sacred helper has given me warning that I am not to see the sunset of tomorrow's sun."[9] Billy's Aboriginal heritage gave great credence to such a prophecy, and he was chilled at the prospect of his last night on Earth.

The next day, Custer divided the 12 companies of the 7th Cavalry into three attacking battalions. Major Marcus Reno was to cross the Little Bighorn River with 142 men and charge into the southern end of the encampment in the valley. Custer rode north with 208 officers and men, circling around the east of the camp, planning to attack from the north and catch the camp in a pincer between himself and Reno. Captain Frederick Benteen and about 100 men were to stay on the hilltop and cut off any attempted escape from either end. One company of 50 men was left behind as a rearguard, while 84 soldiers and teamsters accompanied the slow-moving supply train bringing up the rear.

With 10 scouts, including the Jacksons, Reno's troop crossed the river. The scouts pulled ahead of Reno, galloping down the valley for a mile toward a grove of trees, and came upon the odd Sioux running to escape, but in the trees, they began to take fire.

Letting Reno catch up, the scouts and company came upon the south end of the village—still 500 yards short of the camp. Reno ordered a dismounted skirmish line, but that order weakened his position, leaving a quarter of the force holding horses and unable to fight. After 20 minutes of crossfire, the Sioux and Cheyenne charged the skirmish line. "Then came the rush of the enemy, all of five hundred well-mounted riders in all of their war finery, eager to get at us. Their shots, their war-cries, the thunder of their horses' feet were deafening."[10]

Robert and Billy noticed an enemy coming straight at their position. "Robert exclaimed 'Look! That one on the big white horse! He's Black Elk!'"[11] The boys knew him from his appearances at Fort Buford, and both fired at him. Both missed, or so they thought, but as he swung around the Jacksons, Black Elk tumbled off his mount.

The skirmish line was effective until opposing numbers overwhelmed them. Outgunned, Reno's men took cover in the trees on the riverbank and were in danger of being pinned into the river. Bloody Knife was at Reno's side when a gunshot to the head killed the Crow scout, spattering Reno with blood. Lonesome Charley Reynolds also fell. With the Sioux setting the brush and grass on fire, a panic-stricken Reno mounted up and ordered retreat. His bloodied and beaten troopers galloped through the river after him toward the bluffs, chased all the while by warriors. Reno lost a quarter of his command. Thirty-two men were killed, and some 13 to 18 men were cut off from retreat. Left behind were the Jacksons, Fred Girard and a couple of soldiers.

As Reno retreated, Billy dueled with a warrior who tried to pull him out of the saddle. Just then, a fellow soldier fell off his horse, and Billy slowed to allow him to jump up behind him, but the soldier was shot down. Girard grabbed Jackson's attention and pulled the scouts and stranded soldiers into some heavy trees. They found a small depression to use as breastworks. Hidden from view, the Jacksons were safe while all hell erupted in the valley, although Billy's horse fell dead, shot through the lungs. In the meantime, Reno and the remains of his command joined Benteen's company on the bluffs and were saved from total annihilation. Occupied in holding off an attack, both dug in to hold the hill and could not come to Custer's aid.

Too late, Custer had realized that he was not at the north end of the camp, but in the middle, and that the assembly was much larger than he'd anticipated. It was, in fact, exactly as large as Billy Jackson had said it was: four miles in length along the river. Crazy Horse from the north, and Gall, galloping up a deep coulee that hid his advance, led their warriors in a classic pincer movement. By the time Custer realized his errors, he was pinned on the crest of a ridge, unable to dig in to establish breastworks. A mounted charge broke through Custer's lines, and the rest is history: 208 officers and troopers panicked, dismounted, swiftly ran out of ammunition and died the ultimate death of the warrior. With casualties from Reno's fight, the death toll ran up to 268.

Trapped in the timber, Robert and Billy Jackson, Fred Girard and the two soldiers waited out the day, unable to move, not knowing if any of their blue-coated comrades had survived. At dark, the scouts ventured out to rejoin Reno. Crossing the river silently took skill, and passing by the sentries near the Sioux victory camp took even more. At some points, Billy Jackson was so close to the Sioux, he could hear them talking. He told historian Walter McClintock that he'd even spoken directly to the unwitting enemy: "Under cover of darkness, Siksikakoan (Billy Jackson) ventured upon the battlefield and stripped from the dead Sioux sufficient leggings, moccasins and blankets to disguise themselves. Then, in the dead of night...he led his companions safely through their sleeping enemies, to the bluffs north of the river, to which Major Reno had retreated for safety. During the movement Siksikakoan answered the challenges of the Sioux by giving satisfactory replies in the Sioux language."[12]

By the evening of June 26, the scouts arrived at the camp at Reno Hill.

After General Alfred Terry's column arrived at the battle site, the soldiers and the Jacksons were put to the grim task of burying the dead and transferring the wounded survivors. The steamer *Far West*, which had been following the expedition up the Yellowstone and Bighorn rivers, was assigned to return the wounded 700 miles to Fort Abraham Lincoln. Billy Jackson made litters and helped to transport the soldiers to the boat.

Since that fateful day, when a vainglorious daredevil gambled the lives of his troops and lost, the Battle of the Little Bighorn has been a flashpoint of history and emotion. It was no different in the days after when, around campfires and councils, those with an opinion began to vent, poke fingers and assign blame. It reached the ears of the scouts that "...Reno had made a cowardly retreat, and that if he had held the position where he was first attacked, he could then have rejoined the battle."[13]

The Reno scouts derided the accusation, but Robert Jackson exploded. Girard and William had to restrain him physically from storming into the officers' tents and probably saved him from court martial. Though Reno had many failings as a man and an officer, the opinion of his guides, as noted by James Schultz, stands the test of time: "It was and is the firm belief of us scouts and soldiers who were with Reno that 25th day of June, 1876, that the day was lost by General Custer himself."[14]

The Battle of the Little Bighorn made Montana a hot place to be, and the Jacksons were transferred to General Nelson Miles' command with the remnants of the 7th Cavalry. They scoured the plains, pursuing Sitting Bull through the fall and winter of 1876 and 1877. Billy was an interpreter for Miles with Sitting Bull in the fall of 1876 at Cedar Creek, although their attempt to bring about surrender failed and resulted in an indecisive two-day battle. In 1877, Billy Jackson was attached to the 22nd

A Fred Russell studio portrait of a Blood, *circa* 1885. The rifle and knife contribute to the "aura of savagery" photographers tried to evoke, even though weapons were often props. GALT PI9770155000

(Top left) Crowfoot of the Blackfoot. He kept
his people on neutral ground throughout the
rebellion. His alliance with the Bloods ensured
food for his starving people.
GLENBOW ARCHIVES NA-3700-3

(Top right) Ox-at-et-Pua, a Blackfoot warrior,
circa 1885. Crowfoot had difficulty keeping his
warriors from heading north to join the
insurgents. GALT PI9770154000

(Bottom) Red Crow of the Blood. He steadfastly
chose to remain loyal and reject Cree and Metis
calls for rebellion. That decisiveness guided
Crowfoot to do the same.
GLENBOW ARCHIVES NA-668-53

Fred Russell portrait of unidentified Blood man and woman. Note the Hudson's Bay capote, evoking ties to that historic company. Again, the weaponry is used to add drama to the studio pose. GALT PI9770158000

North Axe of the Peigan, *circa* 1885. During the rebellion, North Axe maintained his tribe's neutrality and was rewarded with a medal and a trip to Ottawa in 1886. GALT PI9770161000

(Top) James Schofield in "mufti," the buckskin clothing of the NWMP for everyday patrol. He would join the Rangers in 1885.
GLENBOW ARCHIVES NA-1602-6

(Bottom) Alfred Lynch-Staunton (far right) and his brother Richard (third from left) in an 1899 polo match. Alfred helped establish the remount farm that would become the basis of the Stewart Ranche.
GLENBOW ARCHIVES NA-184-73

(Clockwise from top left)
Louis Riel, Metis leader in two
rebellions, was brought to trial and
executed for treason. This execution
brought out deep divisions in
Canada. GLENBOW ARCHIVES NA-504-3

Young John George "Kootenai"
Brown. Upon hearing the news of
the Rangers' activation, he rode
40 miles in a single day to volunteer
his services as a scout.
GALT PI9760230113

"Honest John" Herron during his
days in the NWMP. His experience
and military background proved
useful in his occupation as manager
of the Stewart Ranche.
GALT PI9770285079

(Clockwise from top left)
At 27, John Stewart embarked on his 50,000-acre cattle operation in Alberta.
GLENBOW ARCHIVES NA-1827-2

John Stewart, in the dress uniform of the Princess Louise Dragoons, *circa* 1885. From the *Canadian Illustrated War News*.
GLENBOW ARCHIVES NA-1353-36

The 22-year-old John Stewart in Highland attire for a Governor General's dress ball.
GLENBOW ARCHIVES NA 1827-1

(Top) Duncan John D'Urban Campbell, a prominent Fort Macleod businessman and civic politician. GALT PI9770285007

(Bottom) Campbell as he was depicted in April 1885 while serving as adjutant of the Rangers. GLENBOW ARCHIVES NA-1353-23

Infantry out of Fort Ellis and helped track down the Sioux and Cheyenne.

Billy Jackson left the military in 1879 to build a trading post at Flat Willow, Montana. He later took a homestead on the Cut Bank River, on the Blackfeet reservation, building up a sizable herd of horses and cattle, while Robert moved first to south-eastern Montana and then finally ended up in the mining country of Colorado. Of Billy's scouting abilities, it was said: "[He] had an intimate acquaintance with the tribes of Montana, the chiefs and their habits, and his services were highly commended by every officer under whom he served. He was an intelligent, observant and shrewd scout, never hesitating to undertake any mission and never failing to accomplish what was desired."[15] In 1885, Billy would transfer that professionalism to the Dominion of Canada and the Rocky Mountain Rangers.

CHAPTER FIVE

The Ranchers: John Stewart and John Herron

In 1873, Reverend John McDougall bought a bull and seven cows at Fort Edmonton and drove them south to his Morleyville mission. That small herd was the first domestic breeding stock for cattle ranching in the South Saskatchewan basin. The arrival of the NWMP created a market for beef and milk. Soon American traders and ranchers were bringing Texas longhorns across the line to fatten for market on the lush virgin buffalo grass. Discharged police members extolled the virtues of the native prairies and boasted of the moneymaking potential. Over the next three decades, many a Mountie fulfilled his term just to obtain a land grant and parlay it into a home on the range.

In 1881 the Macdonald government passed legislation granting any applicant a grazing lease of up to 100,000 acres at the annual rate of one cent per acre. That set the impetus for the golden age of the big open-range ranches dominated mostly by investors from eastern Canada, Great Britain and the United States. Among the financiers was a young militia officer, Captain John O. Stewart.

Stewart was the scion of a socially well-established Ottawa family. The patriarch, Scot William Stewart, was a prosperous

Bytown businessman during the 1830s and 1840s and a ste-
reotypical pillar of the community. A successful merchant,
real estate speculator and lumber industry capitalist, William
Stewart was also heavily involved in civic activism and pre-Con-
federation politics. He befriended future prime minister John A.
Macdonald, who would have a profound influence on Stewart's
ninth child, John Stewart, born in 1854, just two years before
his father died. John inherited his father's business acumen and
bent for public service. As a boy, he lived through the American
Civil War and the Fenian raids, during which British garrisons
and volunteer militias in the Canadian colonies stood in military preparedness against belligerence from the republic to the
south. Confederation would establish sovereignty and some
measure of safety, and Bytown (renamed Ottawa) would be
the capital of Canada and the heart of the country's military
command.

Although every young man in early Ontario and Quebec was
brought up with the notion of duty, John Stewart viewed it as a
vocation. By the time he turned 18 in 1872, the Volunteer Militia
Troop of Cavalry organized. John joined, first as a sergeant,
but by that fall he'd been named 2nd Lieutenant. The troop
provided escort for Governor General Lord Dufferin at the
opening of Parliament in 1873 and 1874. In 1877, John Stewart
was promoted to 1st Lieutenant, maintaining his duties while
working at Strathroy, Ontario, as an accountant for the Bank of
Commerce.

In the 1878 election, having lost the House in 1874, Sir John
A. Macdonald made a comeback bid to retake the government
from incumbent Alexander Mackenzie. At one of Sir John's
famous campaign picnics at Strathroy, John Stewart carried on
the family tradition as a political ally, rallying the troops as a
ceremonial escort for the candidate. The boisterous Macdonald
was returned to power and subsequently remembered Stewart's
gesture.

When John Campbell, Marquis of Lorne, consort of Princess Louise Caroline Alberta, was suggested for Governor General, the British Colonial Secretary raised concerns. Louise was the daughter of Queen Victoria, so she and Lorne were royal family, and the Secretary posited that the rough-hewn volunteer cavalry was incapable of providing protection. The canny Sir John had a solution. He procured $4,700 to reorganize the volunteer cavalry into the grandly redubbed Princess Louise Dragoon Guards—an escort fit for royalty. The Dragoon uniform was stunning in its military flair—a blue tunic, pipe-clay belt and haversack, dark blue trousers with white stripe, and a Prussian style cork helmet complete with spike and horsehair plume. The duty itself was also pomp and ceremony: accompanying the vice-regal carriage whenever it left the Governor General's Rideau Hall to attend Parliament or performing duties about the capital. The job was also serious. The threat of political assassination was real, as evidenced by the violent death of cabinet minister D'Arcy McGee, gunned down by a Fenian sympathizer right in Ottawa. Any rabble-rouser would have to get past the lance point.

Stewart was appointed to take the front saddle and assume command, giving up a banking position to accept the task. Offered the commissionership of the Dominion police as further enticement, Stewart declined, satisfied with the reins of the Dragoon Guards. Other recruits in the Dragoons included William F. Powell, son of a high-ranking staff officer, and Duncan John D'Urban Campbell, a fellow banker.

Born at Mont-Saint-Hilaire, Quebec, in 1855, Campbell was educated at Bishop's College School in Lennoxville, entering Bank of Montreal employ in 1873 and transferring to Ottawa in 1878 to join Stewart's unit. From the business district, Stewart recruited Thomas Bates and John Herron, partners in a wholesale grocery. The acquaintance of Campbell and Herron in particular would become crucial for all of their futures, as close friends, as partners and as members of the Rocky Mountain Rangers.

John Herron was appointed sergeant major of the Dragoon Guards. Herron was no weekend warrior. His military pedigree was unique and specialized, and he had just returned from four years of rough riding service in the NWMP, in a land barely understood by anyone in Ottawa.

Herron was born in 1853 to an Irish farm family near Ashton, Ontario. With little formal education, he went to work in a logging camp at age 12. At 16 he apprenticed to a blacksmith, and in November of his 21st year, Herron enrolled in the NWMP as a farrier. He was posted to Fort Garry, Manitoba, a month later.

Herron didn't participate in the March West, enlisting too late to join the trek. Soon after arrival in Manitoba, his troop was ordered to Swan River, an HBC fort being converted to an NWMP post. Just days out on the trail, the column was met by Commissioner George French and reassigned to Fort Dufferin for the remainder of the winter. In the spring of 1875, Constable Herron was detailed to patrol duty in Winnipeg, and again ordered to Swan River. While on the trail, the force received word its operations were to be inspected by militia general Edward Selby-Smythe.

General Smythe's entourage of officers and wagons was to travel the west to report on the progress of the NWMP and confer with American military officials on the Missouri River. Smythe ordered a special escort for the inspection tour, and Herron was among the troop. The strong escort alluded to rumours of trouble. Lawrence Clarke, an HBC factor, reported that the Metis at St. Laurent had set up an independent government, which upon investigation was found to be merely a local council with the famed hunter Gabriel Dumont at its head. Clarke's letters had blown the situation out of proportion. Smythe was given a warm welcome, but Dumont was warned not to attempt further regional control. In 10 years' time, however, Metis self-government would again become an issue.

The tour continued to Edmonton and south to cross the Red Deer River, meeting a troop headed by Assistant Commissioner James F. Macleod and Inspector Ephrem Brisebois, who had been ordered north in the event of trouble at St. Laurent. En route, Brisebois' F Troop ran into terrible difficulty fording the Bow River and had to float their wagons across the reach. Brisebois was ordered to return south to establish a new police fort at the site of the perilous crossing.

The Smythe party continued on to meet Crowfoot at Blackfoot Crossing, inspect Fort Macleod and travel to Fort Shaw in Montana to confer with US Army commander Colonel John Gibbon. Then it was back to Fort Macleod to outfit a pack train to climb the South Kootenay Pass into British Columbia. At Wild Horse Creek, Smythe released the police escorts, save for Herron, and turned into Washington Territory, bound for Fort Walla Walla. There Smythe addressed his police escort: "Herron, I don't think we'll need your services any longer. I am going to take the boat [to the Pacific], and as it is too late [in the year] for you to return by the [Kootenay] Pass, I'll give you your pay."[16] Herron was given $300 in gold for wages and return expenses. Smythe may have had Herron in mind when he penned, "Too much value cannot [be] attached to the [NWMP]; too much attention cannot be paid to their efficiency."[17]

Herron boarded a stagecoach for a 700-mile trip to Kelton, Utah, then on the Southern Pacific Railroad to Salt Lake City, where he purchased two horses for a dangerous, solo return to the Bow River. That he came back at all says something about his character. Mounties didn't make a lot of money; a pocketful of gold and free reign in wild boomtowns filled with deserters from Her Majesty's service would have been a sore temptation for anyone. Herron said that when Smythe "...gave me $300 in gold pieces...I thought I would never see a poor day again."[18] But Herron returned with the gold and all receipts accounted for, leading to his moniker of "Honest John."

Herron arrived at the Bow River post around Christmas, in time to witness the fall from grace of the detachment's founding officer Ephrem Brisebois. When Brisebois had ordered his men to build cabins for Metis interpreters, three of them refused, and Brisebois had them arrested for insubordination. The rest of the post mutinied, refused to carry out the order and drew up a list of charges against their commander. The incident attracted the attention of his superiors, and he tendered his resignation. To add insult to injury, Brisebois' previous orders to name the post after himself were rescinded, and the fort was renamed Calgary, after Macleod's ancestral home in Scotland.

In the spring of 1876 a message was received that a young Blackfoot named Nataya had killed another Blackfoot near the fork of the Red Deer and South Saskatchewan rivers. A patrol, under Sub-Inspector Cecil Denny and Herron, now a sergeant, was sent to apprehend the suspect. Several days out, they spotted a group of Blackfoot riders, 100 strong, bearing down on them. Nataya was believed to be among them. As the riders neared, Denny ordered his men to dismount, arm their carbines and stand in a skirmish line six paces apart. As the ponies approached, half of the band broke free and charged forward. Herron remembered, "I never realized a horse could come so fast."[19] About 100 yards from the line, the charge halted, and one of the mounted riders extended his hand in peace.

Denny and Herron held council with the chiefs, and Nataya was surrendered, but the council had news of a graver threat from south of the border. The US Army was moving against the Sioux, who had been ordered by the Grant administration to report to their agencies. Those who did not comply were considered hostile, and punitive expeditions had been dispatched. Herron's patrol was told Sitting Bull had contacted the Blackfoot chief Crowfoot and asked him to join their alliance to destroy the Long Knives. The policemen's hairs rose on their necks upon hearing that Sitting Bull had offered Crowfoot a deal. If the

Blackfoot assisted in destroying the Army, the alliance would turn north and wipe out the redcoats, but Crowfoot had rebuffed the Sioux and affirmed his friendship with the police. Still, when the Mounties left with their prisoner, they covered the first 50 miles at full gallop—lest someone change his mind. On the basis of Denny's report, the NWMP strengthened communications with the US Army, and later that spring they learned the news of the Battle of the Little Bighorn.

John Herron was discharged from the force in May of 1878 and bought into the Ottawa grocery store with Tom Bates. He also married Ida Lake, a tiny woman of barely a hundred pounds but with a determined spirit. After befriending John Stewart in the Dragoon Guards, Herron longed for the west. When his commanding officer came looking for an investment, Herron followed other of his redcoat comrades; in 1881 he returned to the buffalo grounds he'd ridden across to turn them into cattle range.

In time, Stewart, Campbell and Herron left the Guards and, by design, reunited in the Rocky Mountain foothills. The land they would find their fortune in was named by their charge, Lord Lorne, in honour of their unit's patron. On his widely acclaimed vice-regal visit to the prairies in 1881, Lorne wrote a poem to the land he fell in love with, christening it with one of Louise's given names:

In token of the love thou hast shown,
For this wide land of freedom, I have named
A province vast, and for its beauty famed,
By thy dear name to be hereafter known,
Alberta shall it be!

And Alberta it was. The verse received wide distribution, and the name was applied to an organized district of the North-West Territories in 1882. For Lorne's tour, the Mounted Police required the purchase and delivery of more than 100 horses to various forts, and John Herron accepted the contract. Lorne's tour romanticized the west. As representative of the Queen, his office was taken very seriously, and his activities followed with great fanfare. His statement, "If I were not the Governor General of Canada, I would be a cattle rancher in Alberta,"[20] became a symbolic flashpoint in the development of the cattle industry.

While Lorne didn't drop the Great Seal of Canada to pick up a stock saddle, his remark piqued the curiosity of venture capitalists throughout the Empire. Those so inspired reached for their chequebooks, made the penny-per-acre application and headed west. A good example of the British and Canadian ranch capital involved as a direct consequence of the Lorne influence could be found in a college class in Guelph, Ontario. The marquis' aide-de-camp, Colonel Francis De Winton, determined to get in on the grazing boom, enrolled his son Frederick in a three-month livestock course at the Royal Agricultural College. Fred's class was full of bright-eyed, would-be land barons who had eagerly lapped up Lorne's romanticism—among them, future Rocky Mountain Rangers like Prince Edward Islander Fred Ings and a pair of plucky Irish aristocrat brothers.

Henry and Richard Boyle were the sons of Henry Bentinck Boyle of Cork, fifth Earl of Shannon, with a long pedigree steeped in the English gentry. The London-born sons, Richard (1860), and Henry (1862), were both educated at Eton and at Royal Military College at Sandhurst to become junior officers. Richard served two years as a lieutenant in the Royal Fusiliers, and Henry served in the Yorkshire Regiment. As the heir to the earldom, Richard Boyle carried the title of Viscount, or "Lord." The use of titles was as far as affectations went with the Boyles. Completing the Guelph course, the Boyles formed a quartet with Ings and De Winton, and travelled together to their respective ranching adventures. They rode the rails until the developing CPR ran out of track and then pooled their cash to purchase horses and a Conestoga wagon. The party split up at Medicine Hat, Ings going to the Nanton area to found the Midway Ranche, while De Winton and the Boyles concentrated on Pincher Creek to set up the Alberta Ranche Company syndicate. Investors included Richard Duthie, Lord Lorne's canoe man, who became the ranch manager. The syndicate bought land from Mose La Grandeur for a base and took out combined leases of some 50,000 acres in the name of the company and partners. They also operated the Brecon sheep farm near Calgary.

Like the Boyle boys, John Stewart wasted no time in relocating to Lorne's "wide land of freedom." The financial prospects were enough for the former Dragoon Guard to parlay his family fortune into ranching. Stewart sought partners in the venture as much for knowledge as for depth of pockets. John Herron was a seasoned veteran of the Canadian west, when few such men existed. Stewart persuaded him to stay in the west and show him the ropes. With contacts in the NWMP, Herron knew of a failing police project, where a canny investor could pick up the pieces and build the base of a working stock farm. That turned Stewart's attention to the burgeoning town of Pincher Creek to negotiate the purchase of the NWMP Remount Station.

The Remount farm was founded as a breeding program to produce sturdier horses for the force. A lack of conditioned, in-country-bred mounts had been a factor in the force's near demise on their 1874 March West. In 1878 a police post and a farm were founded to care for horses not in use and also grow enough hay and oats to nourish mounts at other outposts. The lush green foothills alongside the mountain creek were an ideal location, and constables Charles Kettles (see Appendix), William Reid, Jack Johnson and Peter McEwen (see Appendix) were sent up into the foothills to cut timber for building construction.

To stock the Remount Station, more than 200 head of horses were driven from Fort Macleod by a detail commanded by Inspector Ephrem Brisebois and staffed by Sergeant William

Parker and constables James Bruneau and Alfred Hardwick Lynch-Staunton (see Appendix). Lynch-Staunton related details of the horse drive and the farm's operation:

> From 1874 to '78, the people, consisting of Indians and a few traders, became fully aware of the law in the form of the Mounted Police. Orders were issued at Fort Macleod to establish a police farm and detachment on Pincher Creek. With no idea how it was to be done, eight of us set out from Macleod and this trip was not as it is now. There were no roads, no fences, no bridges, and only one ranch, at the mouth of the Pincher Creek...All around us stretched the prairie, a sea of grass reaching to our stirrups. Ahead wandered our 200 head of horses and behind came the wagons and implements. The whole country swarmed with duck, [prairie] chicken, antelope and deer. The nearest railroad was the [Grand Trunk Railway] ending at Sarnia, Ont. and the Union Pacific in the U.S. It was not till we crossed Freeze-out Flat and Ridge, that we saw the land of our endeavors.
>
> It was not called Freeze-out then. Some years after, Dave Grier, a gentleman named Scotty, and myself had a supply of hay on the flat for the Police in Macleod. I was in Macleod getting supplies when a bad storm came up. I managed to make the shack before I found Scotty and Grier almost frozen. We had to stay the night but the next morning we left for Pincher Creek with the Christmas supplies for the police—groceries and a cheering liquid not subject to frost. Before we left, we tacked a board, with 'Freeze-out' written on it, to the door of the shack, thus it was named.
>
> Pulling into Pincher Creek in the year 1878, we turned the horse herd out to graze on the flat below what is now the town and we proceeded to build the barracks which was a fine structure in those days—a log shack with a sod roof and a dirt floor being the accepted habitation. Our work was to police

the country from the boundary line to the Porcupine Hills and west to the Rockies, to raise horses for the Force and to keep our buttons shined.[21]

The horses were turned out to graze, and the policemen constructed the barracks and outbuildings. Living conditions were typical: the roof leaked, and the food consisted of sowbelly pork and dried apples. Liquid refreshment was in ample quantity, according to Lynch-Staunton. The local settlers were adept at making bootleg whisky—an interesting admission in light of the fact that the police were mandated to enforce alcohol prohibition.

The Remount Station provided the basis for the founding of the town, as did other settlers like James R. Scott (see Appendix), Albert Milton Morden (see Appendix), Maxie Brouillette and Charley and Marie Rose Smith (see Appendix). The land warrants issued to some of the founding Mounties after discharge—Lynch-Staunton, Kettles and Bruneau—led to careers as novice ranchers and roles as cornerstones of the community. Lynch-Staunton purchased 20 cows from former police commanders Alf Shurtliff and William Winder. In the absence of a railroad or local market, he hauled fresh milk and beef to the police and the townsmen at Fort Macleod. Other policemen followed suit into the cattle grazing business, including George Canning Ives, James H. Schofield (see Appendix), Samuel James Sharpe (see Appendix), John Henry Gresham Bray (see Appendix) and even the retired commissioner James Macleod.

Operating the Remount Station was problematic. Though fine herds grew, day-to-day maintenance took too much time and manpower away from the primary function of an undermanned force. The range was unfenced, and supervising the herd was only part of regular duties. Rustling could not be controlled, and horses disappeared into the reserves or were stampeded across the border to be sold off-market. In 1881 the force got out of the farming business and purchased feed and mounts from private ranchers. That provided the opportunity John Stewart was seeking to buy an established farm—a rare find for the time and place.

Stewart purchased the farm from the government and appointed colleague John Herron as manager of the Stewart Ranche Cattle Company. The station was the base of the spread, where Stewart built the ranch house he called "the Bungalow" and leased 23,000 acres from the Dominion government. In an open range environment, common grazing allowed for another possible 50,000 acres to feed Stewart's horses and cattle. To stock the range, Herron arranged for the delivery of 3,000 head of cattle, trailed in from Utah. In 1882, Herron moved Ida and their two-and-a-half-year-old daughter Georgina from Ottawa. They took up residence in a one-roomed log cabin, half a mile southeast of Pincher Creek.

Herron possessed a tenacious personality, and that tenacity came out in his prowess in the wrestling ring. A match widely advertised for the 1884 Dominion Day celebration in Macleod brought fight fans to witness the spectacle of Honest John taking on a fighter far superior in height and weight. Herron was proficient and his neighbours knew it, but the challenger was massive. Wagering was heavy; the gamblers took one look at Herron's small frame and laid their money down accordingly.

As the favourite and Herron, the long shot, stripped to the waist and stepped into the ring, a tall, lanky American stranger jumped onto the platform. Waving a considerable roll of money, the Yank announced his cash was to be placed on "the little fellow." The mysterious American with the bankroll turned out to be George Lane, a stockman on his way to High River to take over as foreman of the North West Cattle Company. He would soon own that spread as the Bar U, and Lane would be one of the most prosperous cattlemen in North America. At the end of the bout, long faces drooped. Herron was declared wrestling champion of the North-West Territories, but would retire undefeated when his toughest opponent intervened. The diminutive Ida Herron objected to his sporting activity, demanding the end of his fighting career. Devoted husband that he was, Herron complied.

Part of Stewart's rationale was to sell horses, beef and feed to the NWMP, thereby privatizing the original purpose of the Remount Station. Sales were phenomenal. Out of 107 remounts purchased in 1884, the Stewart Ranche sold 49 horses, far above the ratio of other ranches that supplied in single digits. John Herron devoted time to importing stallions and breeding Clydesdale workhorses. His acumen was proved when he trailed 1,000 horses from Idaho, herded them into the Crowsnest Pass to winter graze and accounted for every single head in the spring.

With inroads into government, Stewart also fulfilled beef contracts to the nearby First Nations reserves. Stewart held the Blood and Peigan in very high regard and often expressed a deep sympathy for their mistreatment. To fulfill these contracts and obtain fresh stock from the United States, Stewart partnered with Montana cattleman Robert Ford. Two hundred miles to the south, Ford was one of the American territory's first ranchers, building up an operation on the Sun River two decades before the Canadian industry had.

As early cattlemen found, the challenge of southern Alberta was the lack of a market. The industry was one of subsistence, depending on sparse in-country population to consume its wares. A railroad to ship cattle to population centres was but a future promise in 1881. In addition, Stewart could not depend on government connections for long-term success, so to manage his fresh meat outlet, he enlisted the help of another Dragoon Guards comrade.

In 1882, Duncan Campbell moved to Fort Qu'Appelle but soon was urged by Stewart to come to Macleod. He managed the contracting firm and butcher shop of Ford & Stewart, which was responsible for fulfilling meat contracts with the NWMP and the Peigan and Blood reserves. More interested in civil service, Campbell stayed with the firm only 15 months. In 1883 he was appointed postmaster for Macleod and accepted the office of deputy sheriff to the Supreme Court of the North-West Territories.

Another of Stewart's many partners was James Christie, a former employee of the HBC and possibly a relative of William Christie, the long-time factor of Fort Edmonton. He was also a canny cattle and horse dealer. When the NWMP arrived, Christie had left Edmonton to trade in cattle. He also operated a small dairy near Fort Calgary, supplying fresh milk and butter to the police outpost. In 1876 Christie had driven a herd of horses in from Montana and sold them to the NWMP, who were so desperate for good mounts, they paid him $100 per head, an exorbitant price at the time. This was the horseflesh sense that Stewart was looking for when he brought Christie into his operation. When the Stewart Ranche went into business, the livestock bore the brand SC—for the partners' initials—and the spread was often popularly referred to as the Stewart & Christie.

The day-to-day activity at the Stewart was the same as at any other ranch: breaking horses, putting up hay, riding the range and doing roundups. Among the hired hands were future RMR recruits like James Routledge and James Schofield. Jim Christie set up a racetrack, a staple for the aristocratic ranching elite. In early ranching endeavours, it was customary for operations to be visited by friends, relatives and investors. The guests were impressed by the horse stables and extensive number of buildings, much of them remnants of the police farm. Among the visiting entrepreneurs was Captain Stewart's brother, Macleod Stewart, mayor of Ottawa.

A major financier was one of the world's most powerful banks: the Baring Bank of London. One Baring family member visited the Stewart Ranche. When Herron arranged a tour to Cameron

Creek, Baring, an amateur geologist, observed that the formations on the side of the mountain might yield mineral wealth. In time that prophecy was fulfilled; the site became the location of Alberta's first oil well. Other guests were inspired enough by the majesty of the foothills to begin their own operations.

Stewart's business interests did not end at the farm gate. With Duncan Campbell, he set up stagecoach routes between Macleod, Calgary and Pincher Creek. They soon obtained the Royal Mail contract for these routes, a small task given Stewart's government contacts and Campbell's position as postmaster. Stewart shared the Macleod–Calgary mail contract with James Scott and George Kidd Leeson, who operated express lines throughout the territory. Drivers of the four- and six-horse teams pulling the Concord coaches included Maxie Brouillette, whose wife, "Mother" Brouillette, also took the reins when Maxie was indisposed. Stewart also speculated on land in Calgary and in mining ventures.

Such diverse partnerships, associations and interests were reflective of the 19th-century way of doing business: taking risks on experienced people, offering share capital and using every contact. As his father had pioneered the Bytown lumber trade, John Stewart employed the techniques of venture capitalism in the frontier of the Rocky Mountains, but big business was about to clash with a way of life as old as time itself.

With traditional ways of life eroding, the prairie First Nations bargained with the government. The rights to hunting grounds were exchanged for reserves of land, annuities of food, money and cattle, along with the promise of assistance with education, farming instruction and health benefits. Treaty 7 was meant to ease the pain of the disappearing buffalo herds for the plains people, but they were no longer alone. Ranches, mines, railroads, surveyors and towns brought change to the stark landscape more shocking than anything they or their ancestors had ever experienced. In coming years, the First Nations would be disappointed by increasing government control of their lives. As prairie bands weighed their options, the Metis to the northeast also faced encroachment. Their leaders drew comparisons to the Red River revolt and the tragic violence that resulted. The big question: would it happen again?

CHAPTER SIX

Propaganda and Paranoia

In 1884, Ida Lake Herron, the wife of Stewart Ranche foreman John Herron, was an unwitting early witness to the sort of fear that the entire west would experience within a year. On a hot July day, pregnant with Katie, her second daughter, Ida was home alone with three-year-old Georgina. Working in the kitchen of their cabin south of Pincher Creek, Ida looked up to see an armed warrior, decked out in war paint, standing in the doorway. The visitor made signs that he wanted something to eat. Ida patiently fed the man, and he left as quietly as he had arrived, without a hint of harm to Ida and her child.

Ida was in no danger, but as a girl growing up in eastern Canada, she would have been subject to tales of the Great Lakes wars and weaned on the writings of James Fenimore Cooper and the concept of the Native as "savage." Nevertheless, Ida did everything right: she didn't panic, scream or flee. She was learning about her new neighbours and showed the hospitality she would offer any traveller. Still, in a time of classism, her grace was guarded. In the retelling, incidents like this gained drama and contributed to white settlers' paranoia.

Throughout history, word of an outbreak of armed conflict has prompted deep psychological shock. Oceans away from the events, dour radio voices told the home front of Hitler's invasion of Poland and the Japanese attack on Pearl Harbor. At once the collective soul of a nation was terrorized, angered and moved to react. More recently, Canadian Forces dealt with the FLQ kidnappings, the Oka-Mohawk Crisis in Quebec, the Gulf War, the Balkan conflict and the mission in Afghanistan—all brought to our living rooms through television. The ultimate dread was punctuated with the destruction of the World Trade Center in New York, right in our collective, virtual living room. An entire planet witnessed mass slaughter and further horrors in the subsequent "war on terror."

Transplant those war nerves back to 1885, a time with little or no communication with the governing authority. The conflict was not a few thousand miles away across the ocean, but a few hundred miles down the river. The inherent threat was not some foreign power, but the neighbour across the creek. Added to this mix was a changing landscape, a clash of cultures, an evident and official prejudice, remoteness of living, starvation, boredom and a generous helping of gunpowder. The recipe for general panic was complete.

During the early part of 1885, Charley Smith left his Jughandle Ranche to make a little cash by trapping timber wolves. His hunting party was plagued through the expedition by bad, wintry weather. While waiting out a blizzard, the party holed up in a shack near Big Valley Creek. To amuse themselves, the boys engaged in a poker game. Charley caught an opponent holding a large number of aces and demanded the return of the cheat's ill-gotten gains. The gambler took exception and thrust a hunting knife into Charley's shoulder. The assailant was kicked out of the camp, but Charley's shoulder was partially crippled for the rest of his life.

More pertinent to the story, Charley's party lost some of their horses to two Sarcee during the storm. They tracked and fired on the thieves. Rather than initiate their own massacre by going after the horses—as Charley's friend, Ad MacPherson, wanted—

Charley recommended a retreat to Edmonton. When the snow thawed, the wolfers returned to the shack to retrieve the dead animals they had cached beneath the snowbanks.

Reaching the shacks, they were again surprised by the Sarcee party, who had found, skinned and taken possession of the wolves. Led by Bull's Head, the Sarcee burst into the shack, guns in hand. Charley Smith had had the foresight to bring several cans of plug tobacco, which he offered in peace. The pelts were surrendered back to the trappers without further incident. While this may have just been a minor fracas over hunting turf, the timing is important. When Charley got home, his neighbours would tell him of a few more examples of such scuffles, examples of the restlessness that would soon threaten the peace.

Indeed, as 1885 wore on, rumours and innuendo escalated the issues from political squabble to military threat. The NWMP increased their strength to 550 men, of which Superintendent Lief Crozier commanded 200, concentrated in the Battleford, Fort Carlton and Prince Albert regions. On March 18, Commissioner Acheson Irvine pulled together 90 reinforcements from southern postings and marched out of Regina, bound for Prince Albert.

By March, Riel was resigned that the government intended to settle only with force. As he had at Red River, Riel declared a provisional government, and with frontiersman Gabriel Dumont as his adjutant-general, prepared his people for war. As expected, the federal government refused to recognize Riel's government, accepting the declaration as an act of war. Soon, militia forces were moved west from Ontario on the almost completed Canadian Pacific Railway. Major-General Frederick Middleton was given command of all forces in the North-West Territories and ordered to Fort Qu'Appelle to set up a headquarters for assault.

On March 26, the situation finally came to a head. The previous week, Riel had ordered the police to abandon Forts Carlton and Battleford. Crozier would not be cowed. He decided to settle the matter personally and had challenged Riel and Dumont on their own turf. He had assembled a brigade of 52 policemen and 43 armed volunteers from the Prince Albert community and marched them down the trail to Hillyard Mitchell's trading store at Duck Lake.

A mile and a half from the store, Crozier saw men moving on the ridges around his troop and realized he was surrounded and outgunned. Barricading behind sleds, the police and volunteers readied for battle while Superintendent Crozier and a scout, "Gentleman" Joe McKay, rode into an open field to meet with Isadore Dumont (Gabriel's brother) and Assiyiwin, from the nearby Beardy reserve. During the conversation, Assiyiwin grabbed McKay's rifle and, whether on purpose or accidentally, the gun discharged into Assiyiwin's stomach.

From there, Crozier and McKay beat a hasty retreat as all hell broke loose across the field. The ensuing battle took over half an hour, with the police and volunteers taking the heaviest casualties. Wounded, Crozier ordered a retreat to Carlton. Only the grace of Louis Riel, brandishing a crucifix to order a ceasefire, allowed Crozier to escape unmolested. Overwhelmed by superior numbers, the police–volunteer team suffered 12 men dead and 11 wounded. The Metis lost 5 men, including Isadore Dumont.

By March 24, Irvine had reached Prince Albert and the next day pushed on to Fort Carlton, ignorant of the Duck Lake battle. Upon reaching Carlton on March 26, Irvine found his column was a day late to be of any use to the situation. Carlton was indefensible, situated at the bottom of a sharp hill, its compound exposed to the top, and the high ground all around covered in thick brush. The location was a sniper's dream, and the Metis had many a skilled rifleman among their numbers. Irvine ordered the fort abandoned and a retreat to Prince Albert. In the midst of the evacuation, the fort was set afire accidentally, and no efforts were made to put the blaze out. The force, with Crozier's dead and wounded loaded onto sleighs, made their way to Prince Albert.

News of the first conflict spread quickly and told of a resounding Metis victory. At Blackfoot Crossing, Crowfoot received reports of the clash from Riel's messengers, keeping tribal leaders up to date on the events taking place. Often this unique system of message runners brought word to encampments faster than telegraph wires could flash bulletins to white settlements. In less than 24 hours, both the people of Calgary and the Blackfoot reserve knew the outcome of the first battle of the Northwest Rebellion. No one knew what might happen in the coming weeks, but most were aware that a peaceful dynamic had changed.

When Louis Riel sought allies for his coalition, he could not help but consider the charismatic and respected Plains Cree chieftain Poundmaker. The son of a Stoney father and a Metis mother, and raised a Plains Cree, Poundmaker (*Pito-kanow-apiwin*) was a natural bridge between many of the Aboriginal bands. Riel also understood Poundmaker's unique bond with the Blackfoot chief. In the years of inter-tribal wars, Crowfoot had lost a son in battle. After the truce between the rivals, Crowfoot met the young Poundmaker near the Battle River and was struck by the resemblance to his dead son. Crowfoot came to be extremely fond of Poundmaker and took him in as his own. Poundmaker returned with his new family and lived for many years as a Blackfoot and was given the name Wolf Thin Legs (*Makoyi-koh-win*). Over time, Poundmaker returned to the Cree but always remained in contact with his adopted father.

Although neither a hereditary nor a war chief, by 1876 Poundmaker's charm, eloquence and leadership were recognized as desirable qualities in a tribal hierarchy that was growing political in scope. His people were among the throngs following the buffalo herds into Montana, where he became acquainted with Louis Riel. In 1879 his bands accepted a reserve under his name at the junction of the Battle River and Cut Knife Creek, east of Battleford. The relationship between Crowfoot and Poundmaker was common knowledge among those in the world of prairie diplomacy and not lost on Riel, who sought to use their father–son bond to his advantage.

After the Thirst Dance incident, Poundmaker gained influence among the various small reserves around Battleford, and young warriors took to his authority. He initially rejected the overtures of Riel, but after the Metis victory at Duck Lake, the war councils of minor chiefs considered new options. Over time, a growing number of Cree, Stoney and Metis gathered into Poundmaker's camp at Cut Knife Creek, spawning a movement that threatened to swell into a fighting force.

No warrior, Poundmaker tried to cap the ferment, but on March 31 farming instructor James Payne and farmer Bernard Tremont were killed in separate incidents. Those murders, along with the looting of several Indian department houses, sent the townsmen and farmers of Battleford and area fleeing to the safety of Fort Battleford, the NWMP barracks. To bring some sanity to the situation, Poundmaker went into Battleford to speak to the Indian agent, James Rae. Poundmaker waited patiently at the agency office, but the startled Rae would not leave the safety of the fort to see him. Unfortunately, warriors had followed Poundmaker into town, and he was unable to restrain the hungry, anxious young men as they looted Battleford and set several buildings afire.

As the days went on, white settlers in the area were taken prisoner and cattle were stolen. Poundmaker used the little power he had to dissuade his people from riding to Batoche to reinforce Dumont's troops. The messengers of Riel tugged at Poundmaker's ties to Crowfoot and told wild stories of Blackfoot attacks in the south—even that the US Army was riding to the relief of Batoche. Poundmaker wasn't buying any of it. The news was even more troublesome from the settlement of Frog Lake. The village consisted of a Catholic church, log dwellings, NWMP outpost, HBC store and a central Indian agency for several reserves on the North Saskatchewan. The leader of the

Cree tribes in the area, Big Bear, had always been keenly suspicious of the motives of the police and the Hudson's Bay traders in relation to the Indian department. He'd grudgingly signed Treaty 6 but refused to accept his reserve, putting the legality of the agreement in question. His band camped near Frog Lake in anticipation of accepting land, but remained at odds with the Indian department agent, Thomas Trueman Quinn.

Quinn and Big Bear were known to have quarreled often, Quinn withholding rations unless the Cree leader accepted his reserve. Back in October 1884, the annual treaty payment ceremonies at Frog Lake had very nearly led to war when Quinn refused Big Bear's demands for fresh beef. A war dance, firing of weapons, and spoken threats ensued. Quinn finally acceded in part and provided a steer for the ceremony. Big Bear agreed to accept his treaty payments, and violence was temporarily postponed.

Quinn had jurisdiction over the NWMP, and now, fearful that a police presence would aggravate Big Bear, he ordered the NWMP detachment commanded by Inspector Francis Dickens moved to the HBC post of Fort Pitt. The trouble between Big Bear and Quinn was finally tested when Riel's messengers came knocking and got an audience with unpredictable minor leaders Wandering Spirit and Big Bear's own son, Imasees. The rumour was repeated that Riel's provisional government had support from the US military. On April 1, 1885, Frog Lake heard of the Battleford raids, but Big Bear was away from his camp hunting and unable to keep Wandering Spirit and Imasees from initiating the grisliest episode in the history of the rebellion.

On the evening of April 2, Wandering Spirit and two warriors entered the home of Thomas Quinn and pulled him from his bed. Weapons and horses were appropriated, and the HBC store was entered for the purposes of looting it; however, the store had been threatened some weeks earlier, and the canny trader William Cameron had transferred most of his inventory over to Fort Pitt.

Cameron and about 10 men were ordered to Quinn's office, where Wandering Spirit yelled at Quinn and let the agent know exactly who was in charge. He then had the men taken to the church, where the rest of the citizenry had assembled. Big Bear was there, trying to gain control of the situation. The villagers and several Metis were kneeling in prayer when Wandering Spirit broke in and ordered everyone out of the church and over to the Indian department buildings.

Before the night was over, Thomas Quinn was shot and killed by Imasees. Despite Big Bear's protests, nine others were also brutally shot and killed in the street. William Cameron and several others were spared their lives. Two white women, Teresa Gowanlock and Teresa Delaney, wives of slain men, were captured and dragged off to the Cree camps. Big Bear later apologized to the women for the warriors' actions, but Wandering Spirit and the others had taken a fateful course from which there was no return.

In southern Alberta, the whole of the Blackfoot Confederacy was in serious decline. Treaty 7 was to have been a means of survival as buffalo herds dwindled, but the transition seemed to bring only boredom, disease, death and discontent to the reserves. Despair made young men, who'd been born to the hunt and lived the way of the warrior, difficult to hold back. Red Crow heard the wild stories of the Duck Lake, Battleford and Frog Lake incidents. Some of the tales were related by police scout Joe Healy (the adopted Blood son of John Healy), a fluent speaker of English and privy to all of the news and rumours. Healy lost little time spreading the word. The confused Blood chief approached William Pocklington and demanded the truth.

While Red Crow had no sympathy with Cree or Metis complaints, there were no such guarantees with the younger men itching for a chance to relieve their boredom, establish their war skills and regain the glories that their elders had told them about. Red Crow was losing control, and the rebellion was in danger of snowballing. His reserve was within sight of the American border, where contacts might easily and willingly obtain ammunition.

On April 6, Pocklington and NWMP Superintendent John Cotton visited Red Crow and his council to inquire as to his intentions. The tribal leaders informed Cotton through interpreter Jerry Potts that they had received gifts of tobacco and messages from Riel and from the Cree councils. To entice Blood neutrality further, Pocklington opened the government's wallet and increased the band's flour rations. The Bloods refused the tobacco and sent the messengers away, indicating a refusal to join the insurrection. Red Crow even refused tobacco from Crowfoot so there could be no misunderstanding as to the Blood's position of neutrality. The smaller tribe of Eagle Tail's Peigan soon followed suit and proclaimed their neutrality. Both Blood and Peigan were traditional enemies of the Cree; without Red Crow's support, there was little chance of the Peigan joining the fray. One dissenter, Running Wolf, urged the Peigan to drop their plows in the fields and arm for battle. Nothing came of it, and the Peigans continued to work on their potato crop.

The Blood war chief, White Calf, used all his influence to cast off any notions of young warriors joining the Cree, and the Blood council even offered Pocklington their services in fighting on the side of the government. That offer of fresh troops was considered by many, including the *Macleod Gazette,* Lieutenant-Governor Edgar Dewdney and even Prime Minister Macdonald.

After Duck Lake, Crowfoot's loyalties were not as clear-cut. He continued to welcome Cree and Metis messengers into his camp, but always refused to smoke the tobacco given him. The agitators boasted of victories in the north and how easy it would be to rid the prairies of the white menace, warning that if the Blackfoot refused to assist, they would be considered the enemy and would be attacked after the militia was dealt with.

Early in April rumours of a Blackfoot attack reached Calgary from a panic-stricken telegrapher at Langdon station. Father Albert Lacombe, accompanied by NWMP scout Billy Gladstone as interpreter, was summoned to approach Crowfoot and convince him to choose peace. On April 16, Crowfoot met with Lieutenant-Governor Edgar Dewdney and Father Lacombe at the Cluny railroad station, just a few miles from the Crossing. For the first time since Duck Lake, a government authority had come to council. Dewdney was diplomatic, promised to deliver more rations and offered to provide military protection for Crowfoot's people, should they face Cree reprisals. Crowfoot accepted these measures, and although he still had grievances, diplomatically chose not to bring them up. He offered to provide his own warriors for defence of the region against marauding war parties, as the Bloods had done earlier. Dewdney resisted temptations to offer these fresh troops to the militia, unwilling to reignite the traditional inter-tribal warfare.

At the meeting's end, Crowfoot dictated a message pledging to reject involvement with Riel and the Cree. Messengers were sent to other tribes with offerings of tobacco, urging them to remain neutral and solidify the Blackfoot Confederacy. The note was circulated by telegram to Prime Minister Macdonald, Governor General Lansdowne and Queen Victoria. The message was rambling, with references praising Dewdney and remarks that made the chief's people seem blindly obedient. There is no way to know how much of it was Crowfoot's actual words, but the tone was of trust:

> On behalf of myself and my people I wish to send through you to the Great Mother the words I have given to the Governor at a Council held at which all my minor chiefs and young men were present. We are agreed and determined to remain loyal to the Queen. Our young men will go to work on the reserve and will raise all the crops we can and we hope the Government will help us to sell what we can raise. Continued reports and

many lies are brought to us and we don't know what to believe, but now that we have seen the Governor and heard him speak, we will shut our ears and only listen to and believe what is told to us through the Governor. Should any Indians come to our reserve and ask us to join them in war, we will send them away. I have sent messengers to the Bloods and Peigans who belong to our treaty to tell them what we are doing and what we intend to do about the trouble. I want Mr. Dewdney to be with us and all my men are of the same mind. Words sent by Father Lacombe I answered: We will be loyal to the Queen whatever happens.[22]

The message sent Crowfoot into the history books as a model of diplomacy and oration. Few knew how torn Crowfoot was behind the scenes—fewer still knew that it was Red Crow who had tipped the scales in favour of maintaining neutrality. But Crowfoot's declaration was not a guarantee, just a bargaining chip to buy the government some time as the militia scrambled to catch up and get its war machine into gear. It was early in the insurgency and a big, big country. Around the corner was the unexpected; any new incident, any stupid move, any gun fired in anger, could yet change the game and destroy the tipsy balance of peace.

With Crowfoot's declaration of neutrality, southern Alberta had breathed a little easier, but defences could not be relaxed, and military organizations could not be disbanded. There were still reports of uncommitted bands in the Cypress Hills and Milk River Ridge country—the border region. On the unguarded Montana border, loyalties among those who had camped and interacted often with Big Bear's Cree were uncertain. Agents faithful to Riel on both sides of the border served to keep the pot stirred, and at Wood Mountain and Willow Bunch, Metis hunters-turned-ranchers had their loyalties tested.

The Assiniboine of Piapot in the Cypress Hills and northern Montana were also in question. In previous years they had been a source of concern for the NWMP. In 1879 the US Army built

Fort Assiniboine, a massive brick fortress on the Milk River at the mouth of Beaver Creek, in answer to the plethora of Native bands crossing the border during the buffalo hunts and the Sioux exile. With 680 men at arms, Fort Assiniboine was ready and able for any unpleasantness. After Duck Lake, Fort Assiniboine and other US Army posts along the line, including Fort Snelling in Minnesota and Fort Abraham Lincoln in Dakota Territory, were put on alert, and American cavalrymen patrolled the south side of the Medicine Line.

Misinformation and fear was evident in both Native and white communities. The Sioux wars were a recent memory, as was the so-called Blackfoot War of the late 1860s. Most knew of the overtures made by Riel, and all knew trouble was in the air when the revolutionary submitted his petition to the government. Governing authorities were positioning as well. Even before the battle of Duck Lake, General Middleton had been dispatched to the west in anticipation of armed revolt, and John Stewart had submitted a plan to the federal government for a militia to get a handle on the border frontier.

In Calgary and Fort Macleod, news of Duck Lake was received with both apprehension and fear. Few doubted the Cree would join the fray, but the intentions of the Blackfoot bands, their neighbours, were unknown. That question was answered by the Crowfoot telegram, at least for the government and the military, but the three-week interval between the battle and that fateful message was a period of trepidation and suspicion, owing to general disinformation and the adage that in war, the first casualty is truth.

Unofficial wildfire news delivery stoked rumours—lies that could cost unnecessary panic or even lives. There were tales of Sitting Bull caching 2,000 stolen rifles near the border for Riel's men to pick up and distribute, Sioux "seen" everywhere along the international border and CPR tracks being ripped up. The press listed a plethora of Fenian plots to aid Riel—

from poisoning the canned beef being fed to the troops, to mustering Irish volunteers in New York City to come to his aid. Riel supposedly had 10 artillery guns at his disposal; his Metis forces were said to number 10,000 when estimates of the day put the numbers at "no more than 250 or 300."[23] All of these stories were at once fantastic and chilling, but they made excellent broadsheet copy.

The crucial issue of just how many fighters could be put on the field was also subject to wild speculation. In addition, the combined Blackfoot, Blood, Peigan, Sarcee and Stoney force was rumoured to tally over 5,000 warriors. This was a gross misrepresentation, actually the total population of Blackfoot-speaking men, women and children. In truth, all three bands combined could probably not have mustered many more than 500 warriors. With the numbers incorrectly reported, fear among settlers became very real. As John R. Craig, manager of the Oxley Ranche noted, the cattle country was in the centre of the three most powerful tribes of the North-West Territories, and white settlers were said by Craig to have been outnumbered ten to one.

Fred Ings of the Midway Ranche related an incident that contributed to war nerves at the onset of the rebellion:

> I had ridden into Calgary one Sunday on a big gray horse I called White Eagle, and I found the town in a state of excitement. That morning, while a service was being held for a new little church lately built, quite a bunch of Sarcees in war paint rode up as far as the hill tops overlooking the town. Here they circled around, making considerable noise and letting out fierce war whoops. Someone saw them and rushed to the church, where nearly the whole populace was gathered, and shouted that the Indians were on them. The meeting broke up quickly and the people dispersed to arm themselves with what firearms they could find. The store was opened and the rifles and guns there were distributed among the men. There was talk of barricading

the women and children in the barracks. The Sarcees, quite pleased with the commotion they had caused, rode away without entering the town. It was only a scare, but it showed what could happen if the town was surprised by a band really on the warpath.[24]

In the face of isolation, uncertainty and such occurrences, the Alberta range needed martial mobilization, and among the cow country aristocracy a highly ranked British officer was available. General Thomas Bland Strange, a retired Royal Artillery officer, probably the best high-command material that could be mustered anywhere in Canada, came out of premature retirement. As a cattleman, Strange operated the Military Colonization Company Ranche bordering the Blackfoot reserve and knew he could be called to lead some form of column into action in this rebellion, perhaps on his own back door against uneasy Native neighbours. Reporting for duty via telegraph wire to Militia and Defence Minister Adolphe P. Caron, Strange accepted command of the Alberta Field Force (AFF).

The AFF was a military hodgepodge comprising regiments from Manitoba and Quebec, policemen, British ranchers, American cowboys and Metis scouts. In anticipation of war with the Blackfoot or cross-border raiders, Strange was to ensure the safety of the open range between the Rocky Mountains and the Cypress Hills. Organizing a plan to do so would fall to an important component of the AFF, a regiment organized by the newly promoted cavalry officer, Major John Stewart.

When his train pulled into Calgary on April 4, Stewart found the town in a ridiculous state of panic because of the Langdon telegrapher's messages. A scout was sent out, but nothing was found. The report was the result of an over-anxious imagination. That was fortunate, for Calgary was ill prepared for any kind of trouble. Among the civilians, Mayor John Murdoch and other town officials demonstrated a lack of leadership through displays of public drunkenness, and among the police, ammunition and weaponry were mismatched. On April 5, John Cottingham, a Calgary merchant, sent Minister Caron a lengthy telegram which described the Calgary situation:

> Much uneasiness is felt owing to scarcity of arms. I have with the utmost care examined everything I found in my moving about. In some cases I have found centre fire rifles that were borrowed during excitement loaded with rim fire cartridges and vice versa. Many of the merchants carry stock of mixed ammunition—which becomes badly mixed when issued to men as was the case at Calgary Sunday night. Chief Police Ingram of Calgary received a rim fire Revolver from [storekeepers] Rogers & Grant loaded with Centre fire cartridge. If required to use the same it would have been serious for him, besides arms were placed in the hands of men and boys unfit for the duty assigned them. I am ashamed to admit, nevertheless it is true that some of our leading citizens were much the worse for liquor, Sunday night, those whom we looked to for advise and had the Indian scare been real there would have been serious work done. I am familiar with the doings of the Mayor, Council and a few more of Calgary's drunken beauties; they glory in telling news given to them in confidence by Father Lacombe; in asking Comptroller White for power to barricade the barracks by building bastions and a thousand more foolish and unnecessary requests.[25]

Amidst the fear, one of Cottingham's "drunken beauties," Mayor John Murdoch, declared martial law on the town on April 13. The mayor also appointed retired NWMP officer and farmer James Walker to organize the Calgary Home Guard. On arrival from his ranch near Strathmore, General Strange imposed military authority on the Home Guard, even though his own Field Force existed in name only. Calls for volunteers went out to the area's ranches; Strange awaited raw recruits and for the promised eastern militias to arrive by train.

In the rural area beyond Calgary, homesteaders were not exactly in sympathy with the government line. At Fish Creek, south of Calgary, a settlers' meeting brought a thorough muddling of loyalties while laying bare some of the issues that had caused the entire conflict. As proven by the Prince Albert farmers, settlers had grievances with the government. All the makings for a range war between ranchers and settlers were in place, and at the head of the protest were two of the earliest pioneers.

The *Calgary Herald* of April 9 reported a meeting of 50 disgruntled farmers, chaired by Sam Livingston, at the residence of John Glenn. At the meeting, the settlers speculated that the problem lay with the government protecting all titles on land for purposes other than providing homesteads, in protection of Hudson's Bay and CPR railroad grants, treaty obligations and its friends in the ranching business. They had a point. There was no doubt that the ranching business reeked of political contacts with the ruling Conservatives; one only had to look at the number of politicians like Senator Matthew Cochrane, tycoons like Sir Hugh Allan, discharged Mounties and even professional soldiers like Tom Strange and John Stewart, whose operations benefited from cheap leased land.

For their part, Glenn and Livingston were hardscrabble veterans of a hard American frontier—gold rushers, hide hunters and traders, and determined survivors of many a backcountry battle. Both men, long-haired, brushy-bearded and buckskin-clad, were as tough as their looks. Both Livingston and Glenn allied with the farmers of Calgary against the Dominion Homestead Act administration. For his part, Livingston stated he'd not been able to receive a title on his land, even though he had been on it nine years and fulfilled all legal obligations. Glenn gave a similar story and an assurance that he would guard his claim with deadly force if needed.

Livingston and Glenn went on to relate personal accounts of how their livestock had been forcibly driven off lands claimed by the Cochrane Ranche. Stories were told of newcomers forced to leave because they couldn't find land that hadn't been pre-empted. Settlers threatened to abandoned their spreads and destroy all improvements in their wake. John Glenn threatened even worse: "I will be compelled to burn my place and if I do I will not leave many ranches behind me."

Sam Livingston concurred: "All must either fight for our rights or leave the country and if I am compelled to leave, I will leave marks on the trail behind me."[26]

The gathering organized the Alberta Settlers Rights Association and drafted a petition to Sir John A. Macdonald, embodying the spirit of the group and calling for all lease lands suitable for agricultural purposes to be thrown open for entry and settlement. The message ended with a resolution in support of the grievances of the Metis in the North-West Territories. The homesteader group was no scattered pack of loons: over 200 souls signed the petition. Now southern Alberta—ranchers in particular—faced new peril as homesteaders threatened to support the revolt.

John Stewart was not impressed with the prospect of a local sodbuster revolt. The *Winnipeg Times* reported his view: "The object was doubtless to embarrass the Government, but he was confident that the agitators would be defeated in their purposes."[27] Stewart was right; in spite of Livingston and Glenn's fearsome reputations, the Settlers Rights Association was a tactic to call attention to the issue.

Still, ranchers at the High River crossing met to discuss protection of their range. They discussed the need for construction of a fort to provide safety for white women and children in the area, but such a post never came about. An unnamed British veteran of the Sepoy Mutiny in India stood up bravely and bleated about "how he would deal with these Indians." A few days later, when a band of painted Sarcee came into town, Fred Ings declared that "this brave chap was found hiding down a well."

Ings also stated that at a few of these meetings the "squaw men" (a pejorative referring to frontiersmen with Native wives) were scared, because they knew how the Natives were thinking.[28]

High River organized a Home Guard, and Fred Stimson, the flamboyant manager of the North West Cattle Company (later the Bar U), armed his cowboys unofficially as "Stimson's Scouts." The Scouts included black cowboy John Ware, a former Carolina slave who rode the cow trails north and later became a successful rancher, and a young Prince Edward Islander, Dan Riley, destined to become a Senator.

The town of Macleod and area prepared for the worst. The original Fort Macleod, on an island in the Oldman River, was abandoned in 1882, and the new garrison was situated directly west of the modern town. With no surrounding stockade at the new barracks, defences were reinforced with smooth-wire fence erected around the perimeter. Wooden blockhouses, or bastions, were constructed at opposite corners of the post to provide safe defensive positions in the event of attack.

From the Cochrane Ranche, with its southern range near the Kootenay River, William Cochrane went to Macleod and came back with arms and ammunition for his cowboys. Cochrane had a personal dispute with Red Crow over the boundary of his lease with the Blood reserve, and a lot of his steers had disappeared.

On March 31, Oxley Ranche manager John Craig wired his superior, Alexander Stavely Hill, reporting news of the rebellion and its effects in the area. The Oxley was situated on the trail between Fort Macleod and Calgary and doubled as a stopping house where couriers and travellers changed horses. Craig later wrote of the fear aroused by the Duck Lake battle: "Although the scene of conflict and the general uprising was several hundred miles from us in the Macleod District, yet we were in great peril if the rebels succeeded in even one engagement."[29]

On Sunday, April 5, a rider, believing he was pursued by hostiles, rode into the ranch at full gallop. Excited, he exclaimed:

"Get your family away to Fort Macleod as soon as you can. The Blackfoot Indians have torn up the CPR track for miles. They are all on the warpath."[30] This was yet another classic example of how propaganda begat paranoia, spurred by the misunderstanding that any victory by Riel might send the tribes to arms.

No such destruction of railway property had occurred, but John Craig didn't know that and had no reason to doubt the dispatch rider. He feared for his family, but it was too late in the day to send them the fifty-odd miles into Macleod. Instead, Craig drove his wagon to a cow camp five miles from the main ranch house. The NWMP had left several Winchester rifles and ammunition with Craig, and he now distributed the weapons to the Oxley cowhands. The following day Craig drove his family onto Macleod. On the way there he noticed riders in the distance, heading toward them at a fast gallop. In his fear, he took them for warriors. The faster Craig whipped the team, the faster the threat rode. The riders changed their angle to intercept the Craig family's wagon. In anticipation of a showdown, Craig halted his team, grabbed his Marlin rifle and took aim, but before he could fire, one of his daughters, spying through a field glass, cried out: "Hold on, I think they are cowboys."[31] She was right. Three men rode up to the wagon and identified themselves as scouts for the NWMP. Like Craig, they were uniformed, and had intercepted the travellers just to get the latest news.

Continuing along the trail, the Craigs met the regular stage, one of John Stewart's coaches filled with police officers' wives evacuating from the Macleod barracks to Calgary. It was a bad sign that even the command lacked confidence in their post. The *Winnipeg Times* exclaimed, "There is no use disguising the fact any longer. Fort Macleod is a threatened point and an Indian uprising cannot any longer be prevented."[32]

At Macleod, Superintendent John Cotton met with Craig and debunked the story about the Blackfoot tearing up the CPR tracks. Then, considering his anxiety, spotty information and the inherent danger, John Craig did a very odd thing. He and his family left the relative safety of town and proceeded south to inspect the Oxley's operations on the Belly River near Standoff—in the heart of the Blood homeland. Arriving without incident, he found that even his own cowboys were gone; fearing an attack, they had abandoned the ranch buildings. After spending a night in the deserted house, Craig and his family forded the Belly the next day and carelessly drove through to the Indian agency, which was all but abandoned, with only a few Blood women and children remaining in camp. The Craigs swung north back toward Macleod, stopping at the house of the Anglican missionary, Reverend John Maclean, who was also gone. At Macleod, the police chastised Craig for his recklessness. John Craig had learned his lesson and moved his family into the barracks with most of the other ranch families, but his foolhardy tour did provide much needed information: the Blood warriors and elders were not at their camp.

When several days went by without any communication between the police and the Bloods, the townspeople, ranchers and Mounties drew some disturbing conclusions. There was enough paranoia to go around without repeating every tale on the grapevine. The apprehension was a cause and effect of the times. Despite the myth of the fairness of the NWMP, the 19th century was a time of tribalism and class separation on both ends of the human spectrum. Racism and prejudice were the norm, not the exception. That Canada was "civilizing" the west, in the colonial British fashion, imbued many a settler with a low opinion of the Native North American. The opinion of Anglo society was not much better. With the loss of the buffalo ground, encroachment of the ranches, the heartlessness of the Indian department and the impotence of the redcoats to help, a trust had been broken.

Even so, the *Macleod Gazette* absolutely denied that citizens were seeking safety in the fort, positing that any trouble was spotty and that local residents had long learned how to deal with living among free-roaming Natives. More than likely, Editor Charles E.D. Wood, a former policeman, censored the rumours to stem unnecessary alarm or give credence to wild, unsubstantiated stories. Ironically, the Bloods themselves had not been given any information. Red Crow, who could conceivably command greater numbers than the much-celebrated Crowfoot, approached his agent, William Pocklington, and demanded to know the truth about what was happening. The Cree messengers had been to his camp, telling of victories far up the river. He was skeptical, but without hard information, the same hysteria gripping the white settlers was within his own ranks. Many of the young warriors chafed to go into battle. Their elders were wary, fearing an extension of the warfare many had experienced in Montana.

PART TWO
THE ROCKY MOUNTAIN RANGERS

CHAPTER SEVEN

The Defence of Alberta

One of the reasons behind Sir John A. Macdonald's plan to fill the plains with widespread ranching was national security. His theory was that, if some calamity should arise, the government would have at its disposal ranches teeming with seasoned horsemen trained in arms and conditioned for long hours in the saddle. In other words, a virtual light horse cavalry could mobilize and defend the border region in a heartbeat. His theory was about to get the acid test.

As the Blackfoot threat around Calgary was mitigated, General Strange's brigade was in dire need elsewhere. Somewhere between Battleford and Frog Lake, the telegraph line had gone silent, isolating Edmonton in a region with questions of loyalty that were similar to those of Calgary. Strange was reassigned to march the Alberta Field Force north to the relief of Edmonton, and, once secured, move on to engage the Cree. The defence of southern Alberta was left to the avails and the command of John Stewart.

When hostilities broke out, Stewart was in Ottawa. Whether he was in the capital wintering with his family, or had rushed east for the express purpose of forming a militia unit, is unclear. At any rate, he was acutely aware of the threat—probably through telegraphic contact with someone in Calgary. With great fortune,

Stewart was at the heart of the organizational action, and with his impeccable connections, there were few political barriers.

Stewart was so sure of hostilities that the day before the Duck Lake debacle, March 25, he had filed a plan in the parliamentary office of federal minister of Militia & Defence Adolphe Caron. With the personal recommendation of Sir John A. Macdonald, Stewart requested authorization to form a volunteer mounted militia in the southern extremity of the District of Alberta. Macdonald made mention in his orders to General Middleton: "Captain John Stewart, formerly commanding the Militia Cavalry, and a dashing young fellow, is now a ranchman south of Calgary. He is here just now and is to proceed west where he will raise a corps of Western prairie men—cow-boys and others who can all ride and shoot. They will bring their horses equipments, all but rifles."[33]

With four years' experience in the west, Stewart convinced Caron of the need for an irregular cavalry comprised of men who could defend where they lived and worked. Since so many veterans of the NWMP or the military invested, lived or worked in the region, the unit would be staffed by qualified officers. Fresh volunteers would be required to supplement the NWMP at Fort Macleod to take the place of those leaving with Strange. The troop would have the task of guarding a 200-mile frontier between the Rocky Mountains and the Cypress Hills, protecting cattle herds from thieves and rustlers and keeping an eye out for American bands. Stewart set out conditions for the organization of the Rocky Mountain Rangers in a "carrying out report" submitted as follows:

I have the honour to submit the following Report as requested in private interview today with reference to the formation of a Mounted Force in the Southern District of Alberta, NWT. A Provisional Cavalry Force of the Strength of 150 Officers, Non-commissioned officers and Troopers can be formed in the

District named, having as its northern boundary, High River, its Eastern, Medicine Hat and to Southern the International Boundary Line, of the above strength upon the following basis:

1. Each officer, non-com. Officer and Trooper to supply his own horse and horse appointments (Mexican) consisting of Bridle, Lariat, Saddle and Saddle blanket.

2. The uniform of Officers to be that of an undress Cavalry Officer, supplied at their own expense. The uniform of non-coms and Troopers to consist of, during their provisional enlistment and whilst undergoing their preliminary Drill, of their own serviceable Western apparel, with perhaps some additional inexpensive distinctive equipment supplied by Government.

3. The arms to consist of 1 revolver Mounted Police pattern or any other serviceable Revolver in their possession. One Winchester carbine or other serviceable Carbine or Rifle in their possession. 1 cartridge belt with knife attached (MP pattern) (A limited deficiency in Arms to be supplied by Government, but the conditions of enlistment to require them furnished by the men.)

4. Blankets, 3 per man of NWMP weight and quality.

5. Each officer, non-com officer and Trooper, to be allowed 50¢ per diem for rations. (Camping utensils to be furnished by Government of the description and number required on the Trail.)

6. The forage per horse to be allowed at the rate of 50¢ per day.

7. The pay for horse to be at the rate of 75¢ per day.

8. Pay of Officers to be that of the respective rank of Canadian Cavalry officer with extra Ottawa allowance of 50¢ or:

9. The pay of non-com officers to be that of NWMP non-com officers, viz: – Sergeant-Major, $1.50 – Sergeant, $1.00 and – Corporal 90¢

10. The pay of a Trooper to be that of NWMP Constable, or

75¢ per day. (The total cost of a Trooper, horse, horse appointments, Arms, Equipment, Rations, forage and pay being $2.50 per man and horse per day with the proviso aforesaid that where Arms are totally deficient a draft will be allowed by Government.)

11. The Government to be responsible for loss or destruction of those appointments during Provisional Service, and for the loss by death or stray of horses when established by Board of Officers to have been accidental and not due to neglect or carelessness, validation to be arrived at by said Board of Officers.

12. Cavalry regulations to govern the Discipline and drill and the maintenance to be subject to the aforesaid conditions.

13. If Quartered under Canvas, the prescribed number of tents to be supplied.

14. The enlistment of Officers, Non-com. officers and men to be for a period of 30 or 60 days and during which time they will be subject to orders for Active Service for the period named, and additionally, subject to, and enlisted for if necessary, and received by Government for a further period of 9 months, with the proviso that in the event of Active Service during the additional enlistment, the government will furnish necessary uniforms, Arms and General Equipment for the "trail" with transportation.

15. The Officer in command to be permitted to enlist men of other than British Nationality (Western men of any class) to the extent of say 40, or one troop, provided he has knowledge of their capacity and faithfulness, and will be responsible for their Conduct and Discipline.

In recruiting the aforesaid Contingent it will be necessary to draw the men for Cavalry work and available for any emergency from Ranchers and their employees, a large number of whom are ex Mounted Police of 1 or 2 terms of service in the West together with Englishmen, Canadians & Montanans who have been living a nomadic life and whose home is in the prairie.

In tendering my services to my country and Government to command a force of the nature above described and within the said Territory, I do so with full knowledge of the undertaking and with no fear, [and show] successful results from my experiences in Cavalry work and of the country in which my duties will be required. [34]

Duck Lake rocked the capital, and Caron's office was besieged with activity as the telegraph and messengers rattled off a flurry of innumerable requests for supplies, armaments, arrangements, orders or authorizations. Caron's lobby bulged with favour seekers and contractors. Stewart's thoughtful, organized and detailed plan was a refreshing blast of professionalism, and Caron lost no time pencil whipping his blessing: "Authority is given to raise four (4) troops of Rocky Mountain Rangers on basis and conditions contained in report submitted by Captain Stewart to me."[35]

Shortly thereafter, Caron wired Middleton of his dispensation of forces via Lieutenant Colonel Charles Houghton, commander of the Manitoba Military District: "100 men 'A' Battery, 100 men 'B' Battery, 500 men Queen's Own & 10th Royals; 80 Toronto School under command Col. Otter. Total, 780 moving to front. Authorized Mounted Rangers under Capt. Stewart…Have telegraphed Strange to report himself to you at Qu'Appelle."[36] Of course, General Strange could not report to Middleton and was in the middle of organizing his own column.

On May 29, Stewart sent a telegram to his friend and partner in Macleod, Duncan Campbell. As telegraph lines were yet to reach Macleod, the message was wired to Calgary and expressed by Dominion Mail on Stewart's own stagecoach: "I authorize you to open enlistment roll immediately for mounted force of rangers. Any nationality accepted. Up to 100. Notify Garnet to enroll at Pincher Creek. The saddles arms & horses of men may be required as far as they go by government, & possibly required for active service. [Call on John Cotton] NWMP & approximate number [of] available armed & mounted any description & approximate number available unarmed & with out saddles. Notify Herron & others to have mounts available."[37]

Stewart's comment, "any nationality accepted," referred to the authority to enlist American citizens for Canadian militia service. Americans accounted for a large fraction of the regional population. Some were left over from the whisky and robe trade, some were range riders who remained after delivering cattle herds to southern Alberta, some were freighters working new homesteads. Stewart had a rich resource of homegrown talent that knew the prairie and knew how to ride and shoot. The "Garnet" referred to in the letter was probably one of the Garnett Brothers, a ranching family of Pincher Creek—though the Garnets do not appear on pay lists or rolls.

With Stewart's organization underway, Adolphe Caron reassured Calgary mayor John Murdoch—who had written the prime minister of the situation—that mobilization was in progress: "Your telegram was handed me by Sir John—Authority has been given to raise four troops in Alberta to Major-General Strange and Captain Stewart. I understand this will meet your wishes."[38] Major-General Frederick Middleton, awaiting his troops at Qu'Appelle station, was also informed: "Telegram about Boulton received—Think it is advisable for the present to enroll men furnishing their own horses and rifles. Strange on his way to Qu'Appelle, and Stewart, left tonight to organize four troops at Calgary. He says he can give you 50 mounted men in ten days."[39]

By March 30, John Stewart left Ottawa for Winnipeg on a westbound train of the Chicago, Minneapolis & St. Paul Railroad. Riding with him was James K. Oswald, a failed Montreal businessman who was able to wrangle a military commission as a captain in Steele's Scouts through the influence of his brother, Lieutenant Colonel W.R. Oswald, commander of the Montreal Garrison Artillery. Stewart also brought with him from Ottawa two well-experienced militia officers, Edward Gilpin Brown and William F. Powell, to assist.

Brown (see Appendix) was a British officer to the core, having served on general staffs in campaigns around the globe—Afghanistan, the first Boer uprising in South Africa and the abortive Nile Expedition to the Sudan in 1884. Awaiting application to the NWMP in Canada, Stewart co-opted Brown to add a little professionalism to his corps of irregulars.

Powell was a good friend of Stewart's, another of the Princess Louise Dragoon Guards and the son of Colonel Walker Powell, the Canadian militia's senior Canadian-born officer and adjutant-general. Having Powell in his rolls gave Stewart an edge in getting the attention of the Militia & Defence Department. Stewart used his connections; Powell's name on a message or a telegram got prompt attention. That allowed Stewart to make the most of his train passage west, and through telegraphic contact at whistle stops, he set forth his arrangements en route. From Toronto, Stewart wired Colonel Powell to implore the need for 150 NWMP pattern revolvers.

Layovers to change trains gave Stewart an opportunity to go shopping to equip the mounts of his new cavalry. At the Chicago merchant firm of Ortmeyer & Son, 60 Mexican-style saddles were ordered, at $25 each; bridles and halters at $3 each; and 5 dozen Mexican-style spurs. With no time to waste, he had the tack expressed to Winnipeg. That Stewart ordered this gear, when his own general orders specified volunteers were to provide their own horse and tack, indicates Stewart had some doubt as to how many troopers could make that commitment.

Stewart had time for some second thoughts and feared that he may find himself holding the financial bag for new saddles for an entire regiment. At his next stop, he made another trip to the telegrapher to confirm his expenditures with Militia & Defence. His telegram indicates Stewart was uncertain whether he yet had complete command in southern Alberta and whether the government would provide arms and ammunition. His departure from Ottawa was so fast that approval status for his Rangers had not entirely been cleared.

At Winnipeg, Major Stewart took delivery of the saddlery and tack from Chicago. While waiting for the equipment to catch up to him, Stewart received a wire from Caron, advising him he was to provide his own arms and equipment. The spirit of the telegram indicates Caron evidently did not read the carrying out report closely. Stewart reminded the minister of Section 14 of his report, wherein provision had been made for emergency requirements. Confident of eventual reimbursement, Stewart purchased, at his own expense, a quantity of Model 1876 Winchester rifles and ammunition.

Probably weary of Stewart's string pulling, Caron advised him he was not alone in the request to commission a regiment; applications from other parties to form militias in the same area were on file. But Caron had other news: as a brigade commander, Captain Stewart received a promotion to Major, tendering full command of the troop and full command of southern Alberta, second only to General Strange.

The NWMP Artillery contingent at Fort Macleod—24 men, 43 horses and a 9-pounder cannon—was summoned to join General Strange's column at Calgary. Faced with an emergency and shorted on men, on April 6 Superintendent John Cotton sent a dispatch to Strange requesting 250 infantrymen to garrison Macleod and Pincher Creek and for 100 mounted men to supplement the NWMP patrols. Cotton's request played directly into the hands of Major Stewart as he arrived in Calgary to meet his commander. On April 7, Strange and Stewart forwarded Cotton's request to Minister Caron, together with their own requisitions for 100 Winchester carbines and 10,000 rounds of ammunition. The message was not lost on Caron, who had vacillated on funding Stewart's corps. This time Caron's response was clear and the armaments were finally promised.

In the ensuing days, Strange worked feverishly in Calgary to organize the Field Force, but the promised arms did not arrive. By April 9, Strange could no longer accept Caron's word and sensed there was another issue behind the failure. Strange's troops were still not authorized, even though he was a field general, while those of Stewart's, a subordinate, were. Backed by Stewart's carrying out report, Tom Strange threw his hands up and threatened the minister: "One troop is enrolled for General Service, another is being enrolled for Local service. The conditions for both being [like] those to Capt. Stewart. If you decline to furnish arms and equipments, please let me know at once. I will send you statement of expense already incurred and disband the corps as soon as paid. Part are now guarding the Railroad at Gleichen, the rest at Calgary; I have sent you [a] telegram with my answer to General Middleton."[40] Caron could not afford to dispense with Strange. The AFF was immediately authorized, but the rifles still took time in arriving, and Calgary area troops had to get along with personal weapons.

John Stewart only raised three companies of Rocky Mountain Rangers. However, all early documentation, general orders, telegrams and newspaper stories indicate that he planned for four companies. Caron's telegrams and Stewart's carrying out report confirm this. Articles in the April 11, 1885 edition of the *Macleod Gazette* suggest that, for at least a little while, the "lost company" of the Rocky Mountain Rangers was mustered in Calgary, while the Macleod and Pincher Creek companies were still recruiting. A dispatch from Calgary published in the *Gazette* presented this curiosity: "Our volunteer movement has culminated in the formation of the Mountain Rangers, with Major Hatton as Acting Captain, Lt. Lauder as first [lieutenant] and H.B. Strange, son of the General, as 2nd [lieutenant]. T.B. Dunne, formerly of the NWMP, is acting Sergeant-Major, and your correspondent, besides acting as Orderly Room Clerk is attached to the staff."[41]

A Ranger whose identity is lost to time. The hat identifies the Rangers' one and only concession to military dress code. The 1876 Winchester .45-75 and the Colt pistol tucked in his chaps were the Rangers' weapons of choice. GLENBOW ARCHIVES NA-670-5

(Top) Stockmen and citizens with Bloods, *circa* 1885. The mounted
Bloods may be NWMP scouts. GALT PI9770159000

(Bottom) Louis Riel's Cree allies, Big Bear (left) and Poundmaker.
Big Bear tried to prevent the Frog Lake Massacre but was imprisoned
for treason felony for his band's role in the conflict. Poundmaker
fended off an attack from Colonel Otter's column at Cut Knife Hill.
GLENBOW ARCHIVES NA-1315-18

(Top) RMR members on the porch of "The Bungalow" at the Stewart Ranche, *circa* 1885. (Left to right) Jim Scott, Jack Garnett, William Cochrane, Lord Richard Boyle, Henry Boyle, John Herron, John Stewart, T. Watson, unknown, William Fisher.

(Bottom) Stewart Ranche company buildings.

(Top left) Veronique "Vernie" Hamilton (née Dumant).
GLENBOW ARCHIVES NA-1482-2

(Top right) John Rogers Davis. After the rebellion, he started a ranch that provided provisions to the Blood Indian agency and lumber to Fort Macleod. GLENBOW ARCHIVES NA-3996-3

(Bottom) William Allen Hamilton operating a horse-drawn mower on his ranch in the Porcupine Hills. GLENBOW ARCHIVES NA-1482-5

(Top left) Henry Boyle posing in buckskins. A British barrister, he and his brother, Lord Richard, were investors in the Alberta Ranche. GLENBOW ARCHIVES NA-4452-7

(Top right) Major John Stewart in a combination of Dominion Militia uniform and functional western gear. GLENBOW ARCHIVES NA-1724-1

(Bottom) Lionel Brooke was that odd breed of Englishman known as the "remittance man." Lionel introduced the sport of polo to the cowboys. GLENBOW ARCHIVES NA-1403-1

(Top) Arthur Cox served as Pincher Creek's first teacher and clergyman before becoming a land agent. GLENBOW ARCHIVES NA-2001-07

(Bottom left) Mary Ella Inderwick (née Lees) came west from Ontario with her brother William and became infatuated with Fred Inderwick. GLENBOW ARCHIVES NA-1365-2

(Bottom right) Frederick Charles Inderwick, a former British militiaman, revelled in the life of a cowboy and became founder of the North Fork Ranche. GLENBOW ARCHIVES NA-1365-1

John M. Robson.
Scout with Major Walsh.
at Fort   Walsh
                    1876

(Clockwise from top left)
John Muntz Robson ("Rattlesnake Jack")
sits at Fort Walsh, *circa* 1878, in a NWMP
uniform. Although the writing at the top of
print says Quarter Master Sergeant, there
is no record to substantiate his enrollment
in the Force.

An extremely rare photo of Rattlesnake
Jack as a Rocky Mountain Ranger. He
is wearing the North West Canada 1885
medal, and the scribbling at the top
suggests he may have acted as a guide
at Fort Walsh *circa* 1876.

Kootenai Brown's service in the Canadian
Militia topped his career as a British
lieutenant, a courier for the US Army, a
scout for the NWMP and a magistrate's
constable in BC.

(Top) John D. Higinbotham, a druggist at Fort McLeod. Although he never served with the RMR, he wrote several articles about them for Ontario newspapers, as well as a book, *When the West Was Young*, which was published in 1933. Artist unknown.

GLENBOW ARCHIVES NA-1352-22

(Bottom) RMR line up for a march near Medicine Hat.

GLENBOW ARCHIVES NA-619-3

The Calgary troop organized by Major Hatton and overseen by General Strange was calling itself "the Mountain Rangers with total strength expected to number 80 men, besides officers, when enlistment closed."[42] The article indicates Stewart was in Calgary at this time, so this troop may have met with his approval. While Duncan Campbell and John Herron were raising Rangers in the south, General Strange sent the Calgary unit on its first manoeuvre. Hatton and 18 men left on a special train to protect frightened CPR workers on the 18th siding at Gleichen as another 18 supplemented the garrison at the Calgary barracks.

The next edition of the *Gazette* brought evidence that a Calgary troop of Stewart's Rangers was not to be named as, or be part of, the Rocky Mountain Rangers. The troop remained together for service, henceforth dubbed as "the Alberta Mounted Rifles," with Hatton, Lauder and Dunne remaining in command. Harry B. Strange would serve as his father's aide-de-camp in the Alberta Field Force.

Strange and Stewart received some jealous political resistance in raising volunteers around Calgary by the local potentates: "A few persons, who are fond of airing themselves on every possible occasion, have been covertly putting sticks in the wheels but they might as well have spared themselves the pains. When Gen. Strange and Capt. Stewart take hold of a movement, they are not going to drop it at the insolence of a few individuals who have neither the right, nor the might to make them."[43]

After ascertaining the situation in Calgary, Stewart left for Fort Macleod to survey the formation and assume command of the Rocky Mountain Rangers. Though he was now officially a major, the eastern press insisted on referring to "Captain Stewart's Cowboy Corps." Stewart warned the general populace to prepare for the worst. Many already had, and William Cochrane, with ranges neighbouring the Blood reserve, moved to protect the interests of his ranch and his company. In a letter to his father in

Quebec, he sniffed at Stewart's ability to put together a regiment, putting his faith in his own foreman and the ranch's hired hands:

"I suppose you are all pretty anxious about [us] here. I do not think we will have any trouble with our Indians but will do everything to be prepared. If there should be an outbreak it would be impossible to hold the ranch on account of position and the amount of hay stocked here, but Dunlop does not intend to connect himself with the militia or anybody, but get all the men he can from across the line if necessary, hiring them as cowboys, and act independently in the interests of the company…We have our horses here in the pasture ready for anything that may turn up…I do not believe Capt. Stewart will be able to raise much of a corps here."[44]

With the aid of more than 100 young horsemen, Stewart would directly prove the pessimistic Cochrane wrong.

CHAPTER EIGHT

Roll Call: The Troops

By necessity, the military is not a democracy, but a benevolent dictatorship, so John Stewart had no qualms about drafting friends into the RMR. As commander, Stewart needed those he could trust and looked to his circle of comrades in business and military organizations, considering it good fortune that such a remote area could produce good staff material. All the skills needed by his amateur soldiers were in ample supply. Three companies or "troops" were formed at Fort Macleod.

Stewart was the only senior officer. Each troop had a captain with two lieutenants beneath him. The units were predominantly non-commissioned officers, with two sergeant majors, ten sergeants and ten corporals. The lowest rank, that of "trooper," was equivalent to an infantry private. The nature of their potential opponents' tactics dictated that the Rangers would have to separate into small patrols for pursuit or to counter hit-and-run manoeuvres. With a high ratio of non-coms, Stewart had greater assurance that field decisions could be made and orders followed.

Save for a surgeon and an adjutant, there were few of the frills of the British regimental staff—no aide-de-camp, no batmen, no bands, not even a veterinary surgeon—despite being a cavalry unit. This campaign was going to be on the cheap and often on the move. As an irregular unit, the Rangers had to care for their own mounts. Stewart Ranche manager John Herron was notified to have mounts ready.

Enlistment opened with a telegram ordering Duncan Campbell in Macleod to begin recruitment. Besides the word of mouth from ranch to ranch, a notice appeared in the *Macleod Gazette* on April 18 requesting volunteers for the new regiment. Campbell was authorized to accept enlistment of 100 Rangers who would be prepared to shoot to kill, or be killed in combat. After conferring with General Strange in Calgary, John Stewart left for Macleod. By the time he arrived, response was brisk. Many volunteers turned out, and the parts of the whole were brought into a sum. Besides the Rangers, Stewart was responsible for the Home Guards in the towns of Pincher Creek and Macleod. Several enlistees served in both the RMR and the Home Guard.

The rolls were made up of rank-and-file cowboys who were working stock hands from the Stewart, Cochrane, Oxley and Walrond ranches. For a free spirit like transplanted Englishman Edward Neal Barker (see Appendix), a hand on the Cochrane Ranche, riding off with a cavalry troop sounded like the thing to do. Even Stewart's cook, Thomas B. Watson, enlisted—not a bad addition, considering the old maxim that an army marches on its stomach. Another recruit who likely handled the skillet as well as a carbine was Ed Larkin, a Fenian Raid veteran and a former Mountie at the Remount Station. In the force, and after his discharge, Larkin became "noted all over the west for his culinary proficiency,"[45] cooking for ranch camps and even across the line at US Army posts.

The irregular nature of recruitment was such that reputations or transgressions of character could be overlooked, ignored or just plain forgotten when some lanky, bowlegged hand who looked like he was born in a saddle rode into the NWMP barracks. A typical example of the range hands who stepped up to take the Queen's shilling was James F. Stock (Alberta Jim). Balancing out his cowboy skill was a taste for whisky—not necessarily a sin, but in 1885 Alberta, it was a crime. Stock was convicted in September 1884 of being illegally in possession of liquor, a common offence under prohibition. He was fined $200, which, by his not paying, granted him six months of hard labour in the Fort Macleod guardhouse. By the next spring, however, when the government needed Alberta Jim's services, all was forgiven.

Several Rangers were Americans, and Stewart received permission from the militia department to allow recruitment of American citizens. Though investors from Ontario, Quebec and Great Britain dominated cattle industry ownership, the hired hands performing the real day-to-day work were from across the line, having driven the herds into Canada for contractors supplying the stock to ranchers. Others were left over from the days of the Montana whisky trade incursions. Some were bullwhackers, drivers of the massive bull teams working for the Fort Benton merchant supply business. Many, like William Allen Hamilton (see Appendix), stayed to make their home on Canadian soil.

John Rogers Davis, an Illinois-born former farmer from California, was also a freighter who found new agricultural prospects on a homestead near the Oldman River, but put off his spring ploughing for military service.

Pharmacist John Higinbotham suggested many Rangers had been US Army veterans of the Dakota wars. Though little primary evidence supports that, Higinbotham knew and talked to the men, and can be given the benefit of the doubt. We know already that William Jackson had experienced the terror of the Little Bighorn. What possessed Jackson to leave the Blackfeet reservation in Montana and again risk his life with another militia has gone undocumented, but a Montana newspaper may offer a financial incentive.

The *Benton River Press* of May 13 reported that several Montana cowboys "left for the north...supposed to join the cowboy contingent now being organized for operations against the half-breeds in the northwest." The article named four of the six: "John Gamble, W.E. Doak, English George, George Seifried and two others." If this were the case, the Fort Benton contingent would have been too late to be mustered to the RMR, and the names did not appear on any of the rolls. The true whereabouts of Gamble and company remained unknown, but this indicates others may have left Montana with similar aims. The *River Press* did identify the motivations of the Americans in accepting the spartan terms of Stewart's pay as somewhat mercenary: "The bounty which is being offered by the Canadian government for volunteers on this service is sufficiently liberal to attract many who desire a life of this kind." The entry level may have been a paltry 75 cents a day, but work was work.

With the outbreak of the rebellion, trader Eugene Patrick (Paddy) Hassan's life experience made him a valuable addition. US Army military training, battle experience with General George Crook's column at the Battle of the Rosebud in Wyoming in 1876, fluency in the Blackfoot language and marriage into the Blood band all made Hassan a primary expert in keeping the peace on a war footing (see Appendix).

Besides American soldiers, the Rangers called on experienced men of the NWMP. Several discharged Mounties who had come west with the force and stayed in the country, working as cowboys or ranchers in their own right, also joined the Rangers. Many had been posted to the NWMP Remount Station, where the Stewart Ranche operated. Among the veterans who signed into the ranks were some of the Remount farm's founders: Alfred Lynch-Staunton, Charles Kettles, William Reid and Peter McEwen. Stewart would have trusted these men to fulfill their duties implicitly.

James Schofield had trading in his heart, not cowpoking, and had built up a successful mercantile business, virtually out of the back of a wagon. After selling goods to CPR construction camps, Schofield opened Pincher Creek's first store in partnership with Henry Ernest Hyde (see Appendix), and after only eight years in the west became the leading businessman of the area. At the top of the learning curve as a plainsman, Schofield was appointed sergeant to the Number 3 Troop.

Retired from the NWMP, John Henry Gresham Bray had been a chief constable, the equivalent of sergeant major in police hierarchy, and a veteran of many key points in the force's early history. Discharged in 1882, Bray farmed near Pincher Creek. With extensive military and police experience, Bray was a valuable contribution to Herron's troop.

Along with the at least 13 discharged policemen who joined the Rangers, Stewart had 5 others who had served as scouts before 1885. There is no doubt then that Stewart had the raw materials of disciplined troops with training in infantry and cavalry tactics and knowledge of the country. Most importantly, he had men who knew how to reason with the Natives of the area with diplomacy and tact. As important as the ability to ride and shoot was the knack for asking a question first to keep the lid on tensions. It helped that the best of the retired redcoats was his old sergeant major, the man who'd taught him about the west.

Home Guards, which were not official rifle companies, were formed in many communities across the territories. They were most often ad hoc units with no stamp of authority from the military and no budget for weapons, provisions or compensation. In many cases, guardsmen were volunteers with the best of intentions, but little training or any idea of what they were doing. There might even be a question of a command chain in the event of an emergency. That was not the case in Pincher Creek, where Mounties and trained soldiers dwelled, and an unofficial Home Guard was organized by Herron. Stewart bypassed the possibility of command confusion by absorbing the Home Guard into the Canadian militia as the Number 3 Troop of the RMR. Herron was commissioned captain in charge of this troop.

Roster of the 1885 Rocky Mountain Rangers[46]

Number after name indicates Ranger's regimental number.
(NWMP) after name indicates Ranger's additional service
with North West Mounted Police.

NUMBER I TROOP, ACTIVE SERVICE CORPS

Major	John O. Stewart
Captain	Richard Boyle
Lieutenant	James R. Scott
2nd Lt.	Henry Boyle
Adjutant	Duncan John D'Urban Campbell
Surgeon	Leverett George DeVeber (NWMP)
Sgt.-Major	William H. Heath
Sergeant	George H.P. Austin
	William Jackson 15
	Howard Lovejoy 43
	Montague Adamson 1
Corporal	Charles Kinlock 16
	Anson Ely 7
	Frank Fisher 8
Scout	John George Brown (Kootenai Brown)
	Aaron A. Vice
	John M. Robson (Rattlesnake Jack) (NWMP)
Trooper	Henry B. Robson 27
	Timothy Quirk 25
	James Wheatley 34
	Albert D. Holbrook 13
	Albert W. Robson 26
	Charles Thornton 32
	John Morgan 21
	George Lewis 18
	George A. Mercier 20
	Charles Wachter 33
	Charles Bowen 3
	William Allen Hamilton 10
	Frederick Charles Inderwick 14
	James W. Carruthers 4
	Arthur Stafford 31
	John Rogers Davis 6
	Peter C. Parker 22
	Patrick Eugene Hassan 11
	Edward Gallagher 9

Albert E. Kertcher 17
Alex W. McBride 19
Charles Hildreth 1
Richard Powers 24
William J. Patterson 59

NUMBER 2 TROOP, ACTIVE SERVICE CORPS

Captain	Edward Gilpin Brown (NWMP)
Lieutenant	William F. Powell
	James Christie
Sergeant	Fred A.R. Mountain 51 (NWMP)
	William McCord .
	Alexander Gordon 55
Corporal	Benjamin McCord 52
	David Joseph Wylie
	William D. Armstrong 53
Trooper	George Welch 63
	John W. Little 57
	Joseph Simmons 61
	James Simmons 62
	Albert Martin 58
	Henry Hall 55
	Frederick S. Elliot 52
	Joseph P. Purviance 60
	Arthur Gray
	Arthur Morris (Baldy) 46
	James T. Routledge 45
	Lionel Brooke 35
	Alfred F. Willis 46
	Edward Larkin 42 (NWMP)
	James F. Stock (Alberta Jim) 47
	Edward Neale Barker 48
	George W. Hall 41
	James Collins 38
	Malcolm McNaught 44
	Thomas E. Dawson 39
	William Edmonds 50
	Frank Fontien 49
	Frank Fetch (*Fitch?*) 40
	Charles Langland 51
	Frederick T. Young 63
	Henry Haymes 54
	William Chute 37

Number 3 Troop, Pincher Creek Home Guard

Captain	John Herron (Honest John) (NWMP)
Lieutenant	George Canning Ives (NWMP)
	Charles Smith (Jughandle)
Sgt.-Major	James B. Brennan 1
Sergeant	James H. Schofield 2 (NWMP)
	Albert A. McCullogh 3
	Charles G. Geddes 4
Corporal	Frank LeVasseur 5
	Harold J. Smith 6
	Samuel Leper 7
Trooper	Alfred H. Lynch-Staunton 8 (NWMP)
	Charles Kettles 9 (NWMP)
	Albert Milton Morden 10
	Henry Ernest Hyde 11
	Arthur Edgar Cox 12
	Thomas Cyr 13
	Thomas Hinton 15
	John Henry Gresham Bray (NWMP)
	William Cox Allen 16
	Samuel James Sharpe 17 (NWMP)
	Charles E. Harris 18
	Adolph Cyr 14
	Albert Connelly 19
	Thomas B. Watson 20
	Peter McEwen 21 (NWMP)
	William Carruthers 22 (NWMP)
	William Reid 23 (NWMP)
	Maxime Brouillette (Maxie) 24
	William R. Lees 25
	Ernest Hausen 26
	John Brown 27
	Frederick Delkinton 28
	Leslie Grey Willock 29
	Daniel Wannamaugher 30
	Eugene Chamberlain 31

Rangers who are shown on Pay List and Medal Rolls, but are not listed in Boulton.

James A. Grant 56
Charles Franklin Norris

Number 2 Troop was assigned to the distinguished British Army officer Edward Gilpin Brown, who took on the added duty of regimental paymaster, responsible to the government for the accounting and distribution of the payroll. With his military combat experience against indigenous opponents in hot spots in Asia and Africa, he was most welcome in galvanizing a roughshod cowboy militia. Number 1 Troop was under the command of resident nobleman, Richard Henry Boyle. His military credentials as a Sandhurst graduate were impeccable, and as an unbridled adventure seeker, he relished the rigorous cowboy life. Lord Boyle is pictured on horseback, his Stetson rakishly folded in a colonial three-cornered fashion and a roll-your-own cigarette gripped in his mouth.

Every regiment needs staff officers to support command. Primary is the adjutant—administrative assistant to the senior officer—responsible for the drafting of reports, duty logs, managing of correspondence and maintenance of records on the rank and file. As a sheriff and postmaster, Duncan Campbell had the clerical and legal skills for the job, combined with previous military experience.

A discharged NWMP doctor, New Brunswick-born, Harvard-educated Leverett "George" DeVeber, was the Rangers' surgeon. After years in private practice, DeVeber accepted a commission in the NWMP as a hospital staff sergeant because the expanding force was desperate for qualified medical professionals. While with the force, DeVeber realized the tremendous extent of his required duties. Besides treating sick and wounded policemen, he was also obliged to care for treaty members and settlers. With the shortage of practitioners, it was not unheard of for a police surgeon to ride 200 miles on an emergency call. Posted first to Fort Qu'Appelle, Dr. DeVeber spent more time in transit than practice. From Qu'Appelle, he was transferred to Forts Walsh, Macleod and Calgary, all in his first year with the force. It was back to Fort Macleod in 1883 and later a return to Calgary.

By early 1885, Dr. DeVeber wearied of the frenetic pace and considered private practice in the town of Macleod. At a police dance, John and Ida Herron introduced him to Rachel Ryan, a charming Australian who had travelled to Pincher Creek to keep house for her brother. After they were married, DeVeber resigned to the quiet life of a country doctor, but two months later, Duck Lake would end his new-found bliss.

The entry-level position into an officer corps, the lieutenant, serves as the captain's second in command. Here, Stewart was creative in the selection of junior officers with a mixture of military, police and equine experience—and prairie know-how. Stewart selected his ranching partner, horse trader James Christie, because of his equine knowledge. Christie supervised the arrangements for the cavalry horses, including feed and stabling, veterinary needs, distribution of mounts and general training of the odd recruit wanting in horse sense.

As a militiaman, William F. Powell was named a lieutenant, referred to on the pay lists as "attached," adding a layer of military professionalism to the rough-hewn Rangers. The connection to Adjutant-General Colonel Walker Powell gave access to the high command in Ottawa, and Stewart used it often. Henry George Boyle was made a second lieutenant. Like his sibling, Richard, Henry was eager to cast off his British bearing for the attire of the westerner. When the RMR went into garrison at Macleod, photographer George Anderton took Henry's photograph outside the I.G. Baker store. Striking a fearsome pose with a cigar firmly clenched in his mouth, Boyle looked like a prototype Clint Eastwood, clad in buckskin shirt and fringed leggings with the store creases still in them.

Aside from Herron, George Canning Ives was the only former policeman on the RMR staff. James Scott, noted as "one of the oldest-timers in the country," had been a whisky trader and wolfer. He probably had military experience in the US Army and was a civilian interpreter at the Remount Station. Those rough credentials were solid enough for Stewart to name Scott a lieutenant.

Returning to his Jughandle Ranche in the early spring after his winter of hunting wolves, Charley Smith learned of the Duck Lake battle. After his recent disastrous encounter with the Sarcee, Smith had reason to believe some of the wild stories. His years of buffalo hunting and familiarity with the plains were recognized as important as any knowledge of military regimen, and he was named a lieutenant under John Herron. James Brennan and William Heath were named as sergeant majors, senior non-commissioned officers responsible for conduct and training.

Including James Schofield and William Jackson, seven sergeants were named at Fort Macleod: George Austin, Howard Lovejoy, Montague Adamson, Albert McCullogh and Charles Geddes. More were added later at Medicine Hat.

Of nine corporals, six were recruited in Macleod: Charles Kinlock, Anson Ely, Frank Fisher, Harold Smith, Samuel Leper and Frank LeVasseur (see Appendix). Many Rangers performed double duty as Fort Macleod or Pincher Creek Home Guardsmen, and upon the assumption of the units, the Pincher Creek pioneers joined the rolls of the Rangers as troopers.

Albert Milton Morden hailed from Barrie, Ontario, where, after a fire destroyed a family business, Morden organized a party of 10 to resettle in the west. After hard luck in the Judith Basin of Montana and the mountain settlement of Morleyville on the upper Bow River, the Mordens bought a simple cabin and plot of land from Jim Scott on Pincher Creek and began to stock their ranch.

Like many a settler who shuddered with fear amid the lurid tales of "savagery," the Morden children related stories: "Father was often away, and it would be a bit startling to have the window darkened with a number [of] wildly painted Indians peering in." Son Tom tempered that nervousness, reassuring that "the Indians never gave us any trouble...On the whole, the morals of the Indians were as good as those of the whites, or better."[47] Even so, incidents such as this, when massacres and battles were occurring in the north, often gave rise to wild rumours and crazy stories at the onset of the rebellion. That inspired Albert Morden to join the Home Guard and, by default, the RMR.

Canada in the 19th century was very much an extension of British colonialism and, as such, home for men like Lionel Brooke, one of that odd breed of Englishmen known as the remittance man: the son of wealth or entitlement, the drunkard, gambler, womanizer or otherwise disappointing dilettante who embarrassed his family. These men were quietly shipped off to some distant corner of the empire and sent the occasional envelope to keep him comfortable. Canada's west, with its ranching leases and homestead acreages, was as good as darkest Africa for noble families to hide away their scions, and Lionel Brooke did not care if he ever saw England again.

With the help of the quarterly stipend from the mother country, he dabbled in cattle, but while aristocrats like the Boyle brothers reinvented themselves for the country, ranching was not Brooke's cup of tea. He saw his Chinook Ranche as an estate, where he could live the life of an artistic country squire, in the ranch country's social register. With his patrician tweed attire, his monocle and his carefree, lackadaisical nature, the natty Englishman was a prime candidate for ridicule among the leathery hired hands. He helped introduce the sport of polo, a game snooty enough for the ranch gentry, yet rough enough for the rowdy cowboys. In time, his ensemble of knickers and long stockings was accessorized with a beaded buckskin jacket and a wide-brimmed hat, but in spite of his lordly facade, there was a thirst for adventure in his soul. Remittance men were generally patriotic. When the Queen called, Lord Brooke put down his idle pursuits and volunteered for the RMR.

Two of the original Home Guard were fortune seekers soon given saddles as troopers in the RMR. Arthur Edgar Cox, a working-class teacher from Camden, England, and Les Willock, a sodbuster from Ontario (see Appendix), were typical of western settlers—young men seeking a new life in their own fashion, building their communities and willing to guard them with their lives. Not surprisingly, in an embryonic community where people from different places came to gather and create a life, they would eventually become family.

Familial connections abounded within the Rangers, stemming from the boomtown atmosphere of the area, within which those of different backgrounds found resources, employment, adventure and even love in the foothills. William R. Lees left Perth, Ontario, in 1881 to manage the McLaren sawmill west of Pincher Creek, but a reunion with his sister, the high-spirited Mary Ella, in September 1883 led to kinship with an unlikely neighbour. Mary Ella's father had been unenthusiastic about her abandoning her comfortable home, and a drama of threats of disinheritance on his part and suicide attempts on hers had carried on until at last she arrived in the logging camp. She did not adapt well to hardship and threw herself into a cleaning frenzy to make Willie's cabin bearable. In time she got used to the loggers, who even let her partake of their poker games.

Mary Ella planned to return to Ontario for a career in nursing after her sojourn west. Infatuation intervened when she chanced to meet an English rancher. Frederick Charles Inderwick came to Canada as aide-de-camp to Governor General Lord Lansdowne. The succeeding vice-regent, the Marquis of Lorne, inspired Inderwick to go west, where in concert with financiers, he established the North Fork Ranch. On April 13, 1884, despite the objections of Willie Lees, Mary Ella married "Charlie," as she called him, and resigned herself to life at the North Fork, a day's ride north of Pincher Creek.

Mary Ella found solace in keeping a diary of her times on the ranch. Mysteriously, she kept references to friends and neighbours in code, probably intending the memoirs for publication.

She wrote lovingly of the isolated foothills, although she was not enamoured of the towns and the weather, describing Macleod as "one of the last places to live in all of the world," and sparing no dislike of the never-ending gale-force winds. Mary was affronted by the class system distinguishing the British from Canadian-born women like her, sneered at as some lower caste of colonial. "Though I have married an Englishman, I have not lost my identity and I am purely Canadian and proud of it."[48]

Her feelings toward her Aboriginal neighbours were another matter. She wrote, "I think the Indians should have been isolated in the mountains and left with their own lives and ways of living and never allowed to eat of the fruit of knowledge as revealed by the white men who came to live among them. They could teach civilization a great deal too, but our inconsistencies are too subtle for his direct mind and when he tries to follow he is lost, and under the circumstance the sooner he becomes extinct the better for himself and the country."[49] As patronizing and degrading as the statement was, Mary Ella's racism was indicative of the times. It was the policy of the Indian department to foster assimilation. Such legislated racism has proven to be not only morally bankrupt but destructive to the individual—and it didn't work. To counter Mary Ella Inderwick, the First Nations today thrive and are not extinct. The same cannot be said for English ranchers.

Besides Americans, Britishers and Anglo-Canadians, the Rangers comprised a few French-Canadian influences, stemming from the "French flats" settlements west of Pincher Creek. Among the Metis was Maxie Brouillette, the overnight stagecoach driver for the Stewart express line between Pincher and Macleod. Maxie packed a six-shooter strapped to his hip at all times. He was probably given charge of driving a transport wagon in the Rangers. Other francophones included the Cyr brothers, Adolph and Thomas, Acadians stemming from New Brunswick.

Though the Batoche Metis were at war with the government, the loyalties of Metis as a people were not unified. It was not a cohesive community and could not be, what with the varied ethnic makeup of the Metis and the various communities they founded. As previously recounted, many of the Rangers were married into Metis society. Whether any felt sympathy for the rebels remains a question, but in southern Alberta, the politics of Riel found little hearing.

Three men who had acted as guides and interpreters for the police, and even as policemen, were hired to serve as scouts; a fourth joined later. The job of the scout was to guide a military unit through unknown country, translate conversations during encounters with Natives who had no knowledge of the English language, and have a working knowledge of Aboriginal cultural nuances. Failure to communicate, or inability to clearly state intentions, could lead to tragedy. The history of the westward movement is full of the pathos of those who shot first and asked questions later.

Aaron A. Vice was no newcomer to the southern plains, having scouted for the police at least as early as 1877 at Fort Macleod. The Commissioner's Report of 1878 notes him as having been charged with assaulting a man named William Lawrence in Macleod in February of 1878, but charges were dropped. The only other details of this case may perhaps have something to do with the complainant, William Lawrence himself having been charged with firing a pistol with intent to kill only five days before the date of Vice's offense.

NWMP constable William Cox recalled: "There was one man in the outfit named Robinson [sic] who wore his hair long. It hung down on his shoulders and was a faded red color; also he wore a buckskin shirt or coat with two revolvers in his belt and was known as Rattlesnake Jack."[50] Two photographs of John Muntz Robson picture him in a NWMP uniform. One, dating to 1878, is captioned "John M. Robson, Q.M.S." (Quarter Master

Sergeant). The second, dated 1886, corresponds with Cox's recollection—a long-haired, bearded plainsman, showing off his North West Canada 1885 medal. The caption describes him as a scout with Major Walsh in 1876.[51] Engaging in Ottawa on June 17, 1878, Constable Robson, Regimental Number 151, served at Fort Walsh, but never actually achieved the rank of sergeant. Due to his discharge, at his own request two years later, Jack did not receive the usual land grant offered other veterans.

Kootenai Brown was out of contact as the events at Duck Lake whipped the nation into a lather. As the events of the rebellion unfolded, he'd heard nothing about it. When he bumped into William F. Cochrane at the ford of the Waterton River on April 20, the excitable rancher brought the guide up to speed on the news. Kootenai's response was clear: he gave his horse a kick and spurred it onward to Fort Macleod, galloping 40 miles in a single day to volunteer. At the barracks, Brown's reputation was solid—a British cavalry veteran, with knowledge of the country and established inroads into the Metis world. Stewart accepted Brown's service and named him to his inner circle as the RMR's chief of scouts.

Many men besides Kootenai Brown saw joining the RMR as a chance at adventure. The winter had been tough on the isolated ranches for those who had work. For those who'd been laid off since the fall roundups, there'd been boredom and lack of money. To ride as a cavalryman in the warm spring sun was enticing to young cowhands. Undoubtedly, racial tension was also a motive. The clash of cultures was bound to produce friction, especially to range riders involved in close calls with raids on cattle herds.

On April 15, 1885, the RMR fell in for their first roll call at the Macleod NWMP barracks. The unit divided into three troops. Boyle and Gilpin Brown's troops would be known as the Active Service Corps. Most of Herron's troop was the previous Pincher Creek Home Guard. The *Macleod Gazette* of April 8 diligently reported the first assembly: "The Rocky Mountain Rangers had their first muster on Wednesday morning and have been drilling since then. The men have got into very creditable shape, considering the short time they have been drilled."

Stewart commandeered the office of the North Western Coal and Navigation Company (NWC&NC) for the district's military headquarters. Three days later, as expected, 20 NWMP members, under Inspector A. Bowen Perry, were ordered north to Calgary to join General Strange, bound for the scene of the Frog Lake massacre. That left the police contingent at the barracks short. Bad enough at any time, it could be catastrophic in a war situation, but the RMR augmented the strength of the few policemen Superintendent Cotton had left. Major Stewart forwarded a dispatch to Calgary for Minister Caron in Ottawa: "Organization complete; withdrawn Police from MacLeod; have put fifty men and mounts in Garrison at request Commandant. One hundred rangers additional on duty at important points."[52]

In organization, Stewart was expected to adhere to the carrying out report approved by Minister Caron. All volunteers were to provide their own horses and be paid for their use, with an expense allowance for feed. From his purchase of saddles in Chicago and his instructions to John Herron to ready mounts, it is obvious that Stewart personally provided horses to many from his ranch's stock.

The per diem pay scale for the RMR was aligned with the NWMP, starting at 75¢ for troopers, 90¢ for corporals, $1.00 for sergeants and a whopping $1.50 for sergeant majors. Nobody would get rich, but at least each Ranger would receive an allowance of $2.50 per day for his own rations and those of his horse.

The expectation that volunteers would provide their own firearms was realistic. Despite the myth of a docile Canadian frontier, there were few in the west not within reach of a rifle or sidearm and the knowledge to use it. For hunting and self-defence, the gun was as necessary as a horse. The biggest problem was uniformity and quality. Stewart wanted to know that if a firefight developed, the weaponry of the troops would be equal to that of the warriors. He also wanted to know that the ammunition provided by the federal government was consistent, and he distributed 50 Winchesters purchased in Winnipeg. As John Higinbotham wrote, the RMR were "armed to the teeth, should occasion require."[53]

The Ranger uniform was anything but. There was no official RMR attire, just the crude but functional clothing of the plainsman, consistent with the hard tasks at hand. Higinbotham described the accoutrements: "a sombrero, or a broad-brimmed felt hat with wide leather band, coat of Montana broadcloth or brown duck (canvas) lined with flannel, a shirt of buckskin, breeches of the same or Bedford cord, a cartridge belt attached to which is a large sheath knife and the indispensable leather chaps. Top boots with huge Mexican spurs completed the equipment."[54]

There were a few concessions to formality. Rangers were encouraged to pin the left side of the wide brim of their felt slouch hat up the crown, in the manner of the bushranger hat that would become a trademark of the Australians. A possibility exists that some Rangers may have worn a hatband of red material signifying them as Dominion militia. Photos show other personal affectations to headgear, such as Lord Boyle's colonial tricorne and Edward Gilpin Brown's hatband of plaid tartan, cut from a Glengarry cap.

With high boots and spurs and white riding breeches in the style of a cavalryman, Stewart made the greatest effort to project comportment worthy of a senior officer. A deep blue woollen tunic, in the pattern of the Dragoon Guards, was completed with a "Sam Browne" military belt and holster and a white haversack slung across his right shoulder, crossed with a leather bandolier off his left. Capped with a flat, broad-brimmed Stetson hat, Stewart looked every inch the commander. That stately bearing was needed, because by all reports it appeared basic training was not taken seriously by the rank and file. Farmers, stockmen and cowboys were not easily willing to submit to rigid military discipline. Any skills the corps needed, it already possessed.

The *Macleod Gazette* of April 25 covered the Rangers' training, taking great delight in the humorous incidents between the officers and the rough-riding, undisciplined conglomeration of individuals they were charged with whipping into fighting shape. The reporter told the tale of when a trooper walked out of drill, "On His Own Hook": "One of the boys left the ranks at the old town the other day to do a little business on his own account. Officer in Command: 'Halt! Where are you going?' Trooper: 'Aw, you fellers go on, I'll catch up to you before you get far.'"

One anonymous Ranger in the Number 3 Troop, identifying himself only as "Old Timer," briefly recounted his basic training. In this account, Charley Smith, a Norwegian, is mistakenly referred to as a "Dutchman"—a pejorative commonly thrown around in reference to Europeans: "In 1885 I joined the Rocky Mountain Rangers in Pincher Creek with Jack Herron, our Officer Commanding. A Dutchman by the name of Charley Smith was our Lieutenant. Charlie would give the order—'Mount, Walk, Trot'—then when we got in front of the little log saloon— 'Halt! Everyone dismount and have a drink.' That was all the drill we got."[55]

John Higinbotham was a druggist in Fort Macleod, a newcomer to the town from Ontario who in later years was a successful Lethbridge businessman. He was also a very good, descriptive freelance writer who drew from the busy activity around his town during the furor. Of the RMR training he monitored: "Discipline is quite unknown to them; a Mountie told me that he heard one of them, during drill today, call out to his commander…" Higinbotham's informant heard a captain call his troop into formation, but one errant trooper did not fall in, preoccupied with his mount's saddle adjustments. The captain repeated the order, but only got an answer of "Hold on, Cap, till I cinch my horse!"[56]

Hard drilling was not going to work on these troops. There was no time and no need. The Rangers knew how to ride and shoot, had the resolve to fight and knew the vast open lands they'd patrol. The *Macleod Gazette* of April 29, 1885, illustrated: "Combined with the order which they had obtained by their brief periods of discipline and drill was that free and easy manner and action which is so characteristic of a border corps and which attaches to them a charm not felt in the rigid movements of the strictly drilled military of the east. Troops for service in the West only require enough drill to be able to act in unison and any efforts to make them mere drilling machines only trammels them and detracts from their efficiency."

In real combat, the Rangers' lack of military discipline could have been concerning. The heavy insertion of friends and associates into command positions contradicts military logic. But in the face of a looming threat, Stewart would have to trust his regiment's ability to deal with whatever it may face. The order of battle had to be creative without the luxury of a complete drill program. The officers simply would have to exercise the western technique of making do with the materials at hand.

CHAPTER NINE

———⟫•❮❮———

The March to Medicine Hat

A fter two harried weeks of drilling, the RMR formed up as a cavalry, mobilizing to protect the railroads, trails and communities east of Macleod and guard the foothills, mountains and nearby reserves. Infantry units that had arrived to Calgary by rail were sent down the trail to bolster the RMR's responsibility to NWMP divisional headquarters. First to arrive was one company of the 92nd Winnipeg Light Infantry. When the 92nd was later ordered to join Strange, it was replaced by two companies of the 9th Quebec Battalion, better known as the Voltigeurs.

On Wednesday, April 29, RMR troops Number 1 and 2 marched out of Macleod, bound for Medicine Hat. Ten officers and 60 troopers, including scouts Aaron Vice, Rattlesnake Jack Robson and Kootenai Brown, were to patrol the narrow gauge railway being built between Lethbridge and Medicine Hat and keep vigil on the Cypress Hills and the American border for hostiles heading to the scene of the fighting.

General Alfred Terry, head of the US Army's Department of the Dakotas, offered reassurances in the matter of American charges making their way across the boundary to join Riel. Terry invoked the American laws of neutrality and vowed to take every precaution to ensure that such an incursion be prevented.

The colourful brigade marching out of the barracks and down

Main Street inspired John Higinbotham to jot out a glowing paragraph, laden with adjectives, and send it to the Toronto tabloid *Canadian Pictorial and Illustrated War News*. The *War News* had plenty of content and did not run Higinbotham's missive until June 20, 1885, nearly two months after the fact. Still, the lapse took no lustre off the pharmacist's words:

> Headed by their youthful but intrepid commander, Capt. Stewart, the Rocky Mountain Rangers presented quite a formidable appearance as they left McLeod, amid the loud huzzas of the garrison. Their tanned faces almost hidden beneath the brims of huge Spanish sombreros, strapped on for grim death... Cross belts pregnant with cartridges, a 'six-shooter,' sheath knife, a Winchester slung across the pommel of the saddle and a coiled lariat completed the belligerent outfit. Mounted on 'bronchoes' good for 60 to 100 miles a day, they soon disappeared in the distance, a loud clanking of bits and jingling of their huge Mexican spurs now gave place to the rattling of the transportation wagons.[57]

Higinbotham's article, written for an audience weaned on James Fenimore Cooper romanticism and the sensationalist novels of Ned Buntline, conjured up visions of dashing young soldiers off to fight for glory and return as conquering heroes. In truth, this is probably what the Rangers thought would be the case as they rode out of Macleod. The unit was proud of itself and, despite the lack of pageantry and any kind of uniform, they looked every inch a formidable fighting unit. Charlie Wood of the *Macleod Gazette* described the "Departure of the Rangers: How The Boys Looked and Where They Are Going" in his May 2, 1885 edition:

> The Active Service Corps of the Rocky Mountain Rangers, under Capt. Stewart, left for the Coalbanks at noon on Wednesday. Leaving the barracks, where they were vigorously

cheered, they rode down past I.G. Baker & Co's store in half sections. Quite a large crowd had assembled, and as they passed the above point, they were given a rousing send off, with a long drawn tiger [yell] at the end of it. In front was Major Stewart, in command, and on either side of him, J.G. Brown and A.A. Vice, the two scouts, both of them men who have seen plenty of Indian warfare, and who will take to scrimmage as a duck does to water. Both these scouts have the advantage of being able to talk the Blackfoot language quite fluently. Next came the men, flanked by Capt. Boyle and Lieut. Scott, then the transport wagon, and last, a rearguard.

The corps is composed of a particularly fine body of men, and as they marched past armed to the teeth with Winchesters, and waist and cross-belts jammed full of cartridges, there was but one opinion expressed regarding them, and that was that they would make it extremely unhealthy for several times their number of rebel half-breeds or Indians, should occasion require action.

Despite his praise of the RMR, *Gazette* editor Charles Wood felt the movement of the corps to Medicine Hat a mistake. NWMP Superintendant John Cotton agreed with Wood, feeling the Bloods still posed a threat. He supported the need for a Home Guard in Macleod subject to the militia. Had there been any action, the Macleod Guard might have been absorbed as another company of the RMR. After election of officers, rancher and former NWMP superintendent William Winder took command as captain, with frontier lawyer Frederick Haultain as 1st lieutenant. The Guard held weekly parades, conducted drills and carried out night watches in the streets.

While troops 1 and 2 left, Captain John Herron kept the Number 3 Company behind to keep watch on the ranch country, triangulating between Fort Macleod, Pincher Creek and High River. The 32 Rangers and 4 officers of Number 3 Troop would provide double duty as Pincher Creek's Home Guard and be eligible for military benefits, as many similar Guard units did not qualify for service recognition.

Others stayed behind at Macleod to replace the 20 police joining General Strange's brigade and man NWMP outposts among the Blood and Peigan. After the deployment of the Rangers, even with the Voltigeurs at the barracks, leading citizens of Macleod thought a separate Home Guard should be formed for their town. An organizational meeting was held on May 5, attended by RMR Adjutant Duncan Campbell to explain the obligations of the Home Guard; prospective guardsmen had to submit for duty at notice, and the Guard was subject to Major Stewart's authority.

The tone of the Macleod meeting may have been out of concern for what seemed a change of the mission for the RMR, from protecting foothill area ranches and settlements to guarding construction of the Dominion government's telegraph line from Medicine Hat to Fort Macleod, and the North Western Coal and Navigation Company Railway from Coalbanks to Dunmore.

Coalbanks, a settlement at the bottom of the Belly (later the Oldman) River coulee, was the future Lethbridge. It owed its existence to the mining activity of NWC&NC, a company initiated by Assistant Indian Commissioner Elliott T. Galt and financed by his father, Sir Alexander Galt, and a syndicate of backers.

To be marketable for the use of railroad steam engines, the coal had to be transported to Medicine Hat, the closest point to the Canadian Pacific Railway. A scheme to float it there by sternwheeler on the Belly River proved unreliable due to fluctuating water levels. Three ships, the *Alberta*, the *Baroness* and the *Minnow*, were slated for sale or destruction but later saw service downriver during the rebellion as supply ships to the military.

To feed a railroad, the Galts had to build a railroad. So, in January 1885, the NWC&NC announced plans to build its own 104-mile-long narrow gauge line, from the mines at Coalbanks to the CPR junction at Dunmore. William Cox, a NWMP constable in Fort Macleod, said: "Construction had started on the Galt railroad from Dunmore to Lethbridge, otherwise known as The Turkey Track. It was thought to be important that the work should be protected so the R.M.R. were sent down to Medicine Hat."[58]

Work began early in the spring. The accompanying telegraph line would be extended beyond Coalbanks to Macleod. The railway workers and telegraph crews were concerned about their safety during construction and threatened work stoppages if they were not protected from the threat of possible attack by marauding bands. The Galts, with deep connections into the government, demanded that protection be provided, and the RMR were assigned.

Despite the high political order to guard the narrow-gauge railroad that many called the Turkey Track, Stewart felt obligated to the ranch country. Upon arrival at Coalbanks, he sent 10 Rangers north to assist NWMP patrols between Fort Macleod and High River, providing a line of communication between isolated ranches. While Macleod awaited the telegraph line that would finally link the frontier town and its government, the Rangers provided a dispatch service from Calgary. Their purpose was to stem the tide of unsubstantiated rumours flooding the country and reassure ranchers their concerns were being heard.

The rebellion did not go unnoticed by cattle and horse rustlers, who attempted to use the reassignments of police and absences of ranchers and cowboys to their own shady advantage. To counter, the NWMP set up a three-man outpost in the Crowsnest Pass to prevent herds being driven off to British Columbia and into the remote, hidden mountain valleys. Outposts operated on the Kootenay (Waterton) River, on the northwest corner of the Peigan reserve, in a rented room in Fort Whoop-Up, at Fort Standoff on the Blood reserve and, of course, at Pincher Creek. Wasting no time, Major Stewart left a detachment of Rangers at Coalbanks and proceeded to march to Medicine Hat on the Turkey Track's route. The troops were a visible guard to calm the nerves of the construction crews, and Rangers were left behind to accompany the progress of graders and track layers at various points.

A detachment was left at Woodpecker Island, where a telegraph crew cut cottonwood trees for poles. Another was stationed where the end of the telegraph line had progressed, just east of modern-day Bow Island. The remainder of the force finished the 130-mile, six-day trek through bleak, treeless country. American, Canadian and British cowboys raised on tales of the Civil War might have wondered what all the fuss was about. The Bloods and Peigan were quiet, and the pledge of Crowfoot to stay out of the fray was widely accepted. There were loose stories of sightings, but it seemed the marauders were heard about, never seen.

Nearing the terminus of the NWC&NC construction route, Stewart's Rangers (as the unit was also informally known) swung off the track and rode into the bustling railroad town of Medicine Hat. Residents took one look at the sun-baked, dust-covered, heavily armed RMR and, in a manner less eloquent than Higinbotham's, nicknamed them the "Tough Men."

Medicine Hat came into existence along the South Saskatchewan River in 1883, the chosen site of a strategic bridge that would carry the Canadian Pacific Railway across the river's broad valley. Crews building the bridge and laying the tracks made Medicine Hat a rough-and-tumble boomtown. Ranching was also becoming prominent, as the area was in the heart of a vast short-grass range and within a day's ride of the lush grazing of the Cypress Hills.

A Home Guard was established in the town with Thomas Tweed as captain. An acquaintance of Stewart's from Ottawa, Tweed had opened Medicine Hat's first store. Bob McCutcheon was elected drill sergeant. The Guard was organized like most others, at a civil defence planning meeting immediately after

Duck Lake, when Medicine Hat received unsubstantiated rumours of a Blackfoot attack. One suggestion made was to place the town's women and children into "the immigrant shed" and bar the doors. NWMP Superintendent John MacDonnell scoffed at the notion, bravely boasting that his detachment could easily stand and defeat Crowfoot.

Another motion was made to open the drawbridge portion of the bridge to prevent a mounted force from crossing the river into town. MacDonnell strongly opposed that plan, fearing his policemen would be cut off from their line of retreat while repelling an invasion. Fed up with the policeman who took on the Blackfoot nation one minute and discussed retreat the next, a cocky young English cowboy, David Joseph Wylie (see Appendix), rose to his feet and called MacDonnell "a disgrace to the Queen's uniform."[59] Whether the superintendent deserved the insult or not, Joe Wylie was no strutting peacock. He'd make his mark and join the RMR.

Medicine Hat storekeeper William Cousins joined the Guard and detailed its organization: "Every man in the community that could walk made up the balance of the Home Guards. We drilled every night and soon got into fighting shape. A night guard was picked out in turns for guard duty. The guardroom was in Bill Anderson's photograph gallery. The women took turns in providing coffee and sandwiches for the guard. While we felt this would help, it was not enough. We wired the government for guns and ammunition, any kind. They sent us cases of Snyder rifles and soft nosed cartridges to fit."[60]

With ready access to the telegraph, Stewart wired Minister Caron of the RMR's arrival and of the postings made en route: "Will render all possible protection to railroad men and Medicine Hat. Indians quiet at MacLeod left one hundred efficient rangers as Home guards."[61] Realizing that the territorial governance would relate better to local reports, Stewart also communicated his findings at Medicine Hat to Lieutenant-Governor Edgar

Dewdney: "Confirm report as to Indians moving North and West of Cypress. Have reported to Gisborne and Grant and arranged for protecting their interest. One reliable report that half-breeds and Crees are at forks of Red Deer [River]. Moving south. Am sending Scouts to ascertain truth."[62]

Major Stewart established a camp near the South Saskatchewan River as the military headquarters for the region, but he faced an immediate morale problem among his ranks. They were bored by the long, uneventful march to "the Hat," protecting railroads. "That did not suit most of the men. They wanted to fight Indians." [63]

Captain Brown's pay lists indicate the names of three Rangers—William Chute, William Carruthers and Lionel Brooke—who evidently ranged too far, although no desertion charges or penalties were levied. "They were hired by the month so at the end of the first month most wandered off to the ranches."[64] Stewart merely signed off the men as "Left." It was even rumoured that a few quitters had headed out for the action at Batoche having "went north on their own." No record indicates that any actually made it, or even tried. Between the drifters and the outposts, as well as the detachments dropped off along the railroad, Stewart was losing volunteers. New recruits from the Cypress Hills ranches were sought out, spurred on by Rattlesnake Jack Robson, the long-haired scout, who "wore a buckskin shirt or coat with two revolvers in his belt and...acted as recruiting officer [to] recruits who thought that [Robson's outfit] was the uniform."[65]

By interpreting the regimental numbers on the pay lists, some of the Medicine Hat recruits (or "Hat" Rangers) can be identified. These included two brothers, Joseph and James Simmons, William D. Armstrong, Henry Haymes, Henry Hall, George Holt, John W. Little, Albert Martin, Alexander Gordon, Frederick Elliot, George Welch, Frederick Young, Joseph P. Purviance and James A. Grant. Little or no information has survived regarding these individuals. More is known of a few others. For example, it is known that William McCord had first-hand experience with Natives. As a farm instructor on the Blood reserve, he had some measure of success in teaching nomadic buffalo hunters to plough and plant, and through that experience had learned the importance of co-operating with and not antagonizing the leaders. When Red Crow refused to accept bacon rations in place of beef, McCord settled the matter without incident. With this experience, he was made a sergeant, although on the pay sheets he is listed as a scout.

Like McCord, Frederick A.R. Mountain (see Appendix) had Indian agency experience. He'd also worked for both the NWMP and British Columbia Provincial Police. Mountain had resigned in disgust from the BC Police due to political shenanigans. In the spring of 1885, he came to Medicine Hat, where he joined the RMR as a sergeant.

With headquarters established and the RMR strength reinforced, patrols were sent farther east. Just out of the original town centre, Seven Persons Creek emptied into the South Saskatchewan. There, the troop found a bit of the history of one of their own. A Ranger patrol rode out to the mouth, where Kootenai Brown recalled the incident in which, 20 years earlier, he had taken an arrow in the back from a band of attackers.

Now, in May of 1885, Kootenai and his fellow Rangers dug five slugs out of the cottonwood trees. More eerie was the discovery of two skulls along the creek bank. Kootenai recollected that the remains were those of two of his ambushers, dispatched by the prospectors accompanying him. The incident was a stark reminder to the younger Rangers of an earlier time and what the unit could face. To Kootenai, one of the few who had such a frame of reference, it was a reminder of how much the country had changed.

Kootenai had another life-changing encounter that spring. While out on a patrol, he met a Cree woman, Blue Flash of

Lightning (*Che-Pay-Kwa-Ka-Soon*). Kootenai more often referred to her as "*Nichemoos*"—"Loved One." She would become his companion for the rest of his life. The details of how their relationship came about were romanticized as a trade deal with the woman's father: "Brown became fascinated by the Cree girl and traded five Cayuses for her on the spot."[66] A colourful tale, but it comes from an interview with a journalist, and Kootenai and his type relished in exaggerations to entertain writers. That the scout met Nichemoos (later known as Isabella) while in military service was documented by Marie Rose Smith, a writer less given to hyperbole, whose husband Charley was likely along on the patrol.

The Cypress Hills were strategically crucial as the traditional home and hunting grounds of the Metis. They also provided a natural shelter for fugitives and a virtual escape route through trails into the United States. In 1883 the NWMP post Fort Walsh was abandoned and eventually burned to the ground by prairie fires. It was replaced by barracks near the new railroad town of Maple Creek. This change left the hills virtually unguarded.

Stewart's Rangers patrolled the Cypress Hills in concert with the Maple Creek and Medicine Hat NWMP detachments, under superintendents John Henry McIllree and John MacDonnell respectively. While in the hills, the RMR linked with the Wood Mountain Scouts, the Metis volunteers organized and commanded by Jean-Louis Légaré. Légaré ran the trading post at Wood Mountain and Willow Bunch, in an area that had gained international attention as the refuge of Sitting Bull and the Sioux Nation. For five years, Légaré and his post had been a focal point for the governments of two nations, as the military and police authorities tried to force Sitting Bull and his band to return to the United States after the Little Bighorn.

Légaré's Scouts were familiar with the Cypress Hills as a hunting ground, and many originated from Red River. Riel had spent a great deal of energy trying to achieve an alliance with them. Given the extinction of the buffalo, the Metis were in a depressed state and said to be packing up, ready to leave the villages of Wood Mountain and join their cousins at Batoche. Légaré appealed to the lieutenant-governor, saying that if some employment were offered, he could convince the Wood Mountain folk to remain. Without sanction from the defence department, an arrangement was made to provide the Metis with commissions as NWMP scouts, paid from police appropriations. That took the southern Metis out of the running as potential Riel allies and gave the police a crucial link in the border watch. Forty-five scouts operated between Moose Jaw and Willow Bunch, watching the US boundary for attempts by the Montana Metis to send arms, ammunition or men north to assist Riel's forces. They also functioned as the eyes and ears of the Maple Creek, Wood Mountain and Regina police posts, keeping the government informed of what was going on in the Cypress Hills Metis and Native communities.

With such allies, the RMR continued a lonely and often boring vigil. Their patrol ranged from the Crowsnest Pass to the Cypress Hills, roaming as far north as High River and as far south as the Montana border. For 114 men on horseback, it was a daunting task. And another two months of grave uncertainty lay ahead.

CHAPTER TEN

Dispatches from the North

Much has been made of the quick success of the government forces in suppressing the Northwest Rebellion. The manoeuvres of Middleton, Dumont, Otter, Poundmaker, Big Bear and Strange are always seen as factors in success or failure. Few of the battles demonstrated textbook tactics, and any victory or defeat was as much by happenstance as by strategy. Two of the crucial elements in any battle, however, are communications and logistics. The CPR was key, as 5,000 troops moved at breakneck speed from central Canada. The telegraph was at least as important, keeping the settlements of the west, and military and government officials, in constant contact. Dispatch riders throughout the prairies, the RMR included, were kept busy delivering new information to various telegraph points.

The telegraph was also important to Major Stewart in dispelling wild rumours in early April while he was organizing the Rangers. It ensured that accurate information was received from those in the thick of the furor. With this 1885 equivalent of email, General Middleton could, from his camp at Fort Qu'Appelle, plan his strategy for wresting control of the territories from the panic gripping them. Besides organizing his own assault against Riel's position, the British officer had to formulate a plan for keeping the country's Native population from forming an unbreakable alliance. Middleton kept constant contact by Dominion Telegraph with his superior, Minister Adolphe Caron, whose office could relay intelligence instantly, or within a few days, from Battleford, Calgary, Swift Current, Winnipeg or other points. With one short wire, Middleton could order troops or supplies, receive acknowledgement of his request and then expect an imminent delivery by railroad.

Few war commanders before him had had such wonders at their fingertips, but Middleton, an arrogant man, often wasted telegraph time complaining to Caron about petty jealousies and prejudices. Middleton made no bones about his disdain for Canadian troops, his junior officers, the NWMP, the Metis and anyone else who didn't please him. In the coming weeks, however, reversals for the Canadian forces would present complications to his well-laid plans and teach the arrogant general some humility.

On April 6, Middleton, bound for Batoche, had moved north past the Touchwood Hills with a column consisting of the A Battery Regiment of Canadian Artillery, the Winnipeg Field Battery of Artillery, Boulton's Scouts, the Dominion Land Surveyor's Intelligence Corps, half of C Company of the Infantry School Corps, 10th Battalion of Royal Grenadiers, 90th Battalion of Winnipeg Rifles, and French's Scouts out of Fort Qu'Appelle. Middleton's plan was to knock Riel out as soon as possible, cutting off the head of the revolt.

When the column arrived at the telegraph station in Humboldt, Middleton learned of the Frog Lake massacre and the surrender of Fort Pitt. Trader William McLean and his family, Catholic priest Father LeGoff, Anglican minister Charles Quinney and his family, and several HBC and Indian department employees and their families inhabited Fort Pitt, along with a 25-man NWMP outpost commanded by Inspector Francis Dickens. The Cree vastly outnumbered the contingent and held the fate of the fort at will. Dickens, Middleton learned, had sent out a patrol before Big Bear's arrival, but as McLean and Dickens were negotiating withdrawal, the patrol had returned. In a rash act, it had charged through the gauntlet of the Cree camp to make for the safety of the fort. It was a disastrous run. A scout had made it to the gate, but a Mountie was wounded and another shot and killed. The charge had angered Big Bear, who demanded immediate surrender. Considering the foolhardiness of the police, McLean had put his chances as a prisoner of Big Bear over the capabilities of the NWMP and had voluntarily given up the civilians to the Cree in exchange for fair treatment.

Outgunned, the hapless Dickens had then ordered his men across the river, where they rebuilt an old scow to make an escape. With a one-day guarantee of safety from Big Bear, under cover of darkness, Dickens' command had ridden the scow downriver to the relative safety of Battleford. He had saved his command from annihilation, but the surrender became a humiliation from which Dickens never recovered.

The massacre at Frog Lake and the surrender of Fort Pitt forced Middleton to change his tactics. He planned for Otter's force to march from the railroad town of Swift Current and board a fleet of steamboats at nearby Saskatchewan Landing. After a short voyage, Otter would then join Middleton's force at Clarke's Crossing for a concentrated attack on Batoche, but three of the four boats were stranded in low water below Medicine Hat; only the *Northcote* became available to Otter. This reversal, brought on by nature and not the enemy, coupled with the panic at Battleford and the tragedy at Frog Lake, ripped Middleton's plans to shreds. Otter would instead form an overland column to cross the South Saskatchewan and reinforce Battleford with 50 NWMP under Superintendent William Herchmer, the Queen's Own Rifles, the Governor General's Foot Guards, Half of C Company of the Infantry School Corps, and A Battery, Regiment of Canadian Artillery. Only the Midland Battalion was sent downriver aboard the *Northcote*.

On April 22, Middleton arrived at Clarke's Crossing. He divided his forces, sending half across the river in an attempt to create a pincer movement in the approach to Batoche, with troops advancing on either bank of the South Saskatchewan. On April 24, as the column approached Tourond Coulee, near the tributary of Fish Creek, shots rang out of the trees. Cavalrymen dropped from their saddles as it became readily apparent that the column was under attack.

Gabriel Dumont's Metis and the Sioux of Whitecap fired from opposing concealed positions as Dumont himself, and several others on swift horses, charged into a ravine, attempting to draw the troops into a crossfire as they traversed the creek. When the bulk of Middleton's force arrived to deploy, Dumont fell back to the trees and started a grass fire to obscure the military's vision of his position. Middleton avoided Dumont's trap by first setting up the artillery, divided between right and left batteries, to lay down shelling fire, but, in so doing, the gunners themselves became the targets in a shooting gallery.

As the howitzer guns were being positioned, the Metis marksmen made easy sport of the exposed artillerymen. They used the backfire smoke from the cannon as a target, guaranteeing a hit on the gunnery crew. Middleton himself was nearly struck down when a Metis bullet whizzed through his fur hat. The infantry advanced in skirmish order and returned heavy fire but also took casualties. Finally, stalemated by the terrain, Middleton, unable to do much, decided against a charge. Before Dumont could be overrun, he retreated, using the smoke from a grass fire as cover. The tiny Metis forces slipped away into the brush, and Middleton called a ceasefire, even as the other half of his column vainly scrambled across the river, arriving too late to assist.

Though Dumont was disappointed by the failure of his plan to trap the soldiers at the creek, he was definitely the victor. Middleton had suffered a crushing 55 casualties, with 9 dead. Dumont only lost 4 men, but more devastating was the death of 55 horses, either by artillery shelling or rifle fire from troops who could not see much else at which to shoot. With animal transportation crucial, the loss was a calamity.

On April 26, 1885, a train of 200 wagons full of troops and supplies entered the town of Battleford. Otter had orders from Middleton to reinforce the NWMP, garrison the town and stand pat. But the townsmen and some of Otter's own staff insisted he attack Poundmaker. Bowing to the pressure, he went around his commanding officer and requested permission from Lieutenant-Governor Dewdney to attack the Poundmaker camp. Dewdney gave his blessing, and Otter assembled 392 men from his own command, the NWMP and the town's militia, the Battleford Rifles. With two 7-pounder cannon and a Gatling gun, Otter moved the 35 miles westward to Poundmaker's reserve on May 1.

The following morning they began their attack on Poundmaker's camp of Cree, Stoney and Assiniboine at Cut Knife Creek, but the soldiers bumbled their approach by splashing around in the creek and on the marshy ground, alerting the camp to their presence. The camp probably had also heard the wheels of the wagons and artillery for miles. The Cree war chief, Fine Day, quickly chose the high ground of Cut Knife Hill to organize a counterattack. With 243 fighters at his disposal, he dispatched two flanks of Cree and Assiniboine warriors into the ravines, to emerge in the trees and brush behind the soldiers. That put the warriors into cover, and the soldiers exposed. The withered limbers of the artillery guns had not stood up to the wear and tear of the trail and broke down. The Gatling gun, with little capability to change elevation, proved useless when the enemy learned all they had to was duck beneath the firing pattern.

After six hours, Otter realized he was failing miserably and ordered withdrawal. The soldiers backed out of their trap and across the marsh. Suffering 8 dead and 14 wounded, Otter retreated to Battleford. That the colonel withdrew without further loss of life was purely due to the charity of Poundmaker, who prevented his warriors from attacking the defeated troops all the way back to town. When Middleton learned of Otter's defeat, hot on the heels of his own whipping by Gabriel Dumont, he was enraged, as much by the loss as by Otter's insubordination and the over-his-head appeal to political masters. Otter was admonished and ordered to contain himself to defending Battleford.

That left the Frog Lake–Fort Pitt front and the Big Bear situation, where the unorthodox General Thomas Strange was moving in to take the offensive. His column was a hasty assembly of militia units: Major George Hatton's Alberta Mounted Rifles, initially called the Mountain Rangers; 20 NWMP from Macleod, commanded by Inspector A. Bowen Perry; Steele's Scouts, an irregular volunteer unit combined with an active NWMP contingent, (fresh from putting down a violent strike of railroad workers in British Columbia); and the 92nd Winnipeg Light Infantry under Colonel W. Osborne Smith.

In what Middleton thought would be a jibe to his old rival, he assigned Strange two French-speaking units from Quebec: the 65th Mount Royal Rifles (Carabiniers) under Colonel J.A. Ouimet and the 9th Battalion (Voltigeurs). Middleton held an irrational fear of putting French Catholic troops up against the Metis, but that blind sight was Strange's delight. Having previously commanded the Royal Artillery in Quebec, Strange spoke fluent French and held the francophone troops in high esteem.

On April 20, Strange's column left Calgary to secure the country to Fort Edmonton. Three forts were constructed en route and manned by the 65th Mount Royal: Fort Normandeau at the Red Deer Crossing, Fort Ostell at the Battle River Crossing (at Ponoka), and Fort Ethier at Pipestone Creek (near Wetaskiwin). As the Mounted Rifles patrolled the Calgary–Edmonton trail, the rest of the column marched on to relieve Fort Edmonton, arriving May 10. After securing Edmonton, St. Albert and Fort Victoria, the Field Force left in several stages, on horseback, and in specially constructed barges down the North Saskatchewan.

As reports filtered into Medicine Hat of the fighting and activity in the north, Major Stewart learned of Middleton's and Otter's reversals. These were significant blows to the Canadian government. If Dumont, Poundmaker and Big Bear consolidated in another area and drew new allies, the danger would be great. The *Macleod Gazette* opined that Riel's people would "make for the Cypress Hills where once established, they can hold out against all the troops of Canada while their supplies last. They could also from that point swoop down on the settlements nearby and the cattle country and put the whole country at defiance."[67]

Stewart thought further ahead and realized that in the event of a Metis defeat, several might escape to blend into the American Metis settlements in Montana. If so, the fugitive route would be through the dense jack pines of the Cypress Hills. The major posted a bounty: "Stated Capt. [*sic*] Stewart in Cypress Hills district has offered one thousand dollars reward for the capture of Riel should he attempt to escape into the U.S. through that district."[68] Across the border, the US Army put the post of Fort Assiniboine on alert.

From RMR headquarters at Medicine Hat, long, monotonous patrols were sent out into the Cypress Hills, and into the vast, stark prairie to the west, south to the Milk River Ridge and beyond to the forty-ninth parallel. In the west, Captain Herron's troop patrolled the foothills in uneventful, drawn-out trail rides. The Blood and Peigan tribes remained quiet, and John Herron experienced little excitement. With the NWMP, the RMR escorted wagon trains and guarded the route of the Whoop-Up Trail between Macleod and the border, Galt's railway and the Dominion Telegraph construction projects.

Supplies continued to pour across the border from the town of Fort Benton, Montana, to Medicine Hat, Macleod and Calgary, as had been the case for nearly 20 years. In fact, the I.G. Baker

Co. briefly expanded its mercantile area. With the Carlton Trail from Winnipeg running down the main street of Batoche, the northern town of Fort Edmonton had its usual lines of supply and communication cut off. To fill in, 9 teams of oxen pulling 63 tons of I.G. Baker goods travelled to Calgary and onward, accompanied by the RMR and the Alberta Field Force along the way. The experiment became a stopgap measure when the black soil north of the Bow River proved too soft for the hefty wagons to make a regular bull-team route practical.

The Rangers were ordered into formation daily and put through mounted cavalry drills. When in towns, their routine was to patrol the streets as other troop members were doing at Pincher Creek, Fort Macleod and Coalbanks. To maintain discipline, Major Stewart moved his headquarters camp upriver. Likely that was meant to keep his troops out of saloons, but there was also trouble with the arrival of another regiment into town.

A few days after the RMR appeared at Medicine Hat, a troop train pulled in to deliver the Halifax Provisional Battalion, a unit of 200 infantrymen from Nova Scotia. Too late to join any of the northbound columns, the Halifax was assigned to guard various points along the CPR. It had deployed squads at Winnipeg, Moose Jaw and Maple Creek, but the main body was ordered to the Hat. Given the assignment of defending the national railway, unit commander Colonel James Bremner was under the impression he had command of the southern Alberta District; however, he was yet to butt heads with John Stewart.

The Halifax infantry encamped above the town on the crest of the hill, where Bremner ordered the men to dig rifle pits into the brow of the hill. Then, looking toward the river, he noticed an odd sight. Several military bell tents, not unlike his own, were set up along the South Saskatchewan. Bremner sought out the local post office, which he found located in Tweed's store. Bremner introduced himself to Thomas Tweed, picked up his messages and then asked about the cavalry troop near the river.

Tweed explained that it was an irregular unit from Macleod. Bremner, considering himself the ranking officer, demanded to know why this "Major Stewart" had not reported to him. Tweed replied, "Stewart is wondering why you have not reported to him. He was here before you were and is entitled to know your standing, whether you are an enemy, or a recruit."[69]

Stewart was taken aback by the challenge to his authority. The RMR and the Halifax Battalion soon became involved in a minor turf war over military responsibility. Minister Caron's telegrams had implied to Stewart that he was in charge, second only to General Strange. The failure of communications between the two commanders came to a head and translated down into the behaviour of the troops. An interregimental rivalry developed, as is often the case with base troops, and soon the disagreement escalated.

After the Rangers finished their daily patrol through town, they rode up the hill to the battalion camp to see if they could cause a little trouble. They turned loose the battalion's horses, and soon the mounts were entangled in the guy ropes of the tents. Eventually the shelters collapsed, and the horses trampled what was left. Then the Rangers mounted up and rode out, all the while catcalling and laughing at the "feet soldiers."

Though they saw no action, the Halifax troops met tragedy. As spring grew warmer, the Nova Scotia boys bathed in the river. Unfortunately, two were caught in an undertow and drowned. A military service was held with Rangers and battalion members attending, and the two boys were buried in town.

Whether the drowning had anything to do with it or not, eventually Stewart and Bremner came to an understanding, and co-operation became the new watchword. The rivalry turned from camp destruction to sporting events such as baseball, cricket, target shooting at the rifle range Bremner set up, and even a tug-of-war. The Rangers won all of these competitions, with the exception of the tug-of-war.

Another casualty was the Medicine Hat Home Guard. With the additional troops in town, its members failed to attend the drills. Bob McCutcheon, the sergeant, complained he had more officers than privates and eventually disbanded the Guard.

At the Fish Creek battle site, General Middleton lay in wait while his force licked its wounds from Dumont's hit-and-run attack. He made camp near the ambush site and spent the next two weeks mapping strategy, gathering supplies and arranging for extra horses and feed. His rival at Batoche, Dumont, took martial control of the townsite and the terrain around it. The Metis dug some 20 to 30 shallow rifle pits, reinforced them with log breastworks and camouflaged them with brush, making emplacements effectively invisible to anyone approaching. The town's buildings were fortified, windows boarded, the women and children evacuated into dugout caves in the river's bank, and provisions made to picket the valuable horses away from the town.

Severely outnumbered, Louis Riel, through his messengers, appealed for aid. But Big Bear and Poundmaker had their own problems. Isolated, Dumont and Riel quarrelled over how to fight the campaign. Dumont was an advocate of pre-emptive, guerilla-style night strikes: haranguing the camps with middle-of-the-night gunfire and war whoops, running off the army's horses and even starting night fires to trap the soldiers in camp. Riel disagreed, arguing that a civilized people should fight a civilized war. Dumont felt compelled to obey his commander.

Middleton spent 15 days waiting for supplies and the Midland troops to come upriver on the *Northcote*. The steamer was fighting its own battle with the South Saskatchewan River: it was stranded in low water and on sandbars. Finally growing impatient and still fearing an ambush, Middleton's and Boulton's scouts reconnoitred the approaches to Batoche. By the time they got there, the steamer had arrived, and the general ordered the vessel to be armoured with thick planking, sacks of provisions or anything else that could be found. On May 7, Middleton moved his regrouped column, 850 strong, to strike for Batoche.

He planned to attack the town from Mission Ridge, the hill above it, with his main force. Simultaneously, the *Northcote* was to sail in and deploy 50 armed troops from the Infantry School Corps on shore. The night of May 8, Middleton's brigade camped six miles from town and was marching by 6:00 a.m. Before Middleton arrived at the hill, the *Northcote* prematurely steamed into the reach beneath it, an hour ahead of time.

Fully aware of the steamer, Dumont had had the ferry cable stretched across the river lowered in hopes of snagging the ship. The cable was still too high, but it ripped off the smokestacks, mast and loading spars. Heavy gunfire ensued from both directions as the crew scrambled to put out fires caused by the careening smokestack. The ship was riddled with bullets, but most injuries came from the crashing stacks and masts; only one crewman was winged by gunfire later on. The steamer's commander, Captain James Sheets, ordered the ship onward, refusing to either make the landing or turn around, despite the orders of the regiment commander aboard. With the *Northcote*'s departure, the Saskatchewan River's only naval battle was over.

Soon Middleton's troops appeared, and the artillery rolled into position. As the infantry advanced, they were bombarded by gunfire from Metis riflemen unseen in the trenches and rifle pits. Middleton tried to flank the Metis but, caught in the smoke and heat of more of Dumont's prairie fires, was forced to back off the ridge. The Gatling gun, manned by Lieutenant Arthur "Gat" Howard, the American representative of the gun's manufacturer, was useless in the smoke.

At nightfall, a dejected Middleton ordered his men to retreat to the zareba, an improvised camp and stockade some distance from Mission Ridge. Throughout the night, the Metis fired erratic, spontaneous shots into the zareba to taunt the troops, keep them rattled and prevent their sleeping. For the next three days, each side held its ground and bided time. Middleton, with 900 men at his disposal, was gun-shy, even as Gabriel Dumont held the field with a little over 200 defenders. Officers pleaded with the general to overwhelm the trenches with a bayonet charge, but Middleton rebuffed all suggestions. In the town Riel wandered the trenches, praying with his followers and steeling their courage. On the fourth day, May 12, Colonel Williams of the Midland Battalion mutinied and ordered a charge. Inspired, the other units joined the fray. Middleton's bugler sounded the retreat, but the soldiers were not listening.

The charge was effective, as the sheer numbers of the Canadian force overwhelmed the rifle pits. The infantry flanked the town, one column driving defenders out to the north as the main force drove a wedge into the heart of the community, clearing the street and the buildings of fighters. By evening the siege was over, with 8 dead and 46 wounded on the government side. Metis tolls were much more severe: 16 dead and 30 wounded, a full 10 percent of the population of Batoche. Government forces rounded up the rest of the Metis as houses in the village were looted and burned by some of the very troops who were supposed to be restoring order.

The area around the town was heavily brushed, well given to escape and subterfuge. When prisoners and casualties were accounted for, neither Gabriel Dumont nor Louis Riel was among them. Given the vengefulness of the Canadian troops, hiding was a good strategy. Dumont had no intention of surrender or capture. As the country was scoured, he found a way to make sure his family was provided for and even found the time to have blankets and food taken to Riel's family. Then he and Michael Dumas mounted two sturdy horses and lit out for the US border.

For three days Louis Riel wandered the brush, alone, hungry, disoriented and on foot. On May 15, two of Boulton's Scouts and an interpreter found him on the trail and took him into custody. In order to get him safely past the guard to Middleton's tent, the prophet was passed off as a cook. The ruse accomplished, Riel walked into the general's tent and offered his hand in surrender.

In Medicine Hat, Major Stewart received the news of Riel's surrender. The RMR and Wood Mountain Scouts doubled their patrols in the Cypress Hills, looking for any fugitive making a break for America or taking refuge: "Despatch [sic] from Medicine Hat states Capt. Stewart's Rangers are covering every trail to south through Cypress Hills country. They are apprehensive that Poundmaker is making for south through that region, and that speedy arrangement of troops with scouts & artillery [is] immediately necessary to prevent lodgement [sic] in Cypress Hills."[70]

Still, the RMR and its allies managed to miss the major escapee from Batoche: the adjutant-general, Gabriel Dumont. Accompanied by Dumas, the 51-year old prairie hunter had a lifelong knowledge of the Cypress Hills, a tremendous advantage over the young flatland cowboys looking for him. To the Metis living in the hills, he was "Uncle Gabriel," sometimes in blood, but especially in their hearts—the generous captain of the buffalo hunts who had filled many a starving family's larder with fresh meat. The settlers may not have thought much of Riel, but Dumont was a man whose respect transcended all thought of risk. They were there when he needed their aid, and he and Dumas were harboured and fed by families all along the route.

Dumont slipped across the border like a wraith, evaded capture and followed the Milk River into Montana. He and Dumas later surrendered to the US Army at Fort Assiniboine. Both applied for asylum in the United States. After much diplomatic turmoil, both were released under an order from President Grover Cleveland.

Six days after the fall of Batoche, the Rangers finally saw their first hint of action. On May 19 a cattle herder in the Medicine Hat area was attacked and fired on by a raiding party of what he thought were Metis and Natives. The Rangers' scouting parties, however, could not locate the raiders. Nor could they determine if the perpetrators were hostile or merely on a horse-gathering expedition—and possibly responsible for the nearby theft of horses from freighters Ezra Pearson and the Connelly brothers 10 days earlier.

Also, in mid-May, about 150 Bloods left their reserve on the Belly River and went north, sending war jitters through the people of Macleod. There was no danger at that point—the Bloods maintained they didn't believe what the Cree were telling them and regarded the Gatling gun as a myth. Just the same, the *Macleod Gazette* wrote that the Active Service Corps of the RMR should be recalled to "deal" with the Bloods. The editor even went so far as to suggest that Medicine Hat take care of itself, raise its own corps and let the RMR come home—ignoring that a third of the regiment was still in the Macleod region, and that at least a dozen Rangers were from the Hat. Even with Riel in captivity and the rebellion winding down, an ill wind of alarm and paranoia blew in ranch country.

By the end of May, the Dominion Telegraph line linking Medicine Hat with Fort Macleod was completed, greatly assisting Superintendent John Cotton and Major Stewart with their movements and communications. Telegraph offices were installed at the NWMP barracks and at the post office. Stewart petitioned for the service to be extended to Pincher Creek, but the request was denied.

South of Medicine Hat to the border was a vast, dry country with virtually no settlement. Even ranching was sparse. It was open territory for horse rustlers. They were generally believed to be Assiniboine or Gros Ventres from across the border, in the country to grab some mounts in the plains tradition, but there were other options to consider. Could the horse thefts be due to the Cree, Metis or some other group looting from ranches, mines, railways or teamsters for a northern ally, in anticipation of some new attack? Or were these just common livestock thieves, rustlers using the unsettled conditions as an opportunity to make some illicit cash in the black market? Few wanted to think it a Blackfoot caper, but inaction was not an option. Before some rash act got someone killed, identity and intent had to be determined. For reliable intelligence, the RMR sent out one of its best, Sergeant William Jackson, a battle-scarred survivor of the Little Bighorn.

Near the end of May, Jackson was out on a solitary patrol "somewhere near Medicine Hat."[71] "Somewhere near" was a relative term; there were virtually no settlements in the area with which to reference, save for railway sidings so new they were yet to be named. Some accounts put Jackson south of modern-day Bow Island; other accounts indicate he was south of the Cypress Hills. Both navigational landmarks place him not far from the border.

Wherever he was, Jackson encountered some three dozen Natives. At first blush, he thought they were friendly Bloods. That hope was dashed when the group fired shots at him. Outnumbered, Jackson prepared to go down swinging, possibly showing more pluck than good judgment. In the cavalry style, he pulled his horse to the ground and crouched behind it to use the massive body as a breastwork. In position for the stand, Jackson levelled his Winchester carbine and returned fire. More volleys countered his actions. As his ammunition depleted, Jackson weighed his options. Then, in an odd development, the brief combat ended with no resolution. The party departed, galloping off. Jackson remounted and rode off in the opposite direction. Jackson returned to the rail line and rode a train into Medicine Hat to report to his commanding officer. Again the Rangers rode off in pursuit.

Treaty 7 chiefs were invited to tour eastern Canada and Ottawa in 1886. Back row: Father Lacombe (left) and interpreter Jean L'Heureux. Seated on bench (left to right): Three Bulls, Crowfoot and Red Crow. Front (sitting): North Axe (left) and One Spot.

Duncan Campbell (left) was a prominent Fort Macleod businessman who petitioned for responsible government in the west. David Joe Wylie became a Conservative member of the first legislature when Saskatchewan became a province. ESPLANADE PC 525.2

(Top) Medicine Hat Home Guard poses with members of the NWMP at the Police Point barracks. ESPLANADE PC 525.10

(Bottom) A Ranger scouting party in the Cypress Hills during the Northwest Rebellion gives its horses a well-deserved rest.
ESPLANADE PC 404.12

(Top) Halifax Provisional Battalion. The battalion arrived too late to join any of the fighting and was relegated to guarding the CPR line.

(Bottom left) General Frederick Dobson Middleton, commander of the North West Field Force, was charged with putting down the Northwest Rebellion. He would leave Canada in disgrace over a scandal related to his troops' looting of Metis possessions.

(Bottom right) Kootenai Brown, 1883.

(Top) Mounties, First Nations and Metis take a break from rebellion tension to enjoy a drink. That's Kootenai Brown sitting in the centre.
ESPLANADE PC 234.2

(Bottom) Members of the 1886 North-West Territories Council.
GLENBOW ARCHIVES NA-1323-1

(Top) One of John Higinbotham's articles on the RMR was accompanied by this illustration, "The Cowboy Cavalry," by J.D. White.

(Bottom) Officers of the RMR (left to right): Lieutenant Henry Boyle; Captain Edward Gilpin Brown; unidentified (in white stable jacket); Captain Richard Boyle; Major John Stewart; and Kootenai Brown.

Gabriel Dumont, Fort Assiniboine, MT, after escaping the militia. He made hopeless plans to rescue Riel from his Regina jail cell. He would end up working as a trick shooter in Buffalo Bill Cody's Wild West show.
GLENBOW ARCHIVES NA-1063-1

(Clockwise from top left)
Major John Stewart in the years before his death.
GLENBOW ARCHIVES NA-1827-3

Isabel Stewart (née Skead), daughter of
Ottawa lumber baron James Skead. After her
marriage to John, the couple resided in an
elegant Gothic-style house that still stands
in Calgary's Inglewood neighbourhood.
GLENBOW ARCHIVES NA-1724-2

John Herron was elected to Parliament as
Conservative member for the Alberta riding
(later the Macleod riding). GALT PI9770285007

Dr. Leverett George DeVeber studied medicine
in the US and England before heading west as
a surgeon for the NWMP. He served as surgeon
for the Rangers, but his services were never
required for combat wounds. GALT PI9694786000

Using the new telegraph link, Stewart instantly coordinated with his counterpart in Macleod. When NWMP commander John Cotton received the telegram from Stewart reporting the episode, the *Gazette* amped up the shooting in headlines as "Rumours Of War."[72] "A message was received…from Major Stewart to the effect that some of his men had run across thirty or forty Indians and that shots had been exchanged."[73] The shooting rang familiar with Cotton, recently hearing from his own scouts of the same marauders. His suspicions confirmed, Cotton personally led a patrol to search for the perpetrators.

Cotton hoped that the Jackson shooting had nothing to do with the Bloods being off the reserve. "It was not known who or what the Indians were," the *Macleod Gazette* reported. "[Superintendent] Cotton and Dr. Kennedy started on [May 25] with twenty men for Lethbridge and points farther east…Cotton was anxious as to what Indians they were. A great many Bloods were away from their reserve and supposed by some to be in that direction. If they turn out to be such Major Cotton will endeavour to get them back to their reserve. It is to be sincerely hoped that no mistaken identity or other cause has resulted in the Bloods being fired on, unless they were committing depredations."[74]

To get to the bottom of the situation, Cotton tied in with Major Stewart's strategy of RMR patrols sent out west and south from Medicine Hat, using the NWC&NC railway to move men and horses more quickly. As the *Macleod Gazette* stated, such use was of mutual benefit to both the railroad and the militia: "The moving about of the forces has had the desired effect of giving confidence to the railway men."[75]

Riding all night, Jackson guided the Rangers to the site of his recent exchange. The *Winnipeg Times* identified the location as Pigeon Creek, but probably actually meant Piegan Coulee. To the satisfaction of the officers, no trace of Jackson's attackers was found. Some were even skeptical of Jackson's word. Perturbed by such suspicions, Jackson insisted the raiders were still in the area and set out to prove himself right. He picked up some brush and started a fire. Using green grass moistened with a bit of water, Jackson made the fire produce columns of smoke. His signal was soon acknowledged with corresponding smoke. The Rangers gave chase, but the quarry gave the RMR the slip. No sign was found anywhere—of the party, or its fire.

It was a big country, and Cotton fared no better in ascertaining the mystery of Jackson's attackers. He left Macleod and arrived at Lethbridge, via Fort Kipp, the same day. The next day, Cotton and his men went east following the railroad to the head of Chin Coulee, where the scouts had heard of raiding parties, thence following the coulee on the old Fort Walsh trail. That put them south of the railroad siding of Woodpecker (Barnwell), to Foley's Camp, a ranch line station, to await further communication from Stewart. But patrols always seemed to be a day behind the rumours. After two uneventful days, they returned to Lethbridge, where the dispatch letters from Stewart waited.

To identify the mystery party, the *Macleod Gazette* turned to quoting the RMR sergeant: "Jackson says the Indians he met and fired on were either Assiniboine or Gros Ventre [*sic*] from the States."[76] A man of his background would know the difference between such, and Blackfoot, Peigan or Blood. Despite the chasing of ghost parties, the *Gazette* still praised the quick action of the RMR and hoped it would cure the problem. "There is no doubt that Major Stewart and his men have done good work, and may make the Indians go south to the United States, as it is presumed they saw the movements of the troops."[77]

The matter remained a quandary. Its connection to the rebellion was unknown and probably non-existent save for the timing. The theft of livestock was nothing new to southern Alberta. The possibility of making a quick buck from horses or cattle persuaded away from their owners remained a problem long past 1885 and was beyond the purview of Native bands.

Much of the routine work usually done by the absent NWMP was accomplished by the RMR, and the troop often performed combined patrols. Many had worn the scarlet, and the routine was nothing new to them. For the cowboys, riding the long distances between camps and outposts was little different than herding or riding roundup, with the dangers and the pay about the same.

Near High River, Stimson's Scouts watched over the range. In addition to future senator Dan Riley and famed black cowboy John Ware, the Stimson ranks included Midway Ranche owner Frederick Ings. They combined patrols with their regular range-riding duties and discouraged any possible depredations of their livestock.

Ings often rode with Ware. One day they came upon a freshly killed beef carcass. Shortly after, they discovered a young Stoney travelling on foot and charged him with the crime. The Stoney protested his innocence. Ings related the rest of the story: "John began to uncoil his rope, saying, 'We'll hang him anyway. If he's not guilty today, he will be tomorrow.' The Indian drew himself up to his full height, presenting an appearance of great dignity. He raised his hand, looking straight at us. There was no fear, no cringing, as he spoke in a clear firm voice: '*N'appeequin Kistra machestee si dpitz.*' [White man, I do not lie.] Convinced of his innocence, we left him."[78]

Ings related another personal experience, one in which his paranoia and a better aim could have threatened the peace. "One day I was alone in my shack, crippled having cut my foot with an axe. I heard a noise of horses running. Four Sarcees ran, Indian fashion, right to the house, throwing their horses on their haunches at the door, which they pushed open and entered. They were decked in war paint and carried carbines. Speaking in Indian [Sarcee], they told me to get some grub in a hurry. I pretended not to understand. They kept at me when they saw that I was on crutches. At least one of them poked me in the ribs with his rifle. With the aid of a crutch, I picked up a stick of firewood and started in on them. What the outcome would have been, I don't know, had they not heard the rumble of an approaching wagon. They ran for their horses with cries of, 'White man coming.' I managed to reach my bunk and grab my Colt revolver from under my pillow and shot at them as they ran; but luckily they were out of range, for had I killed one, serious trouble might have started."[79]

In the corridor between Macleod and High River, an outlaw rustling ring brazenly used the distraction of the rebellion to cover their drives of stolen horses. "On Tuesday, the 29th [of] May, information was received at the [NWMP] barracks that a band of horses had been brought in from Montana and had been taken north, the parties keeping well east of the regular trail." The rustlers appeared to be staying off the well-patrolled Macleod–Calgary trail, a surefire way to avoid reporting their "imports" to the NWMP who doubled as customs agents. But it was difficult to keep the dust from a string of mustangs secret. When "it was subsequently found that they were seen about ten miles east of [Fort] Kipp," the drovers' intentions of evading the police post were clear. A combined Mountie–Ranger team—Sergeant Spicer, Corporal Jarvis and an unnamed Ranger—took pursuit.

The squad followed the Calgary Trail, hoping to catch their quarry trying to sell their ill-gotten gains to ranchers along the way. They had no success at the New Oxley and Mosquito Creek ranches. Finally, Spicer caught up with the thieves at High River, but the horses had been cached. Checking an underused trail, the patrol quickly found 16 stolen mounts farther down the banks of the Highwood River. "The arrest was made, and the men, two in number, together with the horses, were brought back to Macleod."[80]

The rustlers were imprisoned in the barracks jail. On June 8, J. Colville was tried and convicted of horse stealing and sentenced by Colonel Macleod, the stipendiary magistrate, to three months' hard labour. What happened to Colville's accomplice is not known. The outlaws probably should have considered themselves lucky to be apprehended on Canadian soil. If caught in Montana, they surely would have paid the ultimate penalty. Only a month earlier, two Canadians, one a former Mountie, had stolen a herd of mules from the NWC&NC mine sheds at Coalbanks and shooed them to Montana. Arrested by Deputy Sheriff Joe Kipp, the Canadians were taken captive by Montana vigilantes and strung up to the nearest tree.

In the north, General Middleton marched the troops from Batoche to the fortified town of Prince Albert, where he took command from Commissioner Irvine of the NWMP. Middleton distributed his force among the assembled fleet of four sternwheeler steamboats (the *North West, Marquis, Baroness* and *Alberta*) and boarded the *North West* to unite with Otter at Battleford. On May 25 the general received the surrender of Poundmaker at Fort Battleford. Though Riel and Poundmaker had laid down arms, Big Bear's band was still at large and was holding prisoners.

From Battleford, Middleton's brigade converged on Fort Pitt and united with General Strange's Alberta Field Force marching in from the west. Strange arrived at the ruins of Fort Pitt on May 24 and found the remains of Constable David Cowen, the mounted policeman killed in the ill-fated charge through the Cree gauntlet. A patrol sent to Frog Lake discovered the gruesome remains of the 10 men killed in the massacre 7 weeks earlier. On May 26, Sam Steele's Scouts followed a trail to Onion Lake and were attacked northeast of Frog Lake at Pipestone Creek. In the short gun battle that ensued, one Cree, Meeminook, of the Saddle Lake band had been killed.

Hearing of that encounter, Big Bear knew he would have a fight on his hands. He chose to make a stand on the high ground, a heavily treed ridge near the mouth of the Little Red Deer River, not far off the North Saskatchewan. To keep the prisoners out of harm's way, trenches were dug in on the back side of the ridge as shelter. On the front side, warriors dug rifle pits to conceal their position among the thick poplars. The ridge was a mile north of a high, cone-shaped mesa called Frenchman's Butte. The proximity of Big Bear's position to the hill led to the error of the fight referred to as the "Battle of Frenchman's Butte."

On the morning of May 28, the Alberta Field Force moved to the marshy ground at the base of the hill. A nine-pounder field gun opened fire on the Cree rifle pits, but the elevation was a tricky calculation, and the cannon shell overshot the ridge. Shrapnel shells had a little more effect. Steele's Scouts rode up the hill and then descended to a brush patch near a creek. The other units flanked to either side along the creek. But the infantry could not cross the swamps without being exposed, and Steele could not flank the encampments for the same reasons.

A rash field commander might have attempted a charge, but the situation was different here. The terrain was boggy, the incline of the hill steep. Just the ascent would tax frontal attackers. Strange realized that dividing his forces would result in a massacre. He withdrew, risking heavy gunfire, as his force slowly came out from cover. Three men were wounded, one pulled off an exposed area of the hill by the general himself; none were killed. Recalling the recent Custer situation, Strange was convinced of the danger of being surrounded. Rifle and cannon ammunition rapidly depleted, and Strange retreated to regroup at Fort Pitt. The Frenchman's Butte battle was rated as another indecisive stalemate.

A week later, Big Bear released a few of the white prisoners taken from Frog Lake. They were found by Strange's scouts and taken to Fort Pitt. About the same time, Middleton arrived on the *North West*. The next day, knowing Middleton would scuttle plans to pursue the Cree, Sam Steele's Scouts, using information gathered from the released hostages, gave chase, following tracks north from the earlier battlefield, through forests that grew ever thicker.

A sniper ambushed and wounded a scout on their first day out. A day later, on June 3, Steele's brigade trapped some of the Cree when they tried to cross an isthmus that separated the twin bays of Makwa (Loon) Lake. A battle ensued, and six Cree were killed, while two of Steele's Scouts were wounded. The narrow land bridge near the battle has since been known as Steele's Narrows. Following the Makwa fight, the conglomerated war party fragmented and scattered. The Chipewyan band went back to their Cold Lake reserve; the Woods Cree headed out past Beaver River, and the main group, led by Big Bear himself, set off to the northeast.

Middleton took command and followed Steele to Loon Lake, ordering a pursuit across the bog in a vain attempt to cut off Big Bear's retreat. That chase ended immediately after Middleton and his horse sank into a saddle-high muskeg bog. The humiliated general withdrew to Fort Pitt. He ordered Strange to the Beaver River, a pursuit that ended at Cold Lake, where on June 9 several Chipewyan leaders were arrested for their part in the Frog Lake massacre. The Woods Cree surrendered at Fort Pitt.

Finally, the instigator of Frog Lake, Wandering Spirit, along with other ringleaders, surrendered at Fort Battleford. He and eight others were convicted and hung in the compound of the NWMP fort. Many of the remaining Cree were expected to make a break south to their previous hunting grounds in Montana. Gradually, over the next month, scattered warriors and their families realized the war was lost, wandered into army camps and laid down their arms.

In southern Alberta, only the news from Frenchman's Butte and Loon Lake brought any excitement—dramatic events that did not repeat themselves in Treaty 7 country. The Blackfoot, Blood and Peigan were swiftly and accurately told of the defeat of the rebels. Major Stewart and Superintendent Cotton kept their men on alert, both for escapees from the northern battles and for those seeking to take advantage of rebellion hysteria for their own ends. Throughout the rest of June 1885, RMR patrols were uneventful. Rangers continued their police-like duties—delivering dispatches, visiting ranches, escorting freight wagons and keeping general vigilance.

This routine began to grate on Major Stewart. Safeguarding cows and chasing phantoms was not what he had raised a cavalry to do, especially when cohorts like Sam Steele were seeing action. Stewart chafed for battle and felt Middleton was ignoring him. He expressed his frustration in a telegram to Minister Caron: "Cannot get General by wire; no American Indians across line frontier, all quiet, duties can now be filled by Police. My force specially adapted for emergency north—horses splendid condition, transport and packs complete; can join General in few days without injury to stock—expenditure not as much as here. After exertions of myself Officers and men, we all feel that the usefulness of the force is being thrown away there being no such material in the force for Indian work; have wired facts to General—will you kindly recommend myself and force to his notice."[81]

Caron advanced Stewart's concern to Middleton the very next day, but other issues were putting the general in an ungenerous mood, making him unwilling to assist subordinates. His jealousy was working overtime, and he was feeling challenges to his command from Strange and others. In a cranky reply, Middleton gave a litany of complaints, amid them the tart counter to the RMR request: "Will get rid of Stewart's Corps on return to Fort Pitt."[82]

When Stewart made his request, he was evidently unaware that the Cree were in such disarray. He knew only that Big Bear had escaped. Stewart increased his vigilance on the Cypress Hills. But the irony was that Big Bear, unfairly charged as a fearsome villain who could hold a nation spellbound and stand off the might of the Canadian militia, had in fact been reduced to a foot-bound fugitive.

The remainder of his band, including his older son, Imasees, abandoned him, choosing to take their chances south of the border. Several did get through. Imasees led them across the South Saskatchewan, somewhere between Maple Creek and Swift Current. Undoubtedly, Big Bear considered Montana as well. Had he made it, the US Army would have had a reverse Sitting Bull situation. But the pressure on him was too great. Fearing the police, or soldiers, might kill him if caught, he decided to give himself up to the Hudson's Bay Company. In previous years he had traded at Fort Carlton, and he resolved to seek asylum there, oblivious that the post was out of commission. For a month, Big Bear, accompanied only by his youngest son, Horse Child, and an elderly councillor, Two & Two, plodded through the prairies and brush along the North Saskatchewan. They travelled by night, sometimes navigating the river on a homemade raft.

Despite his pathetic state, Big Bear eluded all scouting parties, including one of Commissioner Irvine's NWMP patrols out of Green Lake. He came close to walking into Colonel Otter's Turtle Lake camp at one point and was nearly discovered on an island by the crew of the steamer *Alberta* at another. But always he slipped away unseen. On July 2, 1885, he arrived at the burnt-out shell of Fort Carlton and approached the tent of a ferryman across the river. The ferryman recognized his visitor and notified two policemen posted to the detachment inside Carlton. They took Big Bear into custody.

With Louis Riel and Poundmaker in prison, Gabriel Dumont in exile, and Big Bear arrested, the revolt was broken. Canada's civil war was over.

CHAPTER ELEVEN

The March Home

When news of Big Bear's capture became known in the south, the threat of the Northwest Rebellion was past and the Rangers had little left to justify their existence. In fact, a week after Loon Lake, there didn't seem any point in keeping the men away from their ranches. Captain John Herron's company had seen even less action than its Medicine Hat counterparts, and on June 10, Herron disbanded and paid off the Number 3 Troop. Major Stewart could not argue with getting civilians back to their jobs, but bristled that quick demobilization might squander the potential for the regiment he had raised. With the threat gone as fast as it had emerged, the force and all their efforts would soon be all for naught. Raised in a time and place when military readiness was a way of life, Stewart raised concerns that his adopted region would so quickly be left without a plan of defence or a militia.

Caron deferred the matter to Middleton, who had grumpily wanted to "get rid of Stewart's Corps." Incensed, Stewart knew he was going to have to strike while the iron was hot and do an end run around Middleton. On June 17 Stewart played the patronage card, using his connection with the militia's adjutant-general, Colonel Walker Powell. Stewart telegraphed Powell and requested he recommend the RMR for general service. Time was of the essence. A cash-strapped government spent millions in fighting the insurgency. Every day in the field racked the wages and expenses higher, and Caron was pressured to get troops off the rolls. Eastern troops in the field were to board the steamer fleet for transshipment down the Saskatchewan River and across Lake Winnipeg to the CPR. Units stationed on the railway, like the Halifax Provisional Battalion, would return on the rails. Cavalries were to march to disposition points, in most cases backtracking the trails on which they'd come.

The RMR were ordered back to Fort Macleod. The Medicine Hat recruits did not make the trip and were paid out immediately. Leading the column of troops 1 and 2 back into the setting sun was Commander Lord Boyle. Major Stewart headed in the opposite direction and boarded a train bound for Winnipeg, arriving July 9. He was to meet with Middleton and also wanted to persuade Adolphe Caron to gazette the Rangers as a permanent militia unit for southern Alberta.

The *Macleod Gazette* had no doubts whatsoever about Stewart's chances: "The Rangers have been ordered back to Macleod, where they are expected to arrive on Thursday next. They will be disbanded at once, but two troops, consisting of seventy men, will in all probability be re-enlisted for service until next spring. Major Stewart's offer to obtain this number of men for further service, met with a very gratifying answer from the Minister of Militia. The Major has gone to Winnipeg, having been telegraphed for by General Middleton and the probable result of the interview will be the acceptance of his offer."[83]

When Middleton and his troops arrived in Winnipeg in a drizzling summer rainstorm, the tavern keepers of the city kept their establishments open all night. Across the territories, unless liquor laws applied, passing troops blew off steam and, for the sake of the bartenders, a lot of cash.

Cash was also on John Stewart's mind. His personal accounts had taken a significant hit to maintain RMR funding, and the government owed him a bundle. Stewart had supplied horses, saddles, equipment—even employees—out of his own pocket. Now, if he was ordered to disperse, the troops would have to be paid out—another hit to his wallet. Diplomatically, the major let Defence Minister Caron know that if he did not see some cash advanced, he would refuse to discharge the RMR and let the per diem bill accumulate: "...under order from General Middleton to adjust accounts. Am disbanding here in the West, before General reaches here to authorize small advance in pay to the portion [of] my command on frontier which, in my discretion, I found necessary to make. The difference will be doubled by holding that force until his authority issued. I strongly recommend that authority be wired here to meet advance in Pay sheets to permit of their disbandment."[84]

Though the response from Caron or Middleton remains unknown, Stewart's next telegram to the defence minister was defensive, replying to charges that he had gone above his station in authorizing the Pincher Creek Home Guard to his rolls as members of the RMR. Stewart reminded them that his original carrying out report authorized for 150 men, and even with the addition of the Guard, the RMR were far below full enrollment. He argued that, as district commander, he had the right to decide what troops comprised his unit, and if there was an issue on how to pay them differently, the Principal Supply Officer & Paymaster at base headquarters in Winnipeg should be able to straighten it out.

As Stewart waged a war of dialogue with the bureaucracy and internal militia politics, at home the populace was more interested in dusting off the welcome mat. The Rangers were returning, and in the July 1, 1885, *Macleod Gazette*, Charlie Wood urged citizens to "honor the boys." The RMR rode into Macleod in formation on July 8 to the deafening roar of a celebratory artillery salute. Personally, they were disappointed—not with the reception, but with their own lack of battle honours. They had expected war, but had to be satisfied with home-front security.

As far as the citizens were concerned, however, the Rangers were entitled to a party, and on July 9 were treated to one. The *Gazette* chronicled the events and speeches:

THE WELCOME HOME

The Rocky Mountain Rangers Return to Macleod after an Absence of some Three Months

ADDRESS OF WELCOME FROM THE CITIZENS—
LORD BOYLE'S REPLY

On Tuesday afternoon the Mountain Rangers returned to Macleod, after three months of arduous duty on the frontier between here and Medicine Hat. We have frequently referred to their services before as having been of the most valuable nature, services which entitled them to the gratitude of the citizens of this district.

We suggested last week that there should be some public recognition of their services and on Wednesday it was decided to present them with an address of welcome. The original intention was to visit their camp, some two miles below town, for this purpose, but as it was rather late in the evening it was decided to postpone the matter until the next day, when it was arranged to have the troop paraded in town.

In accordance with this arrangement the men were drawn up in line opposite the post office at twelve o'clock, and the address was read by Mr. Wm. Black [president of the South-Western Stock Growers Association], as follows:

By the request and on behalf of the citizens of Macleod and surrounding country, I desire to extend to you a cordial and hearty welcome home, after the months spent by you in guarding our lives and property from invasion.

That your corps has no record of battles lost or won is a matter of sincere congratulations, and we assure you that the absence of such a record detracts in no wise from the sense of obligation we feel for the protection afforded us.

We are well aware that the country so faithfully watched over by you, offered, by it's [*sic*] exposed condition and peculiar resources, great inducements to savage marauders who wrought such havoc to the north of us, and that our district was not the theatre of such scenes of pillage and murder as there prevailed, is due to alacrity with which you responded to the call of duty at the first intimation of danger.

We regret the absence of the organizer of the corps on this occasion as we would wish to congratulate him personally on the manner in which he discharged his duties, as we now congratulate the country on having such men to depend on in times of danger.

You are western men—you know the undemonstrative character of the western people and you will understand that deep down in the hearts of those you have protected lies a feeling of gratitude to the citizen soldiery none the less genuine for being unobtrusive.

We feel that the danger that menaced us has drawn closer the ties that bound all parts of the Dominion and cemented more strongly the feelings with which we locally regard each other.

And now, as you return to civilian life, we trust that all good things may come to you, and we feel that as [*sic*] the duties of citizenship will be as faithfully discharged as your military ones were.

Once more we bid you a cordial welcome home.

Captain Boyle, on behalf of the troop, replied as follows:

To Mr. Black, citizens of Macleod and the surrounding country:

Gentlemen: On behalf of the troop I have the honor to command, I beg to tender you our sincere thanks for the kind manner in which you have welcomed our return. The address you have just presented, will long be remembered, I am sure, by us all as a mark of appreciation of our efforts to defend our country.

You say truly when you say the country we had to guard offered great inducements to Indian marauders, but as can be told you by a number of our men, we did to a certain extent, drive back numerous parties of Indians from the other side.

I also regret the absence of Major Stewart to-day, as he could assure you of the willing and faithful manner in which every man present with me performed the arduous duties which fell to his lot.

I shall have such pleasure in presenting this address to Major Stewart on his return, and I only regret that he is not here now to personally return you his thanks.

Allow me, once more on behalf of the officers and men of the Mounted Rangers, to thank you most heartily for this kind welcome.[85]

The Rangers camped northeast of the townsite awaiting the return of Stewart days later. Aside from the financial issues, his mission to Winnipeg was a failure. Middleton and Caron turned down his request for a permanent force, since "no American Indians across the line frontier"[86] had been seen. The contention was that a permanent militia unit could not be afforded for an area that had not seen any real trouble.

There was a clear bias in effect. Caron delivered a speech thanking Canada's military volunteers for their service but didn't acknowledge Colonel Otter or General Strange—deliberately snubbing them for actions countermanding Middleton. Any hope of special attention for Stewart's "border guards," amidst the battle honours won by Ontario volunteers, was asking too much.

On July 17, Militia general orders released from service all special corps organized for the rebellion. This included the Home Guards in Yorkton, Battleford, Regina, Birtle, Emerson, Calgary and Qu'Appelle, as well as the Moose Mountain Scouts, Boulton's Scouts, the Dominion Land Surveyors Intelligence Corps and, finally, the Rocky Mountain Rangers.

On July 10, Paymaster Edward Gilpin Brown finalized his pay lists, and the corps received orders to disband. The Rangers could not be paid out or discharged until July 17, so they patiently bided an extra week to receive their pay. When the troops finally were remunerated, they realized the government had only approved payment until July 10. The officers agreed to take the case for the seven lost days to the government, but no records indicate the outcome. When totalled, dispensations were as follows:

Total Paid Out

Preliminary Pay for Stewart, Powell, Gilpin Brown from Ottawa, Mar. 28 to Apr. 12:	$251.20
Paid To #1 & #2 Troops	
April 13th to 30th:	$2,825.30
May 1st to 31st:	$6,384.00
June 1st to 30th:	$3,384.00
July 1st to 10th:	$429.50
Paid to No.3 Troop	
April 14th to June 12th:	$5,620.80
Officers' Field Allowance	
April 13th to June 12th:	$231.71
Paid to Lt. James Christie for	
Pay Rations & Forage	$445.99
TOTAL EXPENSES FOR R.M.R.	$19,572.50[87]

While the Rangers awaited their payout and, especially after they got it, whisky flowed like water in Macleod. Liquor could only be served by special permit from the lieutenant-governor, and under this fiat, hoteliers and barkeepers dispensed liquid refreshment. Celebrations big and small were held. At the Macleod Hotel, Harry (Kamoose) Taylor offered up a gigantic feast, in patriotic victory flair, complete with Canadian Red Ensigns, Union Jacks and colourful bunting. Not a bad display for a trader who just a decade earlier plied his wares illegally.

In the midst of the revelry, trooper Charlie Thornton made a quick exit from Macleod, and for good reason. Examining the pay lists, Edward Gilpin Brown discovered that Thornton had falsified documents, resulting in the doubling of his pay. Mounties soon caught up with and arrested him at the St. Mary's River. While in the Macleod guardhouse, Thornton agreed to return his ill-gotten wages and was released two days later.

A few days after pay distribution, John (Rattlesnake Jack) Robson was charged with having liquor in his possession without permit, a fairly common occurrence under the era's prohibition laws. Jack was fined $50 and court costs and had his liquor destroyed.

In August a banquet and ball was held by the town of Macleod in appreciation of the Rangers' service and to acknowledge the return of the 20 policemen of C Troop from service with General Strange. It's unknown if, beyond the officers, many of the rough-and-tumble crew attended the gala, given the need to keep a job after many had been away from their usual careers. The banquet chair, Lord Boyle, made a toast to the Rocky Mountain Rangers. Then he introduced the keynote speaker, Major John Stewart, who had some choice words regarding charges inferred by General Middleton and the media.

He referred to [NWMP Commissioner Irvine's] high qualities both as a gentleman and a soldier and spoke very feelingly of the scandalous charges which have been made, against him. The noble work which the small body of police had done during the rebellion was touched upon, and the high state of efficiency eulogized. In speaking of the work done by the Rangers, Major Stewart said that it had been their bad fortune not to have any of the fighting to do. What duty they had done, however, everyone said had been done well, and every man among them had been willing and ready to go to the front, if they had been called upon to do so. He then went on to say that in this district a body of Mounted men could be raised superior to ANY CAVALRY IN THE DOMINION. He challenged the Eastern press to take this statement up and deny it.[88]

As southern Alberta returned to normal, voters of the district were treated to one last RMR battle—a political fight. The governing body of the North-West Territories, the North-West Territories Council, held an election to fill a vacant seat. When nominations closed, the two contenders were Ranger veterans, Lord Richard Boyle and rancher George Canning Ives. For a month, citizens endured endless speeches and debates over who could best represent the ranch country and how long ranchers could hold their grazing leases against the rising flood tide of settler farmers. The election was held in late September, and Boyle won the seat with a large majority. Most of the electorate could not have cared less—only 134 people in the entire district of Alberta bothered to vote.

Stewart returned to Winnipeg in September to appear before the War Claims Commission. He sought reimbursement of his many out-of-pocket expenses and explained the claims made by his men and several Macleod area merchants for debts incurred on behalf the RMR. Most claims were approved for incidentals such as forage, knife sheaths and belts (250 were purchased, but Stewart only got paid for 111), gun slings, telegrams, railroad freight charges, waterproof slickers, express charges and hay forks.

In all, $5,836.50 worth of claims were made by Stewart in War Claim No. 26. He was reimbursed $4,452, leaving him over $1,200 in incurred expenses. Among the items refused were barracks furniture, stationary, toiletries, washtubs, crockery, apples and field glasses.

Stewart put in a claim for Ranger-owned horses that were lost or injured during the campaign. The War Claims Commission constantly referred back to Stewart's own carrying out report, in which he had set his own rules regarding claims for mounts. Section 11 of Stewart's report took quite a beating as the War Claims Commission squirmed to save the money owed for replacement costs.

> War Claim No. 28.—M. & D.A.M. 2258.—Rocky Mountain Rangers, 6 claims for horses lost and injured. These claims were considered as to their bearing on the special agreement of organization:
>
> No. 1, Trooper [Malcolm] MacNaught, horse lost, $60.
> No. 2, Trooper MacNaught, horse injured, $60.
> Rejected; not coming under clause 11.
> No. 3, Trooper Robson, horse lost, $60.
> Recommended for payment in full.
> No. 4, Trooper [James] Wheatley, horse Injured, $65.
> Rejected; not covered by clause 11.
> No. 5, Trooper [Thomas] Dawson, horse Injured, $60.
> Rejected; not covered by clause 11.
> No. 6, Trooper [George] Mercier, horse lost, $65.
> Recommended for payment in full.[89]

As the Rangers returned to the lives they had previously known, those who had received saddles and rifles from the government, like schoolteacher Arthur Edgar Cox (see Appendix), were allowed to retain them.

Frustrated in attempts for corps acceptance, Stewart travelled to Ottawa to petition for service recognition for his troops. While there, he sat for the city's renowned photographer, William J. Topley, in the uniform he wore as a Ranger. With his sombrero-like hat, riding breeches and blue Dragoon tunic, Topley posed Stewart in front of a giant matte of a militia encampment, giving the illusion the photo was taken in the field.

In October *Macleod Gazette* editor Charlie Wood summarized the contents of a pamphlet, *Volunteer Land Alberta, Grants, Scrip and Pensions*, by militia staff officer Captain C.W. Allen:

In a comparatively small space a large amount of information is given in a clear and intelligible way, so that any of our militiamen who did service in the late campaign can learn what they are entitled to and how they may obtain it. Full and clear instructions are given how to obtain land grants and scrip, how most advantageously to realize the bounty, how the right to land or scrip may be transferred and on many other points in sections with appropriate titles. In the appendix, the late act granting land to members of the militia force on active service in the North West is given, also sections from the Dominion Lands Act bearing on the subject, together with valuable hints and useful forms. This pamphlet ought to prove a veritable *deus ex machina* to the thousand or two militiamen who are probably in doubts and difficulties over the perplexing and scattered regulations of the land office, and particularly so, the Rocky Mountain Rangers who are so far away from all valuable sources of information.[90]

Through the *Gazette* and pamphlet, members of the Rangers and other commands learned of the obligations owed them by the federal government, which was not in any hurry to inform veterans of their due and proper. In December 1885 the government came through with the announcement the RMR were hoping for:

Land Warrants for the R.M. Rangers—Thanks to the exertions of Major Stewart at Ottawa, the way is now clear for the issue of scrip or land warrants to the rangers. The names are now on file at Ottawa, and upon application, the scrip or warrant will be issued. The application must be made either personally, or by some person issued with a power of attorney. Forms for the power of attorney can now be obtained at this [*Macleod Gazette*] office.[91]

The 114 Rocky Mountain Rangers were awarded the North West Canada 1885 medal, officially acknowledging exemplary performance and the hardships endured, in spite of no real action. The medal came with the rebellion scrip, making each man eligible for either an $80 bonus payment or 320 acres of homestead land. Most chose the land and settled in the Pincher Creek–Waterton area, as well as around Fort Macleod and Lethbridge. At least one took his homestead in the Cypress Hills. The homesteads encouraged the discharged Rangers to stay and become established as the earliest pioneer farmers and small ranchers in southern Alberta.

A clerical error in enlistment left Paddy Hassan registered as "Edward Hasson." In 1886, when Hassan made his application for the rebellion scrip land warrant, he had to appoint Major Stewart to attest that "Edward" and "Eugene" was the same person. Hassan got his land at Pot Hole Creek, near Fort Whoop-Up, but the pay list mistake was carried on into the official record for 125 years. A great-grandson, Spenser Anderson, approached this author in 2010 as this book neared completion and corrected the biographical information.

Those on the losing side did not fare as well. Louis Riel was taken to Regina and charged with treason. In a lengthy summer trial, he dismissed his counsel and submitted his own defence, refusing to take the plea of insanity that might save his life. Riel was convicted of treason, with clemency for his sentence of death left in the hands of Sir John A. Macdonald's cabinet.

Vocal politicians and activists in Quebec pleaded for leniency on the basis that Riel was a target for the anger of Protestant, English-speaking Ontarians. They had a point. The politically powerful Orangemen would not let the Conservatives forget the execution of Thomas Scott. The ministers' ultimate decision ignited a controversy that became a flashpoint for the francophone community and a plank in the debate that has threatened to split Canada ever since. On November 16, 1885, the would-be saviour of the North-West Territories was hanged at the Regina NWMP barracks. Present at the execution was Lord Boyle, attending as a member of the North-West Territories Council.

Although there was no official mention of the gaffe, Gabriel Dumont's escape was an embarrassment for the RMR. He rode right through their bailiwick into the Cypress Hills and on to Montana. After his release from Fort Assiniboine at the order of President Cleveland, Dumont travelled the Metis camps of Montana until settling near Lewiston. From there, he spent five months gathering funds, horses and support for a jailbreak of Louis Riel. An unsubstantiated rumour even placed him in Regina during Riel's captivity.

After Riel's execution and the death of Dumont's wife Madeline, Gabriel accepted an offer from William F. Cody to join his touring spectacle, Buffalo Bill's Wild West. Leaving the show after one season, Dumont travelled the Dakotas and Montana. He went on a speaking tour of the francophone towns of the eastern United States, visiting the same communities that had heard Riel. In 1893, under the terms of a general amnesty issued in 1886 for rebellion participants, Dumont returned to Canada and to Batoche. He gained title to his farm at Gabriel's Crossing, though he refused to live in his former house. He built a cabin on a nephew's farm and spent his days hunting, getting reacquainted with old friends and befriending new settlers, regaling homesteaders with stories of the buffalo hunt and wars with the government. Among those listening at his feet was a young lad who grew up to lead that government: John Diefenbaker. Dumont died at Batoche in 1906.

Big Bear and Poundmaker, the two leaders who had done much to keep the bloodshed down, were tarred by the government and media as co-conspirators of Louis Riel, though historians have proven the events of the Frog Lake and Battleford regions were separate incidents related only by timing and hysteria. Both were taken to Regina and ordered to stand trial on charges of treason felony, levying war against the Queen and instigating rebellion.

In the end, the two leaders were convicted and sentenced to Stony Mountain Penitentiary. They were model prisoners, Big Bear becoming a carpenter and Poundmaker a gardener. Both also enjoyed tending to the warden's private zoo, where buffalo grazed behind a fence and a pair of bears paced back and forth in a cage. The irony of bison unable to roam and a captive bear was not lost on either inmate. The dank prison conditions and the shock of freedom's loss weighed hard on their health. With a badly scarred lung, Poundmaker fell ill within six months. Fearing unrest on the reserves should a leader of his stature die inside prison, the government ordered his release on March 4, 1886. Poundmaker returned to his reserve at Cut Knife, but the world he had left was gone.

New directives made by Assistant Indian Commissioner Hayter Reed included disarming Natives of hunting weapons and confiscating horses, abolishing the tribal system and restricting band members from leaving their reserves without a pass. The rules were most stringently applied to reserves like that of Poundmaker, who was branded by Reed as disloyal. Dejected by conditions at home, he decided to visit his stepfather, Crowfoot, at Blackfoot Crossing. On July 4, 1886, while participating in a sun dance ceremony, Poundmaker burst a blood vessel and died in minutes.

Big Bear was released on January 27, 1887, also in failing health. He had no reserve to call home, so he moved to the Little Pine reserve, where a daughter had married into the band. With his people gone, he became a silent shell and did not participate in ceremonies. His heart broken, he passed away in his sleep during a blizzard on January 17, 1888.

What remained of Big Bear's warrior council, including Wandering Spirit, faced the same penalty as Riel. Six Cree and two Assiniboine with culpability in the Frog Lake Massacre and other killings were convicted of murder. On November 27, 1885, within the confines of Fort Battleford, the eight were executed in a mass hanging.

After Big Bear's followers escaped into Montana, leadership was assumed by Imasees. For more than 30 years, his people lived a miserable, homeless existence—wandering throughout Montana, living off meagre hunting, selling deer hides and gathering and selling buffalo bones. They had no status, citizenship or allies among American treaty bands. Montanans called them a nuisance and blamed them for missing cattle or looted cabins.

In 1896 the Canadian Cree were ordered deported, their repatriation overseen by Lieutenant John Pershing, commander at Fort Assiniboine. In stages, the US Army escorted them to the border at Coutts. Taken by train to Lethbridge, Imasees and Lucky Man were arrested for the murder of Thomas Quinn. The rest were taken to the Bobtail reserve near Hobbema, renamed the Montana reserve. Imasees and Lucky Man were acquitted and rejoined their people at Hobbema. But the band's status was in doubt, and Imasees felt the government owed them treaty money in arrears. Unable to come to an agreement, the Cree returned to Montana.

In 1916, amidst pressure from humanitarians such as artist Charles M. Russell, the Americans agreed to grant the Cree a reservation. Imasees joined Rocky Boy, leader of a similar landless band of Ojibwa from Manitoba, and they settled on the Rocky Boy agency, near Box Elder, Montana.

Poundmaker's military leader, Fine Day, fared better. When Poundmaker surrendered, Fine Day moved to Montana and lived among Imasees' band. He eventually returned under the general amnesty and became a medicine man among the River Cree on the Sweet Grass reserve. Fine Day made his living as a hunter, trapper, horseman and grain farmer, but as a holy man, he never lost his rebellious nature. After the 1895 Indian Act banned Native spiritual ceremonies, he continued to practise them. Risking fines and arrest, Fine Day carried on worshipping traditionally well into his old age. But he did accept the respect of the monarchy. In 1939, at the age of 90, he travelled to Biggar,

Saskatchewan, to meet King George VI on his tour of Canada. He died in 1942, six months after pledging loyalty to the World War II effort.

The government acclaimed the loyalty of Blackfoot leaders who'd held the balance in southern Alberta. Throughout 1885, Crowfoot's camp at Blackfoot Crossing held court to a litany of dignitaries. Governor General Lord Lansdowne, General Middleton and Lieutenant-Governor Dewdney all paid homage to Crowfoot for choosing the side of the Queen. The following year, Crowfoot was visited by Prime Minister Sir John A. Macdonald as he crossed the country on the transcontinental railway he'd struggled so hard to get built. Its access through Blackfoot country was another debt he owed Crowfoot.

As a reward for their neutrality, several leaders were sent on another eastern tour to see the capital in Ottawa and visit the prime minister in his own home. In September 1886 Crowfoot and Three Bulls of the Blackfoot, accompanied by Father Lacombe, rode the CPR to Montreal, where they visited St. Peter's Cathedral, met the CPR executives and shot the Lachine Rapids. In Quebec City they saw the Parliament Buildings and were shown the cannons and strong defenses—another test of force. Finally it was off to Ottawa to meet Blood chief Red Crow and the Peigan leader North Axe. Another meeting with Macdonald brought the usual diplomacy and promises to help the reserves in marketing their grain and vegetables. Crowfoot returned home as Red Crow and North Axe proceeded to Brantford, where the prime minister unveiled a statue of Joseph Brant, the Mohawk war leader of another era.

After the tour, Red Crow and Crowfoot faced new realities on the reserves. Red Crow tried to quell infighting among the Blood and persuaded his people to send their children to residential schools run by the churches in order to learn to read and write English. Red Crow saw education as integral to his people's survival. Crowfoot tried a similar tack and, despite failing health, steered his people into agriculture and away from war. While they were correct in their aims, neither leader lived to see the many eventual abuses of the residential school system. In 1890, Crowfoot died at Blackfoot Crossing.

Red Crow continued to have problems with the government. It banned the sun dance and disputed his reserve's southern boundary when Mormon pioneers from Utah settled an area he'd assumed was Blood land, but the old ways of warfare were long gone, and Red Crow became adept at working with the Indian agent. Though not always successful, he urged peaceful solutions and rarely backed down. Red Crow died on August 28, 1900.

The rebellion was an odd campaign in which the victors won the war after losing the battles, save for the final day at Batoche. Despite lack of numbers, unity and funding, indigenous fighters made a courageous stand, overcoming attacks using sound defensive tactics and terrain. Commanders like Strange, Middleton and Otter were humbled. But in the end, it was a war of attrition as the indigenous forces withered in the face of poverty, starvation, abandonment and loss of will. The victory was hollow, as nobody wins in a civil war. Government commanders, regardless of mixed success, were acclaimed for their efforts.

Despite being chastised by Middleton for his premature attack on Cut Knife Hill, William Otter ended up with his boss' job. The 1885 conflict was midpoint in Otter's military career. In 1899 he commanded the Canadian contingent sent to the South African War, his troops the best infantry battalion in the British command. Otter was named chief of the general staff in 1908 and retired in 1910, but spent the rest of his life in various tasks in consultation roles to the military. He died in Toronto in 1929.

Thomas Strange was also slighted—but Strange never thought much of Middleton anyway. It is said Strange only took command of the Alberta Field Force to irritate his old rival. He claimed Middleton heavily edited his portion of the official report to Parliament on the rebellion, though never offered a counter report. Strange returned to run the Military Colonization Company Ranche near Strathmore, in the locality known as Strangmuir. His son Harry left for the British Army in the autumn. Harry's absence, combined with the complications from a broken leg and a devastating grass fire, made the rest of 1885 a trial. The ranch's fortunes collapsed when its herds were obliterated in the deadly winter of 1886 and 1887. Even a run for Parliament failed; he could not obtain his party's nomination. Cutting his losses, he sold the ranch in 1887 and retired to England, where his health and finances recovered. In 1894 he detailed his life in the British military and Canadian west in a quirky autobiography, *Gunner Jingo's Jubilee*, a book as eccentric as its author. He died in England in 1925.

One of the most controversial figures of the rebellion was Frederick Middleton. As victor, the general came out very well, probably better than deserved. But success can be like a boomerang, an ironic weapon that has a way of coming back upon itself. His *Report upon suppression of the rebellion in the North-West Territories Rebellion* earned the enmity of many westerners and his fellow officers. His scathing attack on Commissioner Acheson Irvine and the NWMP was undeserved and tarnished the image of the force in the eastern press. He also slighted his compatriots, Otter and Strange, and totally ignored the work of other subordinates.

At Battleford, the general offended a Metis trader, an action he would live to regret. Charles Bremner, a captive of Poundmaker, was discovered with a rifle belonging to a slain policeman. Bremner was arrested, and Middleton seized the trader's furs—proceeds of a winter's work. The confiscated skins were ordered bundled for shipping and stowed upon the steamers, intended as souvenir gifts for his officers and political masters, as high up as Defence Minister Adolphe Caron.

Somewhere along the voyage, some troops discovered the bundles in a locked toilet on the ship. The soldiers broke into them, and the furs disappeared. Middleton, who had intended to ingratiate himself with the lavish gifts, was left with nothing. Knowing the source of the furs, Middleton said little of the matter, but Bremner did not forget. After beating the flimsy charges against him, he swore out a complaint against Middleton. The general scoffed off the warrant as he basked in the glow of a conquering hero—knighted by Queen Victoria, awarded several medals and provided a $20,000 bonus. He looked forward to retirement with a military pension and a cushy position as president of a Canadian insurance company.

Then Charles Bremner walked back into his life, serving a plate of cold revenge. Assembling a paper trail of documents, Bremner took his story of high-profile appropriation to the national press and the opposition Liberals. Bremner's plight scandalized Parliament and ended what was left of the general's military career and his civilian job as well. An investigation found his confiscation of the furs illegal, and Middleton left Canada in disgrace, retiring to England. There Canadian matters were on the quiet, and he was Keeper of the Crown Jewels in the Tower of London, where presumably his judgment was a little better. He died in London in 1898.

In July 1886 Pincher Creek held its annual Dominion Day celebrations, with a sports day. With competition and camaraderie, the day was a gathering of neighbours and a reunion of veterans. Ex-Rangers contested fiercely to prove their riding and shooting skills remained up to snuff. Since Pincher Creek was a cow town, many of the sports were equine in nature. Fred Austin won a mile-long race on his horse, Pedro; Lionel Brooke and his steed, Priest, placed second. A novelty was the mounted smoking race, where participants lit a cigar at full gallop. Other horse races included a half-mile dash, a race of half-wild Cayuse ponies, a 200-yard dash and a steeplechase. Several foot races were also held, as well as a tug-of-war and a rifle competition won by the Macleod photographers William and George Anderton, with fierce competition from George Canning Ives.

The highlight of the day for the RMR was when Pincher Creek's most distinguished couple, Colonel James F. and Mary Macleod, invited the veterans to assemble at their home. The Rangers did not disappoint, and though a year had passed since their service, they swung into cavalry formation as though they had never disbanded. The July 6, 1886, edition of the *Macleod Gazette* describes the occasion:

> Perhaps the most interesting and unique part of Thursday's proceedings was the presentation of The Rebellion Medals by Mrs. Macleod to the Pincher Creek home guard, and those of the active service Mountain Rangers present. Capt. Herron mustered his old command early in the morning and proceeded with them to the residence of Lieut.-Col. Macleod. Here the troop was drawn up for escort duty, and Col. and Mrs. Macleod drove up with a four-horse team, accompanied by their guard of honor. After the party had alighted at the Marquee, the troop drew up in line fronting them, having gone through a few preliminary movements in a most creditable manner.
>
> Col. Macleod, accompanied by Major Stewart, went down to the line and addressed a few words to the men in his well-known happy style. The Colonel thanked them for the honor they had done Mrs. Macleod in asking her to present the medals and assured them of her thorough appreciation of it. He continued, saying, that it would have added much to the impressiveness of the occasion if some of them had appeared to receive their medals without an arm or a leg. He did not suppose, however, that it would have been particularly interesting for the mangled heroes. He said that the presentation of the medal was of special interest and significance. They had all felt how difficult it was to learn their drill, and what a long time it took, but though they might forget their drill, one thing they all knew how to do, and that was their duty. That is the great thing for a soldier to know.

[Macleod] assured them that the presentation of the medal was a royal mark of the Queen's great appreciation of the way they had performed their duty. He believed that there were a number of Americans in their ranks. He wished to particularly express his satisfaction at the way they had come forward to protect the honor of the Queen. He felt certain that the Americans who belonged to the Rocky Mountain Rangers would cherish this mark of Her Majesty's favor. He hoped they would live long to wear the medal which the Queen had conferred upon them, and that they would always be ready to serve Her.

The Colonel said that it was usual to have the names of the officers and men on the medals. He was very glad, however, that they had not been put on these for it would give him [Col. Macleod] an opportunity of having the names of the officers and men engraved on the medals, and if Major Stewart would allow him, he would have it done. It would be a source of great gratification to him.

The men then dismounted and came forward one at a time to receive the medals from Mrs. Macleod, who pinned them on the coats of the recipients, saying something pleasant to each one.

The Medal, which is a very handsome one, has the Queen's head on one side, while on the other are the words 'Northwest, Canada, 1885,' enclosed in a wreath of maple leaves. It is suspended from the breast by a red and blue striped [ribbon].

Three rousing cheers were given for the Queen, the Dominion of Canada, the Rocky Mountain Rangers and Lt.-Col. Macleod; the escort reformed and accompanied Col. and Mrs. Macleod home, and the crowd which must have numbered some 300 of the beauty and chivalry of the southwestern portion of Alberta dispersed for lunch, well pleased with the opening part of the programme and eager for the sports of the afternoon, which promised to be both interesting and exciting.[92]

The significance of the ceremony can only be appreciated truly by those who have served as brothers in arms, or waited for them to come home. All of the Rangers came home upright in the saddle. Many could just as easily have arrived in a box. The award of a medal and entitlement to a half-section of good Alberta land was the nation's thank you. With the greatest living honour available to a serviceman, the Rocky Mountain Rangers dispersed to continue their lives, not riding into the proverbial sunset, but building the world beneath it.

Old Rangers Fade Away

The period of service of the Rocky Mountain Rangers lasted no longer than four months, but their significance cannot be ignored. In the Victorian era, military service was considered chivalrous. The cavalry were the equivalent of the ancient knights. When battle honours were everything, Stewart's hastily organized "Cowboy Cavalry" received little glory beyond the gratitude of a population that felt safer knowing a significant defensive force was available, if needed.

The *Lethbridge Herald*'s 1935 commemoration of the 50th anniversary of the Riel Rebellion stated: "They were western men, most of them, good shots, could drink out of their hats if necessary, or sleep under a saddle blanket, and were mobile and effective in the event of having to conduct an Indian campaign."[93] Though the words hint more at skills the Rangers possessed as cowboys, the preceding statement sums up the expectation of a military unit in wartime: "mobile and effective."

Despite the vastness of the prairie, the Rangers guarded communities, quashed rumours and protected. They spent many man-hours in the saddle, all in the name of peace and order. Like their NWMP allies, the RMR walked a fine line between the cultures of First Nations and white settlers, both in a state of radical transition. Their experiences as soldiers, hunters, patrolmen and ranch hands made the land safe, with a lot less bloodshed than was usually associated with the westward movement. Individual rangers left little record of their experiences, perhaps because they didn't consider it anything unusual—just a part of what it took to build southern Alberta into a land of promise.

Henry Boyle returned to England, became a lawyer and pursued a career as a London barrister. His brother, Richard Boyle, continued his interest in the Alberta Ranche and threw himself into politics as a member of the North-West Territories Council, representing the Macleod District. He resigned in 1887 and embarked on an extended tour of adventure travel in the west— hunting, fishing, a little prospecting—just generally getting away from it all. Later that year, his family found out just how far away.

Upon the death of his father, Richard was slated to assume the estate and title of the Earl of Shannon, but the budding nobleman could not be found. Concerned, his brother Henry sailed to New York City to launch a continent-wide search, with ads in all major newspapers. Replies left a trail of faint clues that started the hunt in British Columbia. A letter from a US Marshall in Juneau, Alaska, placed Boyle in the north, stating his intent to head up the Yukon River. This was corroborated by a letter sighting him at Sitka, and another from a miner who saw him panning for gold in the Klondike.

Boyle's aristocracy lent romance to the story of his disappearance. Over two years Boyle remained missing, and the press stories got wilder. He was in the diamond fields of South Africa, hunting tigers in Bengal or dead in Australia. Eventually Richard heard of the search and telegraphed his brother of his whereabouts. The two were reunited in New York. Looking fit and tanned, the nobleman claimed to have spent the two years hunting and fishing in Idaho. Returning to the British Isles, Lord Richard claimed his title. He died in 1910 and Henry in 1908.

Duncan Campbell remained active in civic affairs in Fort Macleod. He served a long term as sheriff of the judicial district of Macleod, as postmaster, on town councils, hospital and school boards, the Turf Association, the Western Canada Stock Growers Association and the Macleod Exhibition. A builder, he raised funds to supply the town with water, drainage and fire protection. Campbell also petitioned Ottawa for responsible self-government in western Canada, part of a movement that culminated in the creation of the provinces of Alberta and Saskatchewan.

In 1894, Campbell married American-born Eleanor Wood of Halifax, a woman with distinct roots in American history—the great-granddaughter of Zachary Taylor, 12th president of the United States, and grand-niece of Jefferson Davis, president of the Confederate States. Eleanor's father, Captain John Taylor Wood, a US Navy officer, defected to the south and commanded the blockade-runner *Tallahassee* in the Civil War. Captain Wood stationed his ship in Halifax, where he brought his young family to live, and retired to Nova Scotia after the war. Campbell likely met Eleanor through her brother, Zachary Taylor Wood, a veteran of Fish Creek and Batoche, who joined the NWMP after the rebellion. Still involved in the military, Campbell briefly commanded H Squadron of the Canadian Mounted Rifles in 1901, was a major in the short-lived 15th Light Horse and commanded the 23rd Alberta Rangers until 1911. He died in Fort Macleod in 1920.

William F. Powell returned to the capital to resume his military career, and in 1896 became chief of police for the city of Ottawa.

James Christie stayed with the Stewart Ranche while pursuing other interests, including a successful coal mine on a ridge in the Beauvais Lake area that he worked with his brother, Andrew. In 1891, Jim Christie pulled out of the ranch and moved his stock to Nose Creek, north of Calgary, where he ran an operation of 100 horses and as many head of cattle. In 1894, Christie was thrown from a wagon near Calgary and died from injuries received in the fall.

Frederick Inderwick was politically active and served as an officer in many stock organizations. He and wife Mary Ella continued on his North Fork ranch, but the 1886 blizzard, the cost of their high lifestyle, Mary Ella's deepening depression and their marital problems caused a reversal of fortunes on the ranch. Inderwick eventually sold his interests in the west, and the couple returned to her family home in Perth, Ontario. In 1890 he dreamed of another colonial adventure and, with the financial help of his father, purchased a tea plantation in Ceylon (now Sri Lanka). In advancing years, Mary Ella assembled her letters and diaries about life in Pincher Creek for intended publication. While no book came about, the manuscripts deposited in the Glenbow Archives have become a vital resource for historians of the ranching frontier.

Dr. George DeVeber, the unit surgeon, helped transform medical service in Alberta during a remarkable career. Active in the community in Macleod, DeVeber spent a lot of time making house calls in the growing town of Lethbridge. In 1891 the Galt Hospital in Lethbridge opened, and DeVeber moved there to assist his colleague, Dr. Frank Mewburn, with surgery and anaesthesia. He also ran a private practice from the pharmacy he owned. In April 1898 he was named the town's health officer. In 1905, DeVeber and Dr. Peter Campbell began a practice; Campbell called his partner "a square shooter, endowed with an abundance of human kindness, always charming, courteous and hard-working. His word was as good as his bond."[94]

The good doctor combined his medical concerns with politics. In 1898 he was elected as a Liberal to the North-West Territories Territorial Assembly, where he introduced legislation on sanitation. In 1905 he was elected to Alberta's first legislature and cabinet. In 1906 Prime Minister Wilfrid Laurier appointed him to the Senate. DeVeber retired in 1915, but came out of repose to assist with the 1918 Spanish influenza outbreak. He set up a 35-bed emergency hospital that treated over 2,500 cases. In

1923, DeVeber retired to Aylmer, Quebec. Dr. DeVeber died on July 9, 1925. Mount DeVeber, at the headwaters of the Smoky River, is named after the frontier caregiver.

John Herron became a vital figure in the development of the cattle business into a national industry. Herron, James Christie and other stockmen helped form the South-Western Stock Growers Association (SWGA), an early agricultural lobby to represent ranchers' interests. In 1886 the SWGA became the Canadian North West Territories Stock Association, and Herron its first president. Under Herron, the association co-operated with the Montana Stock Association to limit the traffic in stolen livestock across the border. Over the next decade many similar efforts were founded, finally culminating in the Western Stock Growers Association in 1896.

In 1888 the Stewart Ranche was sold and its leases divided. Using land grants from NWMP and rebellion service, Herron started his own cattle operation and served as a government stock inspector until 1904. That year the Herrons moved into a large frame house at the eastern edge of Pincher Creek.

In the fall of 1896 the Macleod–Pincher Creek area was alarmed when Blood warrior Charcoal (*Chakko*) began a six-week reign of terror. After murdering a band member, wounding an Indian department employee and threatening the reserve's agent—and Red Crow—the chase was taken up by the NWMP, aided by scouts from the Blood tribe and citizen volunteers led by John Herron, but Charcoal eluded them at every turn. The coulees north of Pincher Creek were scoured, but the trail grew cold near the Porcupine Hills. A week later Charcoal was seen on the Cochrane Ranche, and fresh tracks headed into the foothills.

Herron's party took to combing the mountain passes. Charcoal was spotted near the Waterton River, south of Pincher Creek, and pursuit was taken up NWMP sergeant William Wilde and a patrol of Blood police scouts. The patrol encountered Charcoal, and in the melee that followed, Wilde was shot and killed. Charcoal was blamed for the murder, and the manhunt intensified. On November 11, 1896, Herron's posse, with police scout Tail Feathers, tracked the killer to the North Fork of the Oldman River. The tracks disappeared in the heavy timber, so the posse divided. The main party stayed in the valley as Tail Feathers, John Thibodeau and Herron rode up on the ridge to scout. They passed over to the south fork of the river and followed it downstream. Toward nightfall, they climbed a small rise to get a clear view of the valley—and become the target of an ambush. Directly across from them was Charcoal, his Winchester levelled at Herron from behind a black horse taken from Wilde. The party dismounted and took cover in the brush.

A gunfight ensued, but Tail Feathers' rifle jammed. Herron, with a good position, fired 12 rounds from a revolver, but the fugitive was out of range and easily slipped into the bush. The main party heard the shots and came up the valley to cut Charcoal off, but extreme cold forced the posse to withdraw to a ranch house. The next evening Charcoal was captured on the Blood reserve by two of his own relatives. At the Macleod barracks, he was tried and executed for Wilde's murder.

With a new century, Herron switched the focus of his civics career to national politics. In 1904 he was elected to Parliament in the federal riding of Alberta, one of the largest in Canada. In 1908 he was re-elected to the new riding of Macleod. In the early part of the century, many small communities emerged on the prairies. One such, Herronton, was named in honour of his work to obtain a post office for the hamlet.

In the 1911 federal election, Prime Minister Wilfrid Laurier campaigned on the issue of reciprocity, the opening of tariff-free trade with the United States. It was a popular plank with Herron's region, but his party and leader, the Conservatives of Robert Borden, were against it. Caught between his voters and the party, Herron sided with his neighbours as a pro-reciprocity candidate.

The maverick United Farmers of Alberta (UFA) endorsed Herron as "the Farmers' Candidate." Despite an awkward position, Borden endorsed Herron, but in the actual vote, party trumped person; Borden won the House, but Herron lost his seat and never sat in government. After the UFA entered electoral politics, he ran unsuccessfully against UFA incumbent George Coote in both the 1925 and 1926 federal elections.

In 1912, Herron accepted an invitation from Guy Weadick to be honoured at the first Calgary Stampede as a survivor of the original membership of the NWMP, riding in the inaugural parade with active RNWMP counterparts. In 1924 he attended another reunion of the originals, at Fort Macleod's 50th anniversary. In 1930, Herron's friend, Prime Minister R.B. Bennett, offered him a Senate seat, but he declined. Herron died at Pincher Creek in 1936 at the age of 83.

Scouts Rattlesnake Jack Robson and Aaron Vice have almost slipped through the cracks of history. Robson does not show up on historical record again until March 1888, when the NWMP charged him with selling liquor near Battleford and fined him $50 plus court costs. Aaron Vice married in Lethbridge and adopted two children. He died in July 1891 of heart disease and was buried in a service performed by the Knights of Pythias.

With the end of the rebellion, William Jackson returned to the Blackfeet reservation in Montana, probably cashing in his scrip, as the land option would have held no value in the US. Jackson continued to scout and guide for more peaceable clients than armies. He played host to a variety of scientists, authors, politicians, artists and sport hunters in the foothill and mountain country of what would become Glacier National Park. His clientele included naturalist and writer George Bird Grinnell, photographer Edward Curtis and future secretary of war Henry Stimson.

Photographer and ethnologist Walter McClintock hired Jackson as expedition guide for an 1896 federal commission to study national forests. Afterwards, McClintock stayed on the

Blackfeet reservation, spending the next 20 years amassing thousands of images of the Blackfoot culture and lifestyles of northwestern Montana. In his book, *The Old North Trail*, McClintock credits his friendship with Jackson for his introduction to the Blackfoot community.

Though little was said about his service in Canada, Jackson was always very candid on the subject of the Little Bighorn and in his assessment of the blame for the disaster. Noted author James Williard Schultz, who became a relative by marriage, found Jackson's life compelling enough to capture his story, and Jackson dictated his memoirs to the writer before his death. Schultz published *William Jackson, Indian Scout*, in 1926.

Late in 1899, William Jackson died of tuberculosis on the Blackfeet reservation near Browning. According to McClintock, the years of living dangerously on the edge of his own frontier had caught up to him, and he perished "as the final result of injuries received during his life of adventure and hardship as a scout."[95] His greatest legacies were in introducing his friends, McClintock and Schultz, to the world of his people, who in turn left a vital record of Blackfoot society in image and print. Mount Jackson, in Glacier National Park, was named in his honour.

Chief scout Kootenai Brown took his land grant of 320 acres south of Fort Macleod but later sold it. He was not interested in farming or stock-raising and returned to the cabin on his original homestead near Waterton Lake. He had a better trophy from his wartime service than medals or land: he had an end to his loneliness—his beloved *Nichemoos*, Isabella.

As common-law wife and companion, Isabella was devoted to the old mountain man and adept at hunting, butchering meat, curing and tanning hides. She accompanied him often on his hunting and fishing trips and held down his camp when Kootenai left to do occasional scouting or herding for the NWMP. In 1887, Kootenai cached bags of feed for Superintendent Sam Steele and a company of NWMP travelling through the Crowsnest Pass and guided them through the Pass on their return from assignment at Kootenay Landing.

In 1889, Kootenai accidentally founded an industry when he discovered oozy, black seepages on Cameron Creek, a stream running out of an alpine lake in the Rocky Mountains. It was the first such petroleum found in southern Alberta. In partnership with William Aldridge, a Mormon farmer from Cardston, he collected oil into gallon jars and sold it to local farmers for wagon-axle grease.

Soon speculators began trading in stock and bringing in drilling equipment. A small boom ensued, and a number of claimants poured in, hoping to cash in on the burgeoning petroleum fields at what became known as "Oil City." John Herron was in the thick of the action and represented a number of the claim holders. Based on the favourable comments of a consultant for Standard Oil, a local corporation was founded to consolidate the efforts of those seeking to exploit the resource. But the boom did not last. The remote location of the seepages, halfway up a mountain, and the relatively low volumes of oil, doomed the development.

In 1895, Kootenai began a new project, a battle to have his beloved Waterton Lake set aside as a national park. He recruited several allies, including John Herron, to appeal to William Pearce, the Dominion superintendent of mines at the time. On May 30, 1895, the government set aside the Kootenay Forest Reserve. In 1901, Brown was appointed fishery officer for the reserve, but he was far from finished. As a member of Parliament, John Herron was in a good position to help in the quest for park status. Herron lobbied in Ottawa to expand the reserve to the US border, joining it with Montana's Glacier National Park to create a shared international wildlife preserve. He exerted his influence to have a forest ranger installed, and in 1910, at the age of 71, Kootenai became that ranger.

The Kootenay Forest Reserve was designated a national park in 1911 after 16 years of struggle. However, the name of the park, lake and river where Brown lived for so many years was changed. Though "Kootenay" was the traditional designation, Thomas Blakiston, who had visited in 1858, imprinted the landmarks after English naturalist Charles Waterton. In 1914 Waterton Lakes National Park was enlarged to 423 square miles, making a busy job for the forest ranger. Kootenai supervised road building, trail cutting and the fighting of forest fires, but when Waterton required a full-time superintendent, Brown was passed over because of advanced age.

When not performing his duties or out hunting, Kootenai visited with local ranchers and settlers, entertained visitors, gave advice and swapped tall tales long into the night. Some of his most important bull sessions were with W.D. McTait, a Vancouver journalist who later synthesized those interviews into a series of newspaper columns.[96]

On July 18, 1916, John George "Kootenai" Brown passed away in his sleep, bequeathing all his possessions to Isabella. This legendary man was buried beside his beloved Waterton Lake, next to his first wife, Olivia. There he was later joined by Isabella. Since his death, many articles and books have been written about him. The most important study, *Kootenai Brown, His Life & Times*, by William Rodney, was published in 1969 and has never been out of print. In 1991 a motion picture, *The Legend of Kootenai Brown*, was released. But the greatest legacy of his remarkable life is the perpetual, natural beauty of Waterton Lakes National Park.

John Stewart trained his entire life for the military. He organized three militia regiments in his career, including one during wartime, but he never saw battle. Although politics eluded his grasp (he came in dead last in the election for Calgary's first town council in January of 1884), he did make his mark in business. His name made the papers often, making mention of trips into Montana for business consultations with Montana partner Robert Ford. By 1886 the Stewart Ranche boasted 2,500 head of cattle and 300 horses on its 50,000-acre lease, all marked with the distinctive SC brand. Stewart also was successful with real estate investments in Calgary, but also suffered business reversals. In 1886 he lost the mail contract on his stage lines. But the biggest shock came with misjudging the Canadian Pacific Railway.

When the railroad arrived to fledgling Calgary in 1883, "Captain Stewart" traded on his military identity to capitalize on appreciating property values. Cecil Denny also saw fortune, purchasing a square mile of land where he thought the CPR might build their station. But Denny's pockets were shallow, and he sold off his assets to Stewart for $10,000. Stewart sat on section 14 in speculation. The section straddled either side of the Elbow River, but Stewart gambled the CPR would build their permanent station on the east side, where the tracks approached the town. Stewart subdivided the section into town lots, heavily promoting the eastern lots.

When the CPR laid out its own lots in the adjacent section 15, farther west of the river, Stewart's firm, the Denny Land Estate Company, found itself competing with the railroad. Stewart played catch-up and offered his lots for sale on both sides of the Elbow. To sweeten the deal, he proffered lots to schools or churches at no cost, planned for a park, and used his impeccable contacts to sell to reputable folks like Colonel James Macleod. Stewart even offered to finance a traffic bridge across the Elbow. But he was wrestling with a bear; the CPR had full discretion over where it would place its station and used that advantage to promote its own lots. Predictably, the railroad built on its own property on the west side of the Elbow, ensuring that section 15 would become the hub of town. That left Stewart holding his property on the wrong side of the river. In the end, Calgary was destined to be a community far beyond the limits of rails and river, and Stewart still made back six times his original investment.

The railroad and its hunger for coal were also in Stewart's mind when he and his brother, Macleod Stewart, the mayor of Ottawa, developed the anthracite mine near Banff. John was a leader in the Calgary social scene, president of the dramatic and musical clubs, and often exhibited his pride in his Scottish heritage by wearing the full kilt and tartan of the Stewart clan.

In 1887, Stewart married Isabel Skead, daughter of the Ottawa lumber baron and politician James Skead, at St. Andrew's Church in Ottawa. Best man was Lief Crozier, the Mountie whose troops fired the first shots of the rebellion. The couple resided in Calgary, along the Bow River, in an elegant, Gothic-style cottage that still stands in the city's Inglewood district.

Stewart died young, at the age of 39, leaving Isabel and two children. One evening during the Christmas holidays, he retired to his bed early, apparently not feeling well. Between six and seven o'clock, he called for Isabel and spoke his final words: "Bell, you have been a good wife and mother."[97] He slipped into unconsciousness and expired about two hours later. After a short service in Calgary the next day, the body was shipped back to Ottawa for burial.

The commander of the Rocky Mountain Rangers made his last ride.

APPENDIX

━━━➤•◄━━━

Biographies of Selected
Rangers and Families

James R. Scott, Lieutenant, No. 1 Troop
Scott's friendships with merchant D.W. Davis and hotelier Harry
Taylor (Kamoose), former whisky traders, suggest a link by association with the pre-NWMP Fort Benton trade. The *Winnipeg Times*
had reason to believe Scott, "one of the oldest-timers in the country,"
to be "late of General (Jesse) Reno's Frontier Cavalry" during the
Utah War of 1857 to 1858 and possibly the Civil War.[1]

Scott may be the "Bedrock Jim" who appears in recollections
of John J. Healy as a member of the Spitzee Cavalry, a renegade
band of wolf-pelt hunters who tried to outmuscle the proprietor
of Fort Whoop-Up in the early 1870s. Harry Taylor led that esca-
pade, a bid by the wolfers to force Healy and other traders out
of selling rifles to the Blackfoot. When Healy dismissed Taylor
as "a mad dog among a pack of decent hounds," Bedrock Jim's
ire was raised and he cried, "I suppose I am one of the hounds!"
In his rage, Bedrock blurted out that the cavalry was acting for
the Fort Benton merchant Charles Conrad. That brought up the
countercharge by Healy that the Spitzee Cavalry had stolen or
destroyed the property of his patron, T.C. Power. The confrontation ended with Healy threatening the party, Bedrock Jim in
particular, with a shotgun, and the Cavalry leaving the Fort.[2]

188

The years after the Spitzee incident are a haze, but in 1880, Albert Morden purchased from Jim Scott a plot of land with a cabin and a stable on the banks of Pincher Creek, where the town would grow. Morden identified Scott as a herder with the NWMP.

Scott was married on August 30, 1886, to a Miss Morrow at the Macleod Methodist Church. The best man was Donald Watson Davis, the whisky-trader-turned-merchant and federal politician. The wedding feast and party was hosted at the infamous Macleod Hotel by another trader gone legit: Spitzee Cavalry leader Harry Taylor.

Albert B. McCullogh, Sergeant, Regt. #3, No. 3 Troop

Albert B. McCullogh settled on Pincher Creek sometime in the early 1880s, invested heavily in horse racing and constructed an extensive series of corrals and stables. Besides raising Clydesdale horses, he is also credited as the owner of Scalper, a successful racehorse and offspring of another, War Dance. Tragedy followed McCullogh; his two children drowned in the creek, and his house burned to the ground.

Charles G. Geddes, Sergeant, Regt. #4, No. 3 Troop

Charles G. Geddes was George Ives' ranching partner and an importer and breeder of driving horses, probably brother to NWMP constable Fred Geddes.

William Allen Hamilton, Trooper, Regt. #10, No. 1 Troop

Born in a covered wagon in Princeton, Missouri, in 1845, William Allen Hamilton joined the Union Army during the American Civil War in 1864 as a member of the Sixth Missouri Cavalry. After the war, "Billie" Hamilton took a homestead in Arkansas and, though not long in that state, was forever stuck with the nickname "Old Arkie."

Hamilton followed the Missouri River to Fort Benton in the late 1860s and found employment with I.G. Baker freighting goods into Canada. In October 1874, Hamilton was the first teamster to deliver supplies for the NWMP to Fort Macleod. Eventually Billie took out a homestead south of the Porcupine Hills and freighted throughout the district. Family accounts place Billie as "hired by the NWMP as a scout during the Riel Rebellion."[3] But medal rolls and pay lists prove him a member of the RMR.

On a trip to Fort Edmonton, Billie Hamilton met Veronique Marie Dumont.

Born at the Red River, "Vernie" or "Annie" lost her birth parents as a child. Metis hunt leader Gabriel Dumont and wife Madeline raised her as their daughter. Billie and Vernie were married at the St. Albert Convent in 1883, where she had been schooled. Though conflicted, with Gabriel named as an enemy in the rebellion, Vernie served as a nurse at the Macleod NWMP Barracks hospital.[4] After the rebellion, Vernie cared for her ailing adoptive mother at Lewiston, Montana, during Gabriel Dumont's exile.

The Hamiltons established a ranch along Spring Point Road in the Porcupine Hills. Though railroads cut into his freighting business, the region still had need for short-distance draymen, and Billie exchanged oxen for draft horses to take advantage of hauling freight to farms and ranches. In 1896 he delivered supplies for construction of the CPR's Crowsnest Pass line. The Hamiltons raised six children, one of whom, George, was a seven-time champion bronc rider and joined the Lord Strathcona's Horse (Royal Canadians) in World War I, where he broke ranch horses into cavalry mounts. Vernie died in 1913, William in 1941.

William R. Lees, Trooper, Regt. #25, No. 3 Troop

In 1879 the federal government set up a water-powered sawmill eight miles west of Pincher Creek, on Mill Creek, and reserved a 50-square-mile timber limit to supply lumber for the NWMP and the Indian department. In 1881 the mill and timber reserve were purchased by businessman and future federal senator Peter

McLaren. In 1881, McLaren appointed Lees, a relative from Perth, Ontario, to operate the facility and develop it into a profitable concern that provided many jobs in the area. Lees resigned from the McLaren Company in 1888 and went into the ranching business near Mill Creek. With the coming of barbed wire, he cut down on his range and switched to farming. Later moving into Pincher Creek, he was the town's first owner of a Model T Ford. Lees' date of death is uncertain.

James W. Carruthers, Trooper, Regt. #4, No. 1 Troop

James W. Carruthers had a brief term with the Mounted Police. Born in 1849, Carruthers enlisted in the NWMP on June 7, 1881, and served his few days at Fort Macleod, until invalided out due to injury on June 22, 1881. He moved to Pincher Creek.

John Rogers Davis, Trooper, Regt. #6, No. 1 Troop

John Rogers Davis was born May 29, 1862, at Hoyleton, Illinois. He spent a little time farming in California and Mexico, where he learned the techniques of irrigation. With brother Samuel Hopkins Davis, John came to Montana hauling bull-team freight to Fort Benton and liked what he saw at the north end of the Whoop-Up trail. In 1884 he filed for a homestead near the present-day town of Coalhurst. As he developed the ranch, Davis hauled provisions to the Blood Indian agency and lumber to Fort Macleod.

Fascinated with irrigation, Davis constructed a water wheel in the nearby Oldman River to elevate water to his garden and hay crops on the flats. He built a stone pier in the river and developed a wheel that used gunpowder kegs for buckets to scoop the water into a flume. Just a day after his wheel's trial run, spring floods swept the invention away. Undaunted, the would-be engineer took out an ambitious 10,000-acre lease from the North Western Coal and Navigation Company, near Stirling, where he dammed up a small coulee and backed up water to irrigate his hay. The first year Davis did well, and the plan was flawless, but in 1893 the dam broke, and the resulting flood swept away over half a mile of the railroad's Lethbridge–Great Falls line. Davis' plan to rebuild was halted when the company filed a court injunction against his project.

In 1890 he married Alice Maria Perry, the daughter of English ranchers, in a double ceremony shared with Alice's brother. John lost his eyesight in an accident in 1897, and Alice and their three children were forced to carry on the work. On November 26, 1907, Davis died suddenly of a heart attack.

Eugene Patrick Hassan (Paddy), Trooper, Regt. #11, No. 1 Troop

Born in Dublin, Ireland, May 18, 1855, Paddy obtained a Ph.D. in medicine from Dublin University. For unknown reasons, he apparently never practised as a medical doctor. Like many Irish of his day, he emigrated to America and enlisted in the US Army for service in the west.

This brought him into the punitive expedition set out against the Sioux in the spring of 1876. Hassan was assigned to the column under General George Crook and fought in the Battle of the Rosebud on June 17, 1876, in Wyoming, just eight days before the Little Bighorn battle.

Upon discharge, Hassan stayed in Montana and wandered to the Blackfeet reservation at Browning. Fluent in the Blackfoot tongue, he worked as an Indian agent. Wandering into Canada into the Fort Whoop-Up area around 1880, he married a Blood, Medicine Bird Woman. Hassan and Medicine Bird Woman had five children, all born at Fort Whoop-Up. Only two survived— Daniel Eugene and Jeannie.

His ranch south of Lethbridge, under the brand ED, included his land warrant for RMR service. He ran some 300 head of horses on his own ranch and, because of his connections, also grazed the north half of the Blood reserve. Some of those connections came about from operating a ferry on the St. Mary's River. The ferry enabled many Bloods to travel on and off the reserve, in violation of laws preventing them from moving freely. Like many of his time, Hassan also capitalized on the relationship by selling alcohol, again breaking the laws of the day.

Paddy Hassan developed kilns along the St. Mary's River to purify limestone with burning coal to make cement, which he used to build a concrete barn and two houses. He also showed other settlers how to build similar kilns. His Blood in-laws worked as labourers on the kilns.

In the Indian department bureaucracy of the day, Medicine Bird Woman's marriage to Hassan disenfranchised her children from band membership and land rights. In a desperate bid to obtain more land, Paddy applied in 1900 to the North-West Half-Breed Claims Commission on behalf of his three deceased children, under the Scrip program. His application was denied.

Though Paddy was well liked by many, his cavalier respect for the law was a continuing problem. He once came into conflict for assaulting a CPR telegraph crew, probably on the old Lethbridge–Whoop-Up–Macleod line. Matters came to a serious head in 1903, when he was found with one of several horses stolen from Montana ranches. The actual thief had traded a horse for one of Hassan's, but Paddy was caught applying his brand to the rustled animal. The judge, future Alberta premier Arthur Sifton, sought to make an example and sentenced Paddy to a five-year term in Stony Mountain Penitentiary in Manitoba

He died in prison on March 31, 1904, just weeks after his arrival. His remains were buried at St. Patrick's Cemetery in Lethbridge. The Hassan spread was acquired by neighbour George Russell, and the land remains in the Russell family today. His son Daniel fought in the US Army in World War I, and surviving daughter Jeannie Hassan led a colourful life, with five different husbands, although she remained childless.

William J. Patterson, Trooper, Regt. #59, No. 1 Troop
William J. Patterson came from Montana with Charles Conrad's

Circle Ranch Company, a branch project of the I.G. Baker Company of Fort Benton, of which Conrad was the general manager. The Circle operated its main camp at the confluence of the Little Bow and Oldman rivers, in the same place where Conrad, in previous years, operated a whisky-trading post. The Circle's range ran as far north as the Bow River. Former trader Howell Harris was the foreman, and Patterson was one of his top cowhands. Patterson married Miss Agnes Niven at Lethbridge in 1893.

Edward Gilpin Brown, Captain, No. 2 Troop

Born in Yorkshire, England, in 1854, Brown attended a British military academy, probably Sandhurst. As a captain in the 92nd Gordon Highlanders, from 1874 to 1884, Brown was on the ground of many trouble spots of the British Empire. He was posted to Afghanistan during the Second Anglo–Afghan War (1878–1880), on the staff of Major-General Frederick Roberts. Brown followed Roberts to South Africa in 1881 and fought during the first Boer uprising. In 1882 he was aide-de-camp to General Gerald Graham in the Nile Campaign during the Mahdist War in the Sudan. In 1884, Brown came to Canada. Why is a mystery, however; one can speculate that he may have met Canadian voyageurs on the Nile Expedition who told Brown of their country. His application for an officer's commission in the NWMP was set aside when he was attached to the RMR by Major Stewart.

Gilpin Brown married Laura Boulton of Toronto and capped his military career by joining the North West Mounted Police. Brown was the only Ranger enlisting in the force after the rebellion, whereas 13 comrades in the RMR were discharged from the NWMP before 1885. It was not an easy job to get; the force cut back after the rebellion, and a new commissioner, Lawrence Herchmer, was politically wary of an officer with Brown's high qualifications. Despite letters of recommendation—including those from the Governor General, Lord Stanley, and future prime minister Sir John Abbott—Brown's application was inexplicably turned down in 1891. Brown bided his time until finally, on February 8, 1894, he was commissioned an inspector and served at headquarters in Regina. On December 20, 1904, he died of a heart attack while on assignment in Quebec. In a prophetic aside, Brown had been sent to the Quebec armouries to test and make recommendations on a new firearm proposed for police use. The weapon was the Mark II Ross rifle, a gun that would be rejected by the force for defects. In World War I, the rifle's faultiness proved deadlier for the Canadian soldiers wielding it than for the enemy.

Frederick A.R. Mountain, Sergeant, Regt. #51 No. 2 Troop

Fred Mountain was descended from Jacob Mountain and George Mountain, both Anglican bishops of Quebec in the eighteenth and nineteenth centuries. Fred engaged in the NWMP in 1878, lobbying connections with R.W. Scott, the Canadian Secretary of State, to obtain his appointment. He served a three-year hitch, was discharged at Fort Walsh in 1881 and spent a year working with the Geological Survey of Canada. Mountain had Indian department experience and spent 1882 at the Old Sun agency on the Blackfoot reserve as a rations issuer and farm instructor. He rejoined the Geological Survey in the fall of 1882 and worked in the Slocan mining district of British Columbia. That led to a stint as constable in the BC Provincial Police.

Mountain returned to British Columbia, working in various capacities as a surveyor and Indian agent. While in the capital of Victoria, his North West Canada Medal was stolen from him. Years later, in 1914, after he had retired to Montreal, he applied for a replacement duplicate, but no information was found as to his success.

David Joseph Wylie, Corporal, No. 2 Troop

Born in Shrewsbury, Shropshire, England, in 1859, Wylie came to Canada to seek his fortune in 1880 when he was 21. From

Winnipeg, he travelled by ox cart to the Medicine Hat area, beating the railroad to the new town. He took his land grant in the Cypress Hills. There he managed one of many farms operated by Sir John Lister Kaye at Kincorth, west of Maple Creek. As farm manager, Wylie was responsible for 18,000 sheep and a large grain farm. When Lister Kaye's operation went bankrupt, Wylie moved to Hay Creek and worked on a ranch there. In 1889 he married Rachel Botterhill from Oxfordshire, England. In 1896, Wylie obtained financing from brothers and friends in England and formed the Maple Creek Cattle Company. He purchased the Oxarat Ranche, south of the Cypress Hills, from the widow of Basque sheepherder Michael Oxarat. In 1905, Saskatchewan became a province, and Wylie was elected a Conservative member in the first legislature. Wylie was an ardent proponent for the maintenance of the open range leasing system, a losing battle as the Laurier government sought to fill the prairies with homesteaders. In 1916, Wylie bought out his investors and rebranded as the Lazy Double H Ranche, which he operated until his death in 1932.

Arthur Morris (Baldy), Trooper, Regt. #46, No. 2 Troop
Arthur Morris is spoken of in schoolteacher Thomas Newton's diary as "Baldy" Morris. All that is known is that he homesteaded on the south half of section 9, in township 5, in the Fishburn School District, only a couple miles south of the Stewart Ranche.

James T. Routledge, Trooper, Regt. #45, No. 2 Troop
By all accounts, Routledge was a top rider on the Stewart Ranche, though one-legged. Sadly, he later committed suicide.

Lionel Brooke, Trooper, Regt. #35, No. 2 Troop
Born in 1858, Lionel Brooke was a younger son of Sir Reginald and Lady Brooke of Cheshire County in England. Though the blood was blue in the definition of the times, with familial connections to Queen Victoria, Lionel's sin was the order of his birth.

As a second son, he'd no claim to title or estate. What's more, the Oxford graduate seemed to have little career motivation. Only travel, hunting or art interested him. Then, at the age of 25, some unspecified situation put Lionel in disgrace, and he was shown the door of the mansion and the way to the docks.

After seeing the world—Japan, Iceland, South Africa, California, South America and the Caribbean—Brooke came to the Pincher Creek country in 1882, complete with a cook, butler and coachman. Brooke first went into the Butte Ranche in a partnership and later established the Chinook Ranche near Beauvais Lake, as "Lord" Brooke. The ladies among the ranching set were quick to invite Lionel Brooke to their tea parties, to lend scholarliness to their soirees. But in spite of his lordly facade, Brooke's lifestyle could not keep up with his remittances. He was often broke and occasionally had to depend on friends to stake him until money arrived.

Some sources say Lionel Brooke served in South Africa and was even imprisoned by the Boers. Research into the rolls of the Canadian forces does not prove this, but he may have been attached to the British. Whatever the case, Brooke lived a long life in Pincher Creek, courtesy of his family's quarterly remittance payments, said to be as high as $20,000 annually during the Depression. A younger cousin, the Earl of Athlone, would become a Canadian Governor General, but Brooke remained estranged from the bluebloods, comfortable as the squire in his foothills hideaway, throwing lavish parties for Englishmen and local ranchers alike. He gambled for drinks in bars and deliberately lost, just so he could have an audience for his stories.

He played on the South Fork polo team, in a sport demanding horsemanship and toughness. As a rancher, he was no manager— living a feast-or-famine lifestyle, playing fast and loose with cash and making loans he never expected repaid. A fall from a horse crippled him, giving him difficulties caring for himself. Brooke's heart was not in cattle; he worked the ranch primarily as a horse-breeding operation. When his fortunes were down, he moved in with whichever neighbour would have him. When the cheque came in, he'd rehire a servant and return to his own home. But always, Brooke left a little of himself behind. As payment for room and board, he'd paint an exquisite wildlife mural on a wall or a door in the homes of his hosts.

As Brooke aged, inheritances filtered in from deceased relatives. When a cheque arrived, he usually packed up and headed somewhere like Hawaii or San Francisco. He apparently once commissioned a taxi driver to take him 1,500 miles from Victoria to Pincher Creek and cheerfully paid the $1,000 fare. His drinking and penchant for partying did not diminish. In his 70s, he spent summers at the resort of Waterton Lakes, where "he'd let out cowboy yells, Indian yells and drink an astounding amount of beer...He could drink beer all day long and other than getting noisier he didn't get any drunker."[5] Pincher Creek lost its great eccentric in 1939, when Lionel Brooke died at the age of 81.

John Brown, Trooper, Regt. #27, No. 3 Troop
With his attention divided, Lord Lionel Brooke needed a manager for his ranch. In 1883 he urged Mr. and Mrs. John Brown (no relation to Kootenai), to move from England to look after the day-to-day operations. Under Brown, Brooke's string of thoroughbreds thrived, and much of the stock was auctioned off annually. Brooke's lackadaisical work ethic probably explains why the Browns did not stay. In time the couple was very successful raising thoroughbred horses on their own spread.

Two nieces, Cecelia and Frances Eastman, came out from England to lend a hand. The girls were noted for their English-style riding techniques, including the use of sidesaddles, which 19th-century society considered more ladylike for women's equine etiquette. In later years, the Browns sold their holdings and lived out their lives in the mother country.

Edward Larkin, Trooper, Regt. #42, No. 2 Troop

Ed Larkin was born in Killarney, Ireland, in 1846 and was a member of the Royal Irish Constabulary. Immigrating to Canada, he joined the NWMP , Regt. #185, on April 4, 1874 and participated in the March West. While in the force, Larkin showed proficiency as a cook, a skill that carried him into steady civilian employment. He cooked on the Pincher Creek Remount farm until his discharge in 1880 and then took his skills to many of the emerging ranches, including the Walrond. During his career, he cooked for the engineering and construction camps in the Crowsnest branch of the CPR and in a US Army camp in Montana.

In 1920, at the age of 74, Larkin re-engaged with the police as a special constable, again serving as a cook. Ed was a regular at the many reunions of NWMP veterans, including at the Calgary Stampede and the 50th anniversary of the force in 1924. He died in High River on September 6, 1931, at 84 years of age, the last surviving enlisted man in the March West. The year before his death, Larkin was awarded a medal as "the oldest cowhand in Alberta."[6]

Edward Neale Barker, Trooper, Regt. #48, No. 2 Troop

Born at Spelsbury, Oxfordshire, on August 25, 1859, Barker was the son of an Anglican vicar. With a thirst for adventure, he arrived at Sioux City, Iowa, in 1882 to work on a large farm. Wanting to be a cowboy, he travelled to the rough-and-tumble cattle town of Billings, Montana. He gained employment on a ranch in the Bull Mountains near the Musselshell River, cooking from a chuck wagon in herd camps and fixing line fences. The ranches of southeastern Montana were a source of livestock for the blooming Canadian cattle industry, and young Barker met hands who had delivered cattle herds into Alberta. The thought of a new frontier appealed.

Purchasing a Conestoga wagon and team, Ed Barker and three others left for Canada in April 1884. In a month they reached Macleod and announced they intended to homestead.

Macleod at the time was cattle country, and with little tolerance for fool rookie farmers, the people laughed the would-be sodbusters out of town. Barker was undaunted, and when he met Kootenai Brown, who referred him to the Cochrane Ranche in August of 1884, he got a job putting up hay. He then spent the winter on the Muirhead Ranche.

Barker helped establish the southern line camp on the Cochrane Ranche and took his rebellion scrip homestead warrant near Lee's Creek, where he built a log cabin. Barker was there when a wagon train from Utah, led by Mormon leader Charles Ora Card, settled on Lee's Creek, where the town of Cardston sprang up. As the new arrivals began to establish and break up the sod, Barker saw a market and started a sheep herd, selling the mutton and fleece to the Mormons, the NWMP and the people of Lethbridge. In 1889 he married Clara Dusenberry, and the pair moved to a small farm in upstate New York. Poor health forced the Barkers to convalesce in the warmth of Georgia, followed by a year in England.

In 1905 they returned to Cardston, where E.N., as many knew him, was named collector of customs and sworn in as a Justice of the Peace. Upon Clara's death, Barker moved to Edmonton to work on a newspaper. In 1917 he was named a magistrate of the Alberta Provincial Police court and covered a large district taking in most of southern Alberta. In 1922, Barker presided over the formal charges brought forth on the bootlegger king, Emilio Picariello, and his accomplice, Florence Lassandro, in the infamous murder case of Provincial Police officer Stephen Lawson. Barker tried to retire to England, but not one to settle down, he was back to help with the building of the Prince of Wales Hotel in Waterton in 1926. E.N. spent some years in Victoria and finally retired to Hants, England, where he died at the age of 83 on November 25, 1942.

George Canning Ives, Lieutenant, No. 3 Troop

Ives' career with the NWMP was brief, but his contribution to

Pincher Creek was phenomenal. Born in Compton, Quebec, in 1849, Ives enlisted in Montreal and was engaged at Toronto on June 9, 1879. He served at Fort Walsh and was discharged at his own request at Fort Macleod on October 10, 1880. He and Sam Sharpe took over management of the government cattle herd, raising beef stocks for the Blood and Peigan reserves. In 1881, Ives started his own stock farm west of the town and sent for his wife and two small children, Nellie and William.

George Canning Ives split up his partnership with Sam Sharpe in the summer of 1885 and ended up with the ranch buildings. That eventful year also saw his unsuccessful campaign against Lord Boyle for the North-West Territories Council. Ives' greatest legacy was son William, who grew up on the ranch and later studied law in Quebec. When he returned, "Billy" Ives led a distinguished career, rising to the position of provincial chief justice. The press called him "the Cowboy Judge"—as much for his heritage as his impetuous courtroom style.

Charley Smith (Jughandle), Lieutenant, No. 3 Troop

Just as the Remount Station provided the basis for the founding of the town of Pincher Creek, so too did other settlers like James R. Scott, Albert Milton Morden and Maxie Brouillette.

With a long shaggy beard and round ruddy face, plainsman Charley Smith looked like he was born on the back of a horse. "He suited his buckskins as if he had been born to them…His light-colored hair fell to his shoulders underneath a broad brimmed hat. His fair skin absorbed the brunt of the elements, weathering to a ruddy glow."[7] One utterance of fractured Nordic-tinged English, however, revealed he was not of this continent. Charles Smith (his name probably anglicized) was born on a ship off the coast of the Mediterranean in 1844 to Maerward Smith and Anna Peterson. The wanderlust bit him early. At 12, he left his home in Norway and went to sea. How a Scandinavian waif found his way from a European windjammer to the wilds of Rupert's Land is a mystery, but find it he did. In a land domi-nated by the Hudson's Bay Company, Charley Smith fell into the trade and became a noted frontiersman.

The times often dictated violence, and he did not shirk. Often wounded in skirmishes, Charley proudly carried the scars of knives, guns and fistfights. Despite his skill as a fighter, he was "good natured and friendly."[8] As a wandering, independent trader, he hunted and gathered buffalo furs, shrewdly dealing them wherever convenient and amassing a small jackpot in the currency of the country—furs, livestock and wagons.

In 1877, Smith was camped with fellow traders somewhere along the Carlton Trail when a Metis caravan headed by Cuthbert Gervais happened by. Stopping for the night, Smith's band and the Gervais caravan shared camp and a friendly jug around the fire. Gervais was a freighter, making a living on the trail with Red River carts pulled by oxen, hauling trade goods, supplies and furs between the Red River and the many trading posts in the northwest. Among Gervais' caravan were two girls he had adopted as his own, Eliza and Marie Rose Delorme.

Marie Rose had been born on the White Horse Plains in 1861, not far from the Red River colony. The Delormes had placed their young girls in the convent of St. Boniface with the Grey Nuns, a common practice among Metis travellers. Their father, Urbain Delorme, died in 1870, and their mother, Marie Desmarais, remarried Gervais the following year.

Sixteen-year-old Marie Rose was slender, dark-eyed and attractive. She caught the eye of Charley, but it would be a complicated courtship. The biggest problem was that she wanted nothing to do with a man 17 years her senior. Charley, however, followed the Gervais train to Fort Edmonton in pursuit of the girl. One night, with a dowry of a bottle of whisky and a venison roast, Smith visited the Gervais' fire and asked her parents for her hand in marriage. He sweetened the deal with $50 in cash. Where a dead animal's skin was legal tender, such a sum was more money than most people in the barter system saw in a year, maybe a lifetime. In a pact not far removed from feudalism, Mrs. Gervais accepted the money and gave Smith her blessing. But a protest was made—by the bride-elect.

Eventually Marie Rose came to understand what was being asked of her. Metis children had to grow up fast on the plains, and those entering adulthood had to help with the hunts, the building of the community and the work. Few in the Metis world toiled harder than women, cooking, accompanying the caravans and, most vitally, bearing and raising the children. Despite her trepidations, Marie Rose met the challenge. She married Charley on March 26, 1877, in the Catholic mission at St. Albert.

Despite the forced arrangement, Marie Rose endured and came to enjoy life with Smith, joining other Metis traders in Montana following the last vestiges of the buffalo trade. Something in the mountain air blessed the pair with 17 children, all without the benefit of a doctor attending. The health of the children was a constant concern. Many died in childhood. Marie often used Father Lacombe's lifetime railroad pass to take her sick children to a physician. Good friends of Kootenai Brown, the Smiths visited him often, Charley and Kootenai sharing a hand of cards and more than a few stiff drinks.

With many children dying in childhood, Charley determined that the growing family needed a change of occupation and a more stable home. In 1879, Charley realized the robe business was dying and he acquired a herd of cattle, grazing them on open ground near Fort Edmonton. But he found the winters too severe for grazing and sought a change of scenery. In 1880, Smith purchased more cattle in Montana and drove them north to the lush foothills of southwest Alberta.

In 1881 the Smiths arrived at Pincher Creek and became prosperous from their cattle herd. He registered a quarter-circle S brand, but Charley developed another way of identifying his cattle. A fleshy part of the skin under the neck was slit in such a fashion that, upon healing, it resembled the handle of a stone liquor jug. It was as good as a trademark; in the open-range environment, every cattleman knew the mark of the Smith herd. The ranch, and even Charley himself, became known as "Jughandle."

Marie Rose was a devout Catholic. Father Albert Lacombe, who sponsored a hermitage near Pincher Creek, was a friend of the family and a frequent guest at the Jughandle. She spoke fluent English, French and Cree and taught her children to converse in all three. Many Pincher Creek children came into the world with her attending as midwife.

Marie Rose's Metis heritage influenced her to become an accomplished leather crafter, her acumen leading to her nickname of "Buckskin Mary." She created many articles of buckskin clothing for herself and her family. Her tiny hands adorned shirts, vest, gauntlets, gloves, leggings and moccasins with intricate beading patterns. Charley may have been the hunter, but Marie Rose tanned the leather, dried the meat, made soap and candles from the tallow and sold her surplus products commercially through the HBC in Pincher Creek.

Charley died in 1914. Marie Rose Smith continued her leather business and operated a boarding house with her daughters in Pincher Creek. She captured her family's history in a series of columns in *Canadian Cattleman*, leaving a treasure of information and stories passed down to children and grandchildren. She died in 1960 at 98. One granddaughter, Lethbridge writer Jock Carpenter, recounted Marie Rose's memoirs in *Fifty Dollar Bride*.

James H. Schofield, Sergeant, Regt. #2, No. 3 Troop

Schofield was born in March 1858 in Durham, Ontario, of United Empire Loyalist and Scottish immigrant parents. His family moved to Brockville, where Jim took his early education. Expelled from public school at the age of 11 for fighting with a teacher, young Jim entered a long apprenticeship in retail business. He worked as a delivery boy for a Brockville grocer in an uncle's hardware store in Mount Forest and, finally, in Montreal, in a major department store. In 1876 he returned to his hometown to keep the books for a glove manufacturer.

When Inspector James Morrow Walsh, another Brockville native, returned home to seek recruits for the NWMP, young Jim jumped at the chance. Walsh admitted him to the force on June 17, 1878. He served at Forts Walsh, Macleod and Calgary, until taking his discharge. At Fort Walsh, Schofield was one of many patrolmen charged with keeping the peace among the Sioux on Canadian territory, following the Battle of the Little Bighorn. After leaving the force on June 30, 1881, Schofield and Sam Sharpe accepted a contract to deliver a herd of cattle from the Conrad Brothers' Circle Ranche on the Little Bow to the Blood reserve, after which Schofield took a job on the Stewart Ranche.

Seeing a business opportunity in the advance of the CPR, Schofield left the ranch, purchased trade goods and supplies in Winnipeg and sold them to the railroad workers in the camps that followed the ever-moving end of track westward. At Medicine Hat, Schofield concentrated on hauling and trading into the foothills and also drew from Fort Benton to supplement his inventory. In 1882 the rivers rose in spring thaw, cutting off supply and delivery lines and preventing his teams from crossing,

Undaunted, Schofield sold off his remaining goods at Fort Macleod, and with cash in hand the canny merchant opened Pincher Creek's first store, in partnership with Henry Ernest Hyde (see Appendix). The general store was so successful, the competition came calling to protect its market share. In 1886 the Hudson's Bay Company bought the pair out but only offered to keep one of the partners to manage the outlet. Schofield lost the coin toss and headed into the hills to found the Marna Ranche.

In 1888, Jim married Edyth McClement, a Blood reserve schoolteacher formerly of Kingston, Ontario. In 1894, Schofield opened another store in Pincher Creek, and his business acumen led to a very successful mercantile career. In 1898, with a railway linking southern Alberta with the British Columbia interior, Schofield saw business potential. He branched out with men's clothing stores in Fort Macleod and Cranbrook, a general store in Cowley, a sheet-metal business in Pincher Creek and, finally, a new general store in Pincher Creek in 1905.

As a community leader, Schofield sponsored and managed several local football and hockey teams through the years. In 1911 he sold everything, intending to retire to Brockville, but it was too late. Schofield had "discovered he had lived in the West too long to be content elsewhere."[9] Soon he was back in Pincher Creek with a small farm and winter residences in Calgary and California. In 1928 the Schofields finally retired to Victoria. He passed away in 1939, at 81; Edyth died in 1953.

Frank LeVasseur, Corporal, Regt. #5, No. 3 Troop

LeVasseur was a New Brunswick Acadian who arrived in Pincher Creek in 1885. The trip west made Frank a seasoned westerner. He mined in the Black Hills, worked on Missouri River steamboat barges and steered freight wagons for the I.G. Baker Company. In the casino nature of the west, his brother George won a wagon and team in a poker game. Frank drove for the Stewart stagecoach line and, with his brother George, operated LeVasseur & Steadman, a livery business in Fort Macleod. Frank and George both served as Home Guardsmen, and Frank was absorbed into the RMR.

Later, Frank settled his rebellion scrip on homestead land east of Pincher Creek, where he raised horses and operated a racetrack. The brothers also installed head works on Pincher Creek and dug the first irrigation ditch in the area, though the plan backfired, as the gates washed out and the resulting flood altered the course of the creek. In 1895, LeVasseur married Kate Gallagher. Around the turn of the century, he sold his holdings to J.A. Sandgren. He died in 1930.

Alfred Hardwick Lynch-Staunton, Trooper, Regt. #8, No. 3 Troop

Lynch-Staunton was the progenitor of a proud family ranching tradition originating in the Emerald Isle, from which patriarch Francis Lynch-Staunton was supposedly banished. It is said rather tongue-in-cheek that the exile was "for the good of Ireland." Ireland's good riddance was Canada's fortune. Settling down in Hamilton, Ontario, Francis raised 12 children in poverty. Only one of the brood, George, ever gained an education, but he did become a senator.

For a young man without money or prospects, going west as a Mountie was as good a bet as any. Alfred Lynch-Staunton (Regt. #241) enlisted in the NWMP June 11, 1877, at Port Arthur. Commissioner James Macleod signed his oath of allegiance, but did not catch that Alfred had lied about his age. The official file shows his enlistment age as 19, but his family claims he was 17. The underage rookie was posted to Fort Macleod, and the next year to the Remount Station. Lynch-Staunton took his discharge on June 5, 1880, and began one of the first ranches near Pincher Creek, in partnership with fellow policemen James Bruneau and Isaac May.

Shortly after the rebellion, Alfred travelled to the Cypress Hills to meet up with his father and kid brother Richard, who were working for the Dominion Land Survey. Soon Richard was back, with just $50 in his pocket, to buy into Alfred's ranch. A third brother, Charles, joined them in 1896. The trio furthered their endeavours by parlaying Alfred's holdings and rebellion scrip into a spread near the North Fork of the Oldman River. That was the start of a family cattle dynasty, the Antelope Butte Ranche. To market their beef, the family opened a chain of butcher shops called the A-1 Meat Market, in Pincher Creek, Lundbreck, Blairmore and Fernie, BC. They also contracted to put up hay for the NWMP and move cattle herds to stock other ranches.

The staunchly Conservative brothers were charter members

of the Western Stock Growers Association and the Alberta Wheat Pool. They pioneered grazing of cattle in forest reserves by sending their herds into the Oldman River Gap. In work and in play, the Lynch-Stauntons were no less competitive. The makeup of the early ranching community—British aristocrats, cavalry officers, mounted policemen and buffalo runners—was an incubator for the ancient sport of polo. Local teams formed, and the boys took to the game with fervor, becoming star players.

In 1890, Alfred married Sarah Mary Blake, an artist and the sister of a neighbour. Since Alfred's death in 1932, the Antelope Butte Ranche has remained a continuous family operation. Despite their humble beginnings, Lynch-Staunton descendants have embraced education, becoming lawyers and judges. Frank Lynch-Staunton became the lieutenant-governor of Alberta in 1979.

Charles Kettles, Trooper, Regt. #9, No. 3 Troop

Born near Ottawa in 1851, Charles Kettles was just 19 years' old when he served in the Irish militia during the Fenian Raid of 1870. Six years later, on June 7, 1876, Kettles enlisted in the NWMP (Regt. #184). Posted to Forts Walsh and Macleod, he was present at the signing of both Treaties 6 and 7, before assignment to the Remount Station. Upon his discharge on June 14, 1879, Kettles was appointed the first Indian agent on the Peigan reserve, a position he held until the fall of 1882, when he returned to Ottawa to marry Elizabeth Anderson. The next spring the Kettles took up land west of Pincher Creek to raise cattle.

When Timothy Lebel and Thomas Hinton dissolved their partnership, Charles Kettles joined Lebel in the store and also operated a butcher shop and slaughterhouse. Kettles and wife Elizabeth raised four children. The Kettles' brand, the 70, is believed to be the oldest continuously registered brand held by the same family in Alberta. A leading citizen, Kettles served 20 years on the local school board and from 1909 to 1911 as town councillor.

Charles Kettles retired in 1906 and died in 1923. Elizabeth died in 1932.

Albert Milton Morden, Trooper, Regt. #10, No. 3 Troop
Morden managed flour and lumber mills owned by his father-in-law in Barrie, Ontario. In 1879 the business was destroyed by fire. In weighing their options among the ashes, they decided against rebuilding. Instead, a party of 10 embarked for the west in 1880. It included Albert; wife Sarah; children Thomas, Fred and Adelaide; brother-in-law Thomas Mulholland, Jr.; and a Dr. Brunskill and his family.

On the journey, the party was persuaded to try their luck in the Judith Basin of Montana. They'd no sooner arrived at a suitable location and begun to cut timber for housing when a Helena rancher claimed grazing rights to the land. Soured on America, the Morden party packed up and crossed the Missouri River at Fort Benton. Following a bout with the measles, they got on the Whoop-Up Trail bound for Fort Macleod, and then to the town of Morleyville, near the mountains. After arriving, Morden didn't like the soil conditions and turned his family back toward Macleod to check out a ranch he'd heard was for sale.

The Mordens purchased the Jim Scott place on Pincher Creek and moved into Scott's former cabin. In the spring of 1881, Morden stocked his ranch with 225 head of cattle from western Montana, brought through the Crowsnest Pass by trail boss John Rush and a few of the Nez Perce band who settled near Pincher Creek after escaping the Bear's Paw battle with the US Army.

As the open range around Pincher Creek was cross-fenced and ploughed into farmland, the work of Albert Morden and family was an example of western Canada's potential as the granary of the world. In 1892, Morden took prizes for his wheat, barley and oats at the Columbian Exposition in Chicago. More than individual achievement, such prizes brought attention to an unknown corner of the world, contributing to the explosion of settlement in the Canadian prairies over the next two decades. With that came material success, and in the 1890s, Eugene Chamberlain Morden built "a fine two-storey red brick house just across the creek from the little log cabin."[10]

Fred, Adelaide and Tom Morden were kids when their father enlisted in the RMR, but in the South African War, in 1899, Fred lent his shooting and riding skills to the Canadian Mounted Rifles. In the capture of Pretoria by the British, Fred, along with Pincher Creek pals Robert Kerr and Thomas Miles, were trapped holding an outpost at Honing Spruit. Kerr and Fred Morden did not come home.

Albert Morden was never the same after Fred's death, and he sold his cattle herd. On June 22, 1907, Albert drowned in the high water of Pincher Creek during a spring flood—seven years to the day after Fred's death. Tom and Adelaide's husband, Dr. Samuel Hewetson, carried the military tradition into World War I. Tom made it home, but Hewetson died in France.

Henry Ernest Hyde, Trooper, Regt. #11, No. 3 Troop

Hyde was born in Stratford, Ontario, in 1860, the fourth son of Irish doctor John Galbraith Hyde and Jean Mickle Hyde, granddaughter of poet William Julius Mickle. Educated at Stratford and the University of Toronto, Hyde left college for adventure, working the long, ponderous, 10-mile-a-day, Whoop-Up Trail as a bullwhacker for I.G. Baker and driving freight between Fort Benton and Calgary.

In 1883, Henry moved to Pincher Creek and partnered with James Schofield in his general store. With a busy ranch economy, Hyde and Schofield expanded into a larger store, and in 1884, Hyde became Pincher Creek's first postmaster. The store was sold to the Hudson's Bay Company in 1886. Hyde continued as manager and as postmaster until 1905. He established the town's first bank, in a retrofitted log stable, and sold it to the Union Bank in

1889, staying on as branch manager. He could have risen within the corporate hierarchy, but that would have meant transfers and leaving Pincher Creek. Instead, he reopened his own finance and loan company and operated it until his retirement.

Hyde married a teacher, E.M. Chisholm, in 1896. She died in 1902, giving birth to their second child. In 1905, Hyde married Jean Innes, and they raised three children. During World War I, Hyde administered the government Patriotic Fund, which provided financial assistance to widows and orphans of killed servicemen. Jean founded the local Red Cross, and Henry served one term as mayor of Pincher Creek. He died in 1933.

Arthur Edgar Cox, Trooper, Regt. #12, No. 3 Troop
Cox was born in Camden, England, March 11, 1856. The only member of his family to leave the old country, he crossed the Atlantic in 1876 to teach school at Staten Island, New York, and returned home in 1879. Cox longed to see the world and joined the crew of the *Militades*, a windjammer of the Aberdeen Clipper Line, carrying wool fleece from Melbourne to the mills of Britain by way of the Cape of Good Hope. Cox left the ship in Australia to work on an isolated sheep station in the outback. In 1882 he boarded the *Militades* to return to England, but had a slight delay.

Sailing around Cape Horn in South America, the *Militades* was wrecked near an island off the coast of Chile. The marooned crew survived on sowbelly and hardtack from the hold of the ship, taking great care to keep weevils out of the supply. They nearly became a meal themselves when local cannibals discovered them. The Natives were placated when Cox produced his homemade banjo and plunked out a few tunes, which earned him the nickname "Banjo Man."

After the crew's rescue, Cox arrived in New York and went to Winnipeg to take a job in CPR construction. Then he was hired by the Dominion Land Survey to help plot out the open prairie into square-mile sectional grids. In a throwback to his shipwreck days, Cox was marooned by the crew chief when a co-worker contracted smallpox; Cox was left to care for the patient in a solitary tent on the open prairie near the Cypress Hills. When the affliction passed, Cox burned all the clothing and the tent.

At Maple Creek, Cox purchased a pony cart and drove through a three-day blizzard to Fort Macleod, where he hoped to secure a position as schoolteacher. Finding no work in Macleod, and being out of cash, he sold the cart and rode the pony bareback to Pincher Creek, where he found Charles Kettles organizing support for a school. Cox was hired on the spot, and in the spring of 1884 opened the first school in Pincher Creek. He also performed ministerial duties until an ordained pastor moved to town.

Cox took his land grant five miles west of Pincher Creek, where he established the Mount View Ranche and raised Percheron and Clydesdale horses and Hereford cattle. In 1887, Cox married Mary Elizabeth Willock, sister of fellow Ranger Leslie Grey Willock.

In 1897, Cox was appointed Dominion land sub-agent, helping new settlers in filing for, locating and gaining patent on government homestead lands. He performed a similar service selling and distributing lands for the Calgary & Edmonton Railway and the Hudson's Bay Company. Land agents were often corrupt or shifty at best, but Cox was said to be unswervingly honest in his dealings and never advised a settler to take a piece of land without seeing it first. Cox tried his hand at politics in 1921, unsuccessfully challenging the Pincher Creek provincial riding as an independent. He died in 1946 at the age of 90. The restored Cox home, a two-storey frame house, stands today in Kootenai Brown Pioneer Village in Pincher Creek.

Thomas Cyr, Trooper, Regt. #13, No. 3 Troop, and Adolph Cyr, Trooper, Regt. #14, No. 3 Troop

The Cyr brothers, Adolph and Thomas, were Acadians from New Brunswick. In addition to being small ranchers, the Cyr brothers were involved in the illegal whisky trade. This was hardly shameful. The west was so vast, and the demand for alcohol was so strong, that prohibition was impossible. The law was winked at and unenforceable in the ranks of the NWMP.

Thomas Hinton, Trooper, Regt. #15, No. 3 Troop

Hinton was born in the village of Chalford, Gloucestershire, England, on November 13, 1859. In 1883, with his last £100 and intentions of making his fortune in Canada, he travelled steerage on a steamship to Montreal. A carpenter and cabinetmaker by trade, Hinton found work at a lumber mill near Keewatin, in southern Manitoba. Here he met Timothy Lebel, with whom he formed a partnership. They headed west to Pincher Creek in the spring of 1885, shortly before the formation of the RMR. Hinton and Lebel built and opened a general store in the town. Two years later they split as partners, and Hinton built a hardware store across the street. Around the same time, he brought his wife, Lucy Smart, over from England, along with three brothers. Hinton eventually sold the store to Sam and George Barry.

John Henry Gresham Bray, Trooper, No. 3 Troop

Born January 24, 1840, in Dewdley, Worcestershire, England, Bray enlisted in the British Army at 18 and served 10 years with the 10th Royal Hussars. As a raw recruit, Bray went to India in 1858 to augment the ranks after the bloody Sepoy Mutiny. Bray's unit was ordered to China in 1860 but was called back to England due to a cholera outbreak.

In the early 1860s, Bray and the Hussars were sent to Ireland to deal with the Fenian rebellions. While there, the 10th worked with the Royal Irish Constabulary, the police force that the NWMP was modelled upon. Bray's ankle was shattered by sniper fire, leaving him with a distinctive limp that resulted in the nickname "Turkey Legs." After two years on the staff of Prince Edward of Wales and three years as a drill instructor at the Staffordshire Yeomanary, Bray left Britain for Toronto. In October 1873 he joined the NWMP (Regt. #92) with the rank of chief constable of C Troop. Following the March West, Bray was posted to Fort Macleod, then to Fort Walsh in 1875.

In the Cypress Hills, Bray came to know Jemima McKay, daughter of Metis settler and trader Edward McKay. They married in 1876, and in March 1877 Flora Bray became the first child born to an active member of the force. In 1879, Bray was appointed judicial sheriff, the first west of Winnipeg, and spent much time travelling the prairies to perform court duties. His tact was tested during the force's first murder, when Constable Marmaduke Graburn was gunned down near Fort Walsh. Star Child, a Blood, came under suspicion, but due to his band's travels in Montana, he was not apprehended until 1881. During the high-profile trial in Fort Macleod, the court wished to demonstrate to the Bloods that their people could receive a fair trial from the Dominion and tasked Bray with summoning an impartial jury. Star Child was acquitted.

In late 1881, Bray was assigned to Pincher Creek to take charge of the NWMP's Remount Station. Discharged in November 1882, Bray took his land grant near Pincher Creek and raised horses with the HB brand.

Bray suffered the devastating loss of his cattle herds in the winter of 1887 and was nearly wiped out. In 1892 health conditions left him seeking a lower altitude. He moved his family to Medicine Hat, where he was appointed the foreman of public works. Bray thrived in the growing town and built a house north of the river near Police Point and the NWMP barracks. He also got back into the cattle business and ranched downstream of Medicine Hat, on a river bottom that became known as Bray's Flat. Other landmarks were named for him as well: Bray Street in town and Bray's Trail, the road to the Red Deer River.

Medicine Hat's status as a railway division point created demand for overland freighting. Bray ran a string of teams and wagons to supply ranches and homesteaders from the town and developed a good business from the bare bones of a bygone era—literally—as his crews gathered and stockpiled buffalo bones near the railroad. Bone picking was big business, with thousands of carloads of bones shipped to manufacturers as a source of phosphorous for fertilizer and carbon for gunpowder. At $2.50 per ton, the heavy bones added up fast.

Bray served on many agricultural and stock associations. As a cattleman with experience, born at the dawn of the industry, Bray advised new ranchers on cattle-related problems such as rustlers, mavericks, fires and the organization of roundups. In 1896 he was appointed territorial brand inspector, succeeded to the provincial equivalent in 1905 and held the position until 1919. So well-respected was Bray that upon entering any beverage room, all "The Grand Old Man of Medicine Hat" had to do was clear his throat, and a pint of beer would make it his way.[11] Bray died in 1923.

William Cox Allen, Trooper, Regt. #16, No. 3 Troop

"William Allen" was a common name in the era. Two Mounties went by the name, but both were discharged and left the area before the rebellion. The most likely candidate to be the William Allen in the RMR was William Cox Allen, who in 1886 was appointed collector of customs at Fort Macleod.[12]

Samuel James Sharpe, Trooper, Regt. #17, No. 3 Troop

Born in Clare, Ireland, in May 1850, Sharpe enlisted in the NWMP (Regt. #206) on March 28, 1874, at the age of 24. He was a sub-constable posted at Fort Macleod at its founding. Like many Mounties, Sharpe was impressed with foothills country, and upon discharge he partnered with George Ives, managing the government herd. When the Stewart Ranche took over the herd, Sharpe took out a grazing lease with Jonas Jones between the forks of the Oldman River.

Sharpe took his rebellion scrip homestead land 10 miles west of Pincher Creek and dubbed it The Willows Ranche. In 1888 he married Emma Clarke, a young Englishwoman from London. The Sharpes were sympathetic to the Peigans and Stoneys, having watched much deprivation on the reserves. Sam was noted for giving away supplies such as flour, salt, tea, meat and even Emma's freshly baked bread to aid them in the shortfalls of Indian department rations. The Sharpes had two children: Wallace James and Ethel Sarah. In 1898, nine-year-old Wallace was sent to town to seek medical aid for his ailing father, but the doctor did not get back in time and Samuel died. In adulthood, Wallace Sharpe carried on his father's ranch, military and political traditions. He became a decorated cavalry officer in World War I and a candidate for the provincial legislature. Wallace died in 1923 of complications from his war wounds. His mother Emma died in Pincher Creek in 1950.

Albert Connelly, Trooper, Regt. #19, No. 3 Troop

Connelly was the son of Irish engineer Robert Connelly, who moved his seven sons and a daughter to Quebec in 1870 and shortly afterwards to Fargo, Dakota Territory. As the brothers came of age, Albert, Jim and Alfred started a bull-team service, contracted to I.G. Baker, from Fort Benton to Fort Macleod. In the aftermath of the Battle of the Little Bighorn, a Connelly bull team and wagon was confiscated by a US Army cavalry troop for its own use. Jim Connelly's protests ended in his arrest. He was tied in the back of the wagon, but the officer in command had to retrieve him when the oxen refused to respond to Army teamsters. In the early 1880s the entire family moved to Pincher Creek, where Albert and Alfred Connelly built the Alberta Hotel, the town's first, in 1885.

Albert Connelly operated the hotel until 1892, when he and his bride, Elizabeth Reardon, took out a homestead northwest of present-day Lundbreck. There they raised five children. In 1898, Albert helped organize the Lee School District and built the log cabin school. He also opened a butcher shop in Blairmore, cutting and selling his own beef to the lumber mills and mining camps. The business was sold to the Lynch-Stauntons, and he lived on his homestead until his death on November 20, 1908. Connelly Creek, a tributary of the Crowsnest River, was named for the pioneering family.

Peter McEwen, Trooper, Regt. #21, No. 3 Troop

Peter McEwen of Perth, Ontario, enlisted in the NWMP (Regt. #233) on June 5, 1877, and was posted to Fort Macleod. Sent to the Remount Station in 1878, he often served as teamster, moving freight, supplies and prisoners. Discharged June 5, 1880, McEwen homesteaded near Mountain Mills on the south fork of the Oldman River. There he met and married Mary Gladstone, Metis daughter of William Shanks Gladstone (Old Glad), the carpenter who'd built Fort Whoop-Up. Peter and Mary McEwen had several children, but only three boys survived infancy. Besides ranching, Peter McEwen supplemented his income with freighting work between Pincher Creek, Medicine Hat and Fort Benton.

Mary died in 1890. In 1894, McEwen remarried, and another seven children were added to the family. After 1900 he sold the ranch at Mountain Mills and took up a homestead, possibly a grant from rebellion scrip, near Cowley. He later opened a livery stable and a restaurant and bakery there.

During World War I, and at nearly 60 years of age, McEwen served with the Home Guard at Banff and was posted as a guard at the Kananaskis prisoner-of-war camp. One son was killed in action during the war. McEwen spent his twilight years around Cowley as a foreman on several haying outfits. He died in 1929 after a brief illness. Mrs. McEwen passed away in 1961.

William Reid, Trooper, Regt. #23, No. 3 Troop

Billy Reid was born in 1849. As a volunteer in the 13th Battalion, he served in the Fenian raids in Upper Canada. He joined the NWMP (Regt. #102) on May 29, 1875, and was posted to Fort Macleod. In 1878 he was assigned to cut timber to construct the NWMP

Remount Station. Reid was discharged May 22, 1884, and was granted a quarter-section land warrant, taken near Pincher Creek.

Leslie Grey Willock, Trooper, Regt. #29, No. 3 Troop

Willock was born near Lindsay, Ontario, in 1866. He moved west with his parents, Francis and Margaret Willock, and sister Mary (the future Mary Cox) in 1872, to a homestead in Springfield, Manitoba. After nine years the Willock family was growing, but nothing else was. They were forced off their homestead in 1881 by drought and locusts that left "even the fence posts and fork handles...nibbled."[13] Told of paradise—mild winters and lush grass in the foothills—the Willocks travelled west. They found that paradise at Pincher Creek on a homestead called "The Poplars."

In 1883 they sold off the Springfield holdings and put the family and livestock onto a CPR train. At Swift Current the settlers disembarked and loaded several covered wagons and Red River carts with personal effects. Fifteen-year old Leslie was in the saddle, driving the herd of cattle and horses the 300 miles west. The family lived on buffalo meat during the trek and spent their first winter in a tent, building a log cabin with a sod roof the following spring. The Willocks were ardent farmers, growing rhubarb, peas and seed wheat, harvesting bushels of wild berries and raising Clydesdale horses. Productive and progressive, Willock and son set up a blacksmith shop and did much iron work for their neighbours. They also introduced one of the first steam-powered threshing machines in the area.

The Willocks permitted a small group of American Natives to set up camp on their property. The group of Nez Perce families were led by White Bird, a follower of Chief Joseph, and were the last of the tribe that had fought a running battle with the US Army in 1877. Fleeing their traditional home in western Idaho, they met a crushing defeat in the Bear's Paw Mountains of Montana. From there, they escaped into the Cypress Hills.

They later built cabins nearby the Willocks, where many took employment on ranches and farms, practised subsistence hunting and farming and sold their produce in town. Their numbers were few, and the tiny community was well liked. In 1892 they suffered a severe setback at the hands of one of their own. White Bird was brutally killed by a member of his own band. After the murder, the Nez Perce families left the district and returned to the Wallowa Valley in Idaho, or intermingled with the nearby Peigan.

Leslie Willock took his land grant near the railroad siding of Pincher Station and farmed it with his father Francis. As community leaders, Leslie and Francis organized cattle roundups, schools, churches and the Pincher Creek local of the United Farmers of Alberta. Their twin violins were heard at many a local function. Leslie married Jessie McPherson of Glasgow, Scotland, in 1898. He died of pneumonia in 1909 at the age of 43.

Eugene Chamberlain, Trooper, Regt. #31, No. 3 Troop

Eugene Chamberlain, born in 1860, was a bricklayer by trade and the first such mason in Pincher Creek. He built his own house, the first brick house in the town, and helped construct the Arlington Hotel. Later he ranched near Beauvais Lake in the hills west of Pincher Creek.

Thomas E. Dawson, Regt. #39, No. 2 Troop

Born in 1858, Thomas Dawson and his brother James were the mixed-blood sons of Andrew Dawson (the "last King of the Missouri," a fur trader and chief factor of the American Fur Company at Fort Benton from 1854 through 1864) and a Gros Ventres woman. This would have also made him the foster brother of famed guide Jerry Potts, whom the elder Dawson raised. Tom and James went with their father to Liverpool, England, in 1864, where both were educated. Tom returned to Montana in the 1880s, just in time to serve with the RMR. Tom lived out his life near Glacier National Park and died in his 90s.

NOTES

Prologue, Parts One and Two

1 William Cochrane to Matthew Cochrane, April 26, 1885, *Cochrane Ranche Letter Book*, Glenbow-Alberta Institute Archives—M 234.

2 Frederick Ings, *Before the Fences: Tales Of The Midway Ranch*, 29.

3 Edgar Dewdney to Indian department, letter, July 19, 1884, Sir John A. Macdonald Papers, Library and Archives Canada.

4 Rodney, William G., *Kootenai Brown, His Life & Times*, 83.

5 James Williard Schultz, *Rising Wolf, the White Blackfoot; Hugh Monroe's Story of his First Year on the Plains*, 2.

6 James Williard Schultz, *William Jackson, Indian Scout*, 7.

7 Ibid., 10.

8 Ibid., 95.

9 Ibid., 129–30.

10 Ibid., 135.

11 Ibid., 136. Jackson may have been mistaken in this identification. There was a 13-year-old Oglala boy named Black Elk who fought and survived the battle, later transcribing his memoir of the battle as *Black Elk Speaks* (William Morrow & Company, 1932). He died in 1950.

12 Walter McClintock, *The Old North Trail*, 7.

13 James Williard Schultz, *William Jackson, Indian Scout*, 158.

14 Ibid.

15 "Noted Indian Scout Dead," *New York Times*, January 9, 1900.

16 *Lethbridge Herald*, July 11, 1935.

17 John Peter Turner, *The North-West Mounted Police, 1873–1893*, 1:240.

18 *Lethbridge Herald*, July 11, 1935.

19 Ibid.

20 Marquis of Lorne, *Memories of Canada and Scotland*, cited in McDougall, D. Blake, *Princess Louise Caroline Alberta*, Edmonton Legislature Library, 1988.

21 A. Lynch-Staunton, "Founding of Police Horse Farm," *RCMP Quarterly*, April 1950.

22 Crowfoot to Macdonald, telegram, April 11, 1885, "Outgoing Telegrams of the North-West, 1885," Glenbow-Alberta Institute Archives—M 2286.

23 P.H. Garnot to Bishop Taché, "Metis Present at Batoche. May 9-12, 1885," Fonds Taché, St. Boniface, Archives & Museum.

24 Frederick Ings, *Before The Fences: Tales from the Midway Ranch*, 30.

25 Desmond Morton and Reginald H. Roy, eds., *Telegrams of the North-West Campaign 1885*, 107.

26 *Calgary Herald*, April 9, 1885.

27 *Winnipeg Daily Times*, April 4, 1885.

28 Frederick Ings, *Before The Fences: Tales from the Midway Ranch*, 30.

29 John R. Craig, *Ranching with Lords and Commons*, 156.

30 Ibid., 157.

31 Ibid., 158.

32 *Winnipeg Daily Times,* April 8, 1885.

33 Sir Joseph Pope, ed., *Correspondence of Sir John Macdonald.* Sir John A. Macdonald to General Middleton, March 29, 1885.

34 Sessional Papers of Canada, Department of Militia & Defence for 1886. Stewart to Minister Caron, also known as "Carrying Out Report, Rocky Mountain Rangers," March 25, 1885.

35 Desmond Morton and Reginald H. Roy, eds., *Telegrams of the North-West Campaign 1885,* 28.

36 Ibid., 16.

37 Stewart to D. Campbell, telegram, March 29, 1885, "Outgoing Telegrams of the North-West, 1885," Glenbow-Alberta Institute Archives—M 2286.

38 Desmond Morton and Reginald H. Roy, eds., *Telegrams of the North-West Campaign 1885,* 28.

39 Ibid., 30.

40 Ibid., 146.

41 *Macleod Gazette,* April 22, 1885.

42 Ibid., April 11, 1885.

43 *Winnipeg Daily Times,* April 14, 1885.

44 William Cochrane to Matthew Cochrane, April 12, 1885, *Cochrane Ranche Letter Book,* Glenbow-Alberta Institute Archives—M 234

45 *Lethbridge Herald,* September 9, 1931.

46 Original source: *Reminiscences of the North-West Rebellions* by Charles Boulton, 1886; modified in 1994 and in 2009 by Gordon E. Tolton.

See also: Barbara M. Wilson, ed., *Military General Service 1793–1814 / Egypt Medal 1882–1889 / North West Canada Medal 1885, Index to the Medal Rolls* (London, England: Spink & Son Ltd., 1974).

47 Pincher Creek Historical Society, "Morden," in *Prairie Grass to Mountain Pass,* 126–27.

48 Mary Ella Inderwick, "A Lady And Her Ranch," *Alberta Historical Review,* Autumn 1967.

49 Ibid.

50 William Cox, *Lethbridge Herald,* July 11, 1885.

51 Photographs of John M. Robson, in Southwestern Saskatchewan Old Timers Museum—PC.1.21.

52 Desmond Morton and Reginald H. Roy, eds., *Telegrams of the North-West Campaign 1885,* 187.

53 *Macleod Gazette,* May 2, 1885.

54 J.D. Higinbotham, in *Canadian Pictorial & Illustrated War News,* June 20, 1885.

55 Anonymous (Old Timer), "The Old Log Town of Macleod 1883," in *Canadian Cattleman,* December 1941.

56 J.D. Higinbotham, *When The West Was Young,* 226.

57 J.D. Higinbotham, in *Canadian Pictorial and Illustrated War News,* June 20, 1885.

58 William Cox, *Lethbridge Herald,* July 11, 1885.

59 J.W. Morrow, *Early History Of the Medicine Hat Country.*

60 William Cousins, "Medicine Hat and the Rebellion," in *Alberta History,* Autumn 1985.

61 Desmond Morton and Reginald

H. Roy, eds., *Telegrams of the North-West Campaign 1885*, 236.

62 Stewart to Dewdney, telegram, May 4, 1885, "Outgoing Telegrams from the North-West, 1885," Glenbow-Alberta Institute Archives—M 2286.

63 William Cox, *Lethbridge Herald*, July 11, 1885.

64 Ibid.

65 Ibid.

66 W. McD. Tait, *Recollections of Kootenai Brown*, xvi.

67 *Macleod Gazette*, May 9, 1885.

68 Desmond Morton and Reginald H. Roy, eds., *Telegrams of the North-West Campaign 1885*, 249.

69 William Cousins, "Medicine Hat and the Rebellion," *Alberta History*, Autumn 1985.

70 Desmond Morton and Reginald H. Roy eds., *Telegrams of the North-West Campaign 1885*, 284.

71 *Macleod Gazette*, June 6, 1885.

72 Ibid.

73 Ibid.

74 Ibid.

75 Ibid.

76 Ibid.

77 Ibid.

78 Frederick Ings, *Before The Fences: Tales From the Midway Ranch*, 31.

79 Ibid.

80 *Macleod Gazette*, June 6, 1885.

81 Desmond Morton and Reginald H. Roy, eds., *Telegrams of the North-West Campaign 1885*, 348.

82 Ibid., 349.

83 *Macleod Gazette*, July 7, 1885.

84 Desmond Morton and Reginald H. Roy, eds., *Telegrams of the North-West Campaign 1885*, 378.

85 *Macleod Gazette*, July 15, 1885.

86 Adolphe P. Caron Papers pertaining to the Northwest Rebellion, Volume 199, 1885, Library and Archives Canada.

87 Sessional Papers of Canada, Volume 5, Militia & Defence, fourth session of the fifth Parliament, Report 4, War Claims Commission, 1886, Library and Archives Canada.

88 *Macleod Gazette*, August 11, 1885.

89 Sessional Papers of Canada, Volume 5, Militia & Defence, fourth Session of the fifth Parliament, Report 4, War Claims Commission, 1886.

90 *Macleod Gazette*, October 1885. Date is unclear on microfilm.

91 Ibid., December 15, 1885.

92 *Macleod Gazette*, July 6, 1886.

93 *Lethbridge Herald*, July 11, 1935.

94 Dr. Robert Lampard, MD, *Five Celebrated Early Surgeons of Southern Alberta, 1874–1913*. The De Veber–Campbell practice continues today as the Campbell Clinic in Lethbridge.

95 Walter McClintock, *The Old North Trail*, 14.

96 W. McD. Tait, *Recollections of Kootenai Brown*, (n.d.).

97 *Calgary Herald*, December 28, 1893.

Appendix

1 *Winnipeg Daily Times*, May 15, 1885.

2 "Tappan Adney's Biography of John J. Healy," (unpublished manuscript, Baker Library, Dartmouth College, Hanover, New Hampshire, n.d.).

3 Pincher Creek Historical Society, "William Allen Hamilton," in *Prairie Grass to Mountain Pass,* 844.

4 Ibid.

5 Tom Kirkham, taped interview, Glenbow-Alberta Institute Archives—RCT-329-1.

6 *Lethbridge Herald,* September 9, 1931.

7 Jock Carpenter, *Fifty Dollar Bride,* 42.

8 Ibid.

9 Pincher Creek Historical Society, "Schofield," in *Prairie Grass to Mountain Pass,* 146.

10 Ibid., "Morden," in *Prairie Grass to Mountain Pass,* 126–27.

11 *Lethbridge Herald,* October 28, 1911.

12 William Beahen and Stan Horrall, *Red Coats on the Prairie, The North-West Mounted Police 1886–1900,* 19. The website of Library and Archives Canada was utilized to narrow down the possibility of the other two William Allens (Library and Archives Canada, North West Mounted Police—Personnel Records, 1873–1904, *www.collectionscanada.gc.ca/databases/nwmp-pcno/index-e.html*).

13 Pincher Creek Historical Society, "Willock," in *Prairie Grass to Mountain Pass,* 184.

BIBLIOGRAPHY

Archival Sources

GLENBOW-ALBERTA INSTITUTE ARCHIVES, CALGARY, AB

Cochrane Ranche Company Ltd. fonds M 234. Cochrane Ranche Letter Book.

Riel Rebellion telegrams fonds M 2286, M 4785. "Outgoing Telegrams of the North-West, 1885." Canadian Pacific Railway, Western Division.

LIBRARY AND ARCHIVES CANADA, OTTAWA, ON

Adolphe P. Caron Papers, vol. 199, 1885 (pertaining to Northwest Rebellion).

Dept. of Militia & Defence, Record Group 9:

Militia General Order 21, September 18, 1885.

Field Pay Lists, Rocky Mountain Rangers, adjutant-general's office correspondence, April 23–July 10, 1885. 11, file 7, vol. 8.

Dept. of Veterans Affairs, Ledger of the Militia Force engaged in The North-West Territories 1885, Honours & Awards Division.

Middleton, Major-General Frederick D., et al. *Report upon the suppression of the rebellion in the North-West Territories and matters in connection therewith.* Ottawa: Queen's Printer, 1886.

RCMP File, Record Group 18:

Monthly Report Fort Macleod, April 1885. Superintendent John Cotton. 22634-1885.

North West Mounted Police Annual Reports, 1874–1888.

Scouts of the North-West Field Force. G995-10.

North West Mounted Police Personnel Records 1873–1904. <www.collectionscanada.gc.ca/databases/nwmp-pcno/index-e.html>.

Report of the Auditor General on Appropriation Accounts for the year ended June 30, 1885, and year ended June 30, 1886.

Sessional Papers, fourth Session of the fifth Parliament of the Dominion of Canada. vol. 5, Militia & Defence.

Strange, Thomas Bland. Report of the Major-General Commanding. Report of Operations of Alberta Field Force from March, 1885 to July 2, 1885. Appendix G.

Published Sources

Anderson, Frank W. *Riel's Saskatchewan Rebellion.* Saskatoon, SK: Gopher Books, 1987.

Anonymous, (Old Timer). "The Old Log Town of Macleod 1883." *Canadian Cattleman,* December 1941.

Antonson, Brian, and Gordon Stewart, eds. *Canadian Frontier Annual 1977.* Langley, BC: Antonson Publishing, 1977.

Army Historical Section. *The Regiments and Corps of the Canadian Army: Volume 1 of the Canadian Army List.* Ottawa, ON: Ministry of National Defence, 1964.

Association of Métis & Non-Status Indians of Saskatchewan. *Louis*

Riel: Justice Must Be Done.
Winnipeg, MB: Manitoba
Métis Federation Press, 1979.

Atkin, Ronald. *Maintain The Right.*
Toronto, ON: Macmillan, 1973.

Beahen, William, and Stan Horrall.
*Red Coats on the Prairie:
The North-West Mounted
Police 1886–1900.* Regina, SK:
Friends of the Mounted Police
Museum, 1998.

Beal, Bob, and Ron Macleod.
*Prairie Fire: The 1885 North-
West Rebellion.* Edmonton, AB:
Hurtig, 1984.

Berry, Gerald L. *Alberta-Montana
Relationships.* Edmonton, AB:
University of Alberta, 1950.

Berton, Pierre. *The Last Spike.*
Toronto, ON: McClelland &
Stewart, 1974.

Boulton, Charles. *Reminiscences
of the North-West Rebellions.*
Toronto, ON: Grip Printing
and Publishing, 1886.

Boulton, James J. *Uniforms of the
Canadian Mounted Police.*
North Battleford, SK: Turner
Warwick Publishing, 1990.

Brado, Edward. *Cattle Kingdom.*
Toronto, ON: Douglas &
McIntyre, 1984; Surrey, BC:
Heritage House, 2004.

Brown, Wayne F. *Steele's Scouts:
Samuel Benfield Steele and the
North-West Rebellion.* Surrey,
BC: Heritage House, 2001.

Bundy, Freda Graham. *In The
Foothills of the Rockies.* N.p, n.d.

Burke, Bernard, et al. *Burke's
Peerage & Baronetage, 105th
Edition.* Burke's Peerage, 1978.

Cameron, William B. *Blood Red
the Sun.* Calgary, AB: Kenway
Publishing, 1950.

Cardston Historical Society. *Chief
Mountain Country.* Cardston,
AB: Cardston Historical
Society, 1978.

Carpenter, Jock. *Fifty Dollar Bride:
A Chronicle of Métis Life in
the 19th Century.* Hanna, AB:
Gorman & Gorman, 1993.

Chambers, Ernest. *The Royal
North- West Mounted Police.*
Montreal, QC: Mortimer Press,
1906.

Coalhurst History Society. *Our
Treasured Heritage.* Lethbridge,
AB: Coalhurst History Society,
1984.

Cornish, F.C. "Blackfeet and the
Rebellion." *Alberta Historical
Review,* Spring 1958.

Cousins, James. *Southern Alberta's
Past.* Lethbridge, AB: Historical
Research Centre, 1989. Audio
lecture series.

Cousins, William. "Medicine Hat
and the Rebellion." *Alberta
History,* Autumn 1985.

Craig, John R. *Ranching with
Lords and Commons.* Toronto,
ON: Briggs, 1903; Surrey, BC:
Heritage House, 2006.

Crowsnest Pass Historical Society.
Crowsnest and Its People.
Coleman, AB: Crowsnest Pass
Historical Society, 1979.

Degenstein, Barry J. *The Pursuit of
Louis Riel: A Journey Back in
Time – 1885 – Newspaper
Chronicles.* Battleford, SK: s.p.,
2007.

Dempsey, Hugh. *Big Bear, The End
of Freedom.* Vancouver, BC:
Douglas & McIntyre, 1984.

———. "The Bull Elk Affair." *Alberta
History,* Spring 1992.

———, ed. "Calgary and the Riel

Rebellion." Calgary, AB: *Alberta History*, Spring 1985.

——. *Charcoal's World*. Saskatoon, SK: Western Producer Prairie Books, 1978.

——, ed. *The CPR West: The Iron Road and the Making of a Nation*, Vancouver, BC: Douglas & McIntyre, 1984.

——. *Crowfoot, Chief of the Blackfeet*. Norman, OK: University of Oklahoma Press, 1972.

——. *Indian Tribes of Alberta*. Calgary, AB: Glenbow-Alberta Institute, 1978.

——, ed. *Men in Scarlet*. Calgary, AB: Historical Society of Alberta/McClelland & Stewart West, 1974.

——. *Red Crow, Warrior Chief*. Saskatoon, SK: Western Producer Prairie Books, 1980.

——. "The Rocky Mountain Rangers." *Alberta Historical Review*, Spring 1957.

——. "The Tragedy of White Bird." *The Beaver*, February-March 1993.

Dempsey, James. "Little Bear's Band–Canadian or American Indians?" *Alberta History*, Autumn 1993.

Denny, Cecil. *Riders of the Plains*. Calgary, AB: Herald Printers, 1905.

Dixon, Ann. *Silent Partners: Wives of National Park Wardens*. Pincher Creek, AB: Dixon & Dixon Publishers, 1985.

Doty, James. "A Visit to the Blackfoot Camps." *Alberta Historical Review*, Spring 1966.

Dunlop, Allan C. "Letters from a Soldier Tourist." *Alberta History*, Summer 1975.

Dunn, Jack F. *The Alberta Field Force of 1885*. Calgary, AB: s.p., 1994.

——. "Ripping Off the Soldiers in Alberta, 1885." *Alberta History*, Spring, 1993.

Elofson, Warren M. *Cowboys, Gentlemen and Cattle Thieves: Ranching on the Western Frontier*. Toronto, ON: McGill-Queens University Press, 2000.

English, John, and Réal Bélanger. *Dictionary of Canadian Biography*. Toronto, ON: Sainte-Foy, QC: University of Toronto/Université Laval, 1966. (online: <*http://www.biographi. ca/009004-120-e.html*>).

Evans, Simon, ed. *Cowboys, Ranchers and the Cattle Business: Cross-Border Perspectives on Ranching History*. Calgary, AB: University of Calgary Press, 2000.

Fardy, B.D. *Jerry Potts, Paladin of the Plains*. Langley, BC: Sunfire Publishing, 1984.

Flanagan, Thomas. "The Mission of Louis Riel." *Alberta History*, Winter 1975.

Fort Macleod History Book Committee, *Fort Macleod, Our Colourful Past*. Fort Macleod, AB: Fort Macleod History Book Committee, 1977.

Freebairn, A.L. *Sixty Years in an Old Cow Town*. Pincher Creek, AB: s.p., 2001.

Fryer, Harold. *Alberta: The Pioneer Years*. Langley, BC: Stagecoach Publishing, 1979.

Godsal, F.W. "Old Times." *Alberta Historical Review*, Autumn 1964.

Gould, Ed. *All Hell for a Basement.* Medicine Hat, AB: City Of Medicine Hat, 1981.

Graves, Donald E. *Century of Service: The History of the South Alberta Light Horse.* Toronto, ON: Robin Brass Studio, 2005.

Guttman, Jon. "Revolt of the Métis." *Wild West,* June 1991.

Haig, Bruce. "The Rocky Mountain Rangers." *Lethbridge Magazine,* 1986.

Hart, Herbert M. *Old Forts of the Northwest.* Seattle, WA: Superior Publishing, 1963.

Higinbotham, John D. *When The West Was Young.* Toronto, ON: Ryerson Press, 1933.

Hildebrandt, Walter. *The Battle of Batoche: British Small Warfare and the Entrenched Métis.* Ottawa, ON: National Historic Parks and Sites, Environment Canada, 1985.

Holmgren, Eric & Patricia. *Over 2,000 Place Names of Alberta.* Saskatoon, SK: Western Producer Prairie Books, 1976.

Howard, Joseph Kinsey. *Strange Empire.* New York, NY: William Morrow & Company, 1952.

Inderwick, Mary Ella. "A Lady and Her Ranch." *Alberta Historical Review,* Autumn 1967.

Ings, Frederick. *Before The Fences: Tales from the Midway Ranch.* Nanton, AB: Nanton Historical Society, 1936.

Jackson, H.M. *The Princess Louise Dragoon Guards.* Ottawa, ON: Published by the Regiment, 1951.

Jameson, Sheilagh. *Ranches, Cowboys and Characters.* Calgary, AB: Glenbow-Alberta Institute, 1987.

Jamieson, F.C., ed. *The Alberta Field Force of '85.* Battleford, SK: Canadian North-West Historical Society, 1931.

Johnston, Alex, ed. *Battle at the Belly River.* Lethbridge, AB: Lethbridge Historical Society, 1964.

——. *Boats and Barges on the Belly.* Lethbridge, AB: Lethbridge Historical Society, 1966.

——. *Cowboy Politics.* Calgary, AB: Western Stock Growers Association, 1971.

——, ed. *Lethbridge, Its Medical Doctors, Dentists, & Drug Stores.* Lethbridge, AB: Lethbridge Historical Society, 1991.

Kelly, Leroy Victor. *The Range Men.* Toronto, ON: William Briggs, 1913; Surrey, BC: Heritage House, 2009.

Kilford, Christopher R. *Lethbridge at War: The Military History of Lethbridge from 1900–1996.* Lethbridge, AB: Battery Books, 1996.

Lampard, Dr. Robert, MD. *Five Celebrated Early Surgeons of Southern Alberta 1874–1913.* Lethbridge, AB: Lethbridge Historical Society, 2006.

Light, Douglas W. *Footprints in the Dust.* North Battleford, SK: Turner Warwick Publications, 1987.

Lynch-Staunton, A.H. "Founding Of Police Horse Farm." *RCMP Quarterly,* April, 1950.

MacEwan, Grant. *Colonel James Walker, Man of the Frontier.* Saskatoon, SK: Western Producer Prairie Books, 1989.

——. *Fifty Mighty Men.* Saskatoon, SK: Western Producer Prairie Books, 1958.

——. *Frederick Haultain.*
Saskatoon, SK: Western
Producer Prairie Books, 1985.
——. *Métis Makers of History.*
Saskatoon, SK: Western
Producer Prairie Books, 1981.
——. *Sitting Bull, The Years In
Canada.* Edmonton, AB:
Hurtig Publishers, 1973.
MacGregor, J.G. *Senator Hardisty's
Prairies 1840–1889,* Saskatoon,
SK: Western Producer Prairie
Books, 1978.
Maclean, John. *Canadian Savage
Folk.* Toronto, ON: William
Briggs, 1896.
Macrae, Archibald Oswald. *History
of the Province of Alberta.*
Winnipeg, AB: Western
Canada History Co., 1912.
Malcolmson, Robert. "Northcote,
Paddlewheels and Glory on the
Saskatchewan." *The Beaver,*
August–September 1993.
Mancini, John. "The Pursuit of
Big Bear's Cree." *True West,*
November 1992.
Mardon, E.G. *Who's Who in
Federal Politics from Alberta.*
Lethbridge, AB: s.p., 1972.
McClintock, Walter. *The Old North
Trail: Life, Legends and Religions
of the Blackfeet Indians.* Lincoln,
NE: University of Nebraska
Press, 1968.
McDougall, D. Blake. *Princess
Louise Caroline Alberta.*
Edmonton, AB: Legislature
Library of Alberta, 1988.
McKee, Sandra Lynn, ed. *Gabriel
Dumont, Indian Fighter.*
Aldergrove, BC: Frontier
Publishing, n.d.
McLennan, William M. *The
Hudson's Bay Company in
Calgary.* Calgary, AB: Fort
Brisebois Publishing, 2000.
——. *Tsuu T'ina.* Calgary, AB: Fort
Brisebois Publishing, 2000.
——. *Where the Elbow Meets
the Bow.* Calgary, AB: Fort
Brisebois Publishing, 2005.
Michino, Gregory F. *Lakota
Noon: The Indian Narrative of
Custer's Defeat.* Missoula, MT:
Mountain Press, 1997.
Morrow, J.W. *Early History of
the Medicine Hat Country.*
Medicine Hat, AB: Medicine
Hat & District Historical
Society, 1923.
Morton, Desmond. *The Canadian
General: Sir William Otter.*
Toronto, ON: Hakkert, 1977.
——. *The Last War Drum.* Toronto,
ON: Hakkert, 1972.
Morton, Desmond, and Reginald
H. Roy, eds. *Telegrams of the
North- West Campaign 1885.*
Toronto, ON: Champlain
Society, 1972.
Mulvaney, Charles P. *The North-
West Rebellion of 1885.* Toronto,
ON: A.H. Hovey & Co.,
1885.
Nichols, Ronald H., ed. *Men
with Custer: Biographies of the
Seventh Cavalry.* Hardin, MT:
Custer Battlefield Museum &
Historical Assn., 2000.
Ninastako Cultural Centre. *A
History of Surnames on the Blood
Reserve.* Blood Reserve, AB:
s.p., 1983.
Overholser, Joel. *Fort Benton,
World's Innermost Port.* Helena,
MT: Falcon Press Publishing,
1987.
Pemmican Club of Lethbridge.
Pemmican Club Round-Up,

1885–1985. Lethbridge, AB: s.p., 1985.

Pincher Creek Historical Society. *Prairie Grass to Mountain Pass*. Pincher Creek, AB: Pincher Creek Historical Society, 1974.

Pincher Creek Oldtimers Association. *Pincher Creek Memories*. Pincher Creek, AB, s.p., 1975.

Pioneer Historical Publishing. *Alberta Past and Present, Historical and Biographical*. Chicago, IL: Pioneer Historical Publishing, 1924.

Pope, Sir Joseph, ed. *Correspondence of Sir John Macdonald*. Toronto, ON: Oxford University Press, 1921.

Potyondi, Barry. *Where the Rivers Meet: A History of the Upper Oldman River Basin to 1939*. Lethbridge, AB: Alberta Public Works, Supply & Services, 1992.

Rasporich, Anthony, and Henry Klassen, eds. *Frontier Calgary, 1875–1914*. Calgary, AB: University of Calgary/ McClelland & Stewart, 1975.

Rees, Tony. *Polo: The Galloping Game*. Cochrane, AB: Western Heritage Centre Society, 2000.

Rodney, William G. *Kootenai Brown, His Life & Times*. Sidney, BC: Gray's Publishing Ltd., 1969.

Schultz, James Williard. *Blackfeet and Buffalo, Memories of Life Among the Indians*. Norman, OK: University of Oklahoma Press, 1962.

——. *William Jackson, Indian Scout*. New York, NY: Sprague Publishing, 1926.

——. *Rising Wolf, the White Blackfoot: Hugh Monroe's Story of his First Year on the Plains*. Boston, MA: Houghton Mifflin, 1919.

Sharp, Paul F. *Whoop-Up Country*. Norman, OK: University of Oklahoma Press, 1973.

Shepherd, George. "The Oxarat–Wylie Ranch," *Canadian Cattleman*, June 1941.

Sherlock, Robert A. *Experiences of the Halifax Battalion in the North-West*. Halifax, NS: Jas. Doley, 1885.

Silversides, Brock. "The Face Puller." *The Beaver*, October–November 1991.

Smith, Marie Rose. "Eighty Years on the Plains." *Canadian Cattlemen*, various issues *ca.* 1948–1949.

South-Western Saskatchewan Old-Timers Association. *Our Pioneers*. Maple Creek, SK: s.p., 1982.

Stanley, George F.G. *The Birth of Western Canada*. Toronto, ON: University of Toronto, 1961.

——. *Louis Riel*. Toronto, ON: MacGraw-Hill Ryerson, 1961.

Steele, C.P. *Prairie Editor*. Toronto, ON: Ryerson Press, 1961.

Steele, Samuel Benfield. *Forty Years in Canada*. London, UK: H. Jenkins Ltd., 1914.

Stewart, Donald M. "Leeson & Scott." *Alberta History*, Autumn 1976.

Stonechild, Blair, and Bill Waiser. *Loyal till Death: Indians and the North-West Rebellion*. Calgary, AB: Fifth House, 1997.

Strange, Thomas Bland. *Gunner Jingo's Jubilee*. London,

UK: 1893. Second edition, Edmonton, AB: University of Alberta Press, 1988.

Tait, W. McD. *Recollections of Kootenai Brown As He Related Them to W. McD. Tait.* s.p., 1957.

Tanner, Ogden. *The Old West: The Canadians.* New York, NY: Time-Life Books, 1977.

Taylor, John H. *Ottawa: An Illustrated History.* Toronto, ON: Lorimer & Co., 1986

Thomas, Lewis G., ed. *The Prairie West To 1905.* Toronto, ON: Oxford University Press, 1975.

Thomas, Lewis H. *The Struggle for Responsible Government in the North-West Territories 1870–97.* Toronto, ON: University of Toronto Press, 1956, 1978.

Tolton, Gordon E. *Prairie Warships: River Navigation in the Northwest Rebellion.* Surrey, BC: Heritage House, 2007.

Tolton, Gordon E. *Rocky Mountain Rangers: Southern Alberta's Cowboy Cavalry in the Northwest Rebellion 1885.* Lethbridge, AB: Lethbridge Historical Society, 1994.

Turner, John Peter. *The North-West Mounted Police, 1873–1893.* Vols. I–II. Ottawa, ON: King's Printer, 1950.

Van West, Carroll. *A Traveler's Companion to Montana History.* Helena, MT: Montana Historical Society Press, 1986.

Ward, Tom. *Cowtown.* Calgary, AB: City of Calgary Electric System, 1975.

Wiebe, Rudy, and R.C. Macleod. *War in the West.* Edmonton, AB: Hurtig Publishers, 1980.

Wilson, Barbara M., ed. *Military General Service 1793–1814/Egypt Medal 1882–1889/North West Canada Medal 1885, Index to the Medal Rolls.* London, UK: Spink & Son Ltd., 1974.

Wilson, Garrett. *Frontier Farewell: The 1870s and the End of the Old West.* Regina, SK: Canadian Plains Research Center/ University of Regina, 2007.

Woodcock, George. *Gabriel Dumont.* Edmonton, AB: Hurtig Publishers, 1975.

Wuth, Farley. *The History That Almost Wasn't: Chronicles of Pincher Creek's Ill-Fated Railway History.* Pincher Creek, AB: Pincher Creek Historical Society, 2008.

Zuehlke, Mark. *Scoundrels, Dreamers & Second Sons: British Remittance Men in the Canadian West.* Vancouver, BC: Whitecap Books, 1994.

Newspapers

(Fort) Benton Record
(Fort) Benton River Press
Calgary Herald
Canadian Pictorial & Illustrated War News
Edmonton Bulletin
Helena Herald
Lethbridge Herald
Lethbridge News
(Fort) Macleod Gazette
New York Times
Pincher Creek Echo
Saskatchewan Herald
Toronto Daily Mail
Winnipeg Daily Times
Winnipeg Free Press

INDEX

Lacombe, Albert (Father), 23, 42, 75-76, 80, 169, 204
La Grandeur, Mose, 58
Laramie Treaty of 1868, 44
Larkin, Edward, 100, 105, 199
Little Bighorn, Battle of the, 45, 48, 56, 101, 128, 144, 183, 192, 216
Lone Walker, 43
Lorne, Marquis of, 28, 52, 56-57, 111
Louise Caroline Alberta (Princess), 52, 56
Lynch-Staunton, Alfred Hardwick, 59-60, 102, 106, 207-8, 217
Lynch-Staunton, Francis, 207

Macdonald, John A. (Sir), 18-19, 24, 34, 50-51, 74-75, 82, 88-89, 165, 169
Mackenzie, Alexander, 19, 51
Macleod, James (Commissioner), 23, 54-55, 60, 186, 173-74, 207
Macleod Gazette, 74, 86, 114, 117-18, 120, 136, 143, 145-46, 155-56, 163
MacPherson, Ad, 67
Manitoba, 18, 19, 32, 53, 79, 92, 168, 193
Marias River, 40
Martin, Joe, 38-39
McDougall, John (Reverend), 50
McEwen, Mary (*née* Gladstone), 217
McEwen, Peter, 58, 102, 106, 217
McGee, D'Arcy, 52
Medicine Bird Woman, 192
Medicine Hat (Alberta), 26, 37, 58, 90, 109, 119-29, 136-37, 139, 142-45, 154, 157, 205, 214-15
Metis, 14, 17-21, 24, 26, 31-34, 38-40, 53, 55, 65, 69-71, 73-74, 76, 78-79, 82, 112-14, 128-29, 131, 133, 135-36, 139-44, 166, 171, 190, 202-4, 214, 217
Middleton, Frederick Dobson (General), 68, 77, 89, 92-93, 96, 130-36, 139-42, 149-52, 154-56, 159, 161, 169-72
Midway Ranch, 16, 58, 78, 147
Miles, Nelson (General), 21, 48
Milk River, 17, 77, 136, 142
Missouri River, 14, 53, 189
Monroe, Amelia, 44
Monroe, Hugh, 43, 44
Montana, 8, 17, 20-21, 26-27, 42, 44-45, 48-49, 54, 62-63, 70, 76, 86, 91, 101-2, 109, 116, 129, 136, 142, 148-49, 151, 153, 166, 168, 180, 182-84, 186, 190-93, 199, 203, 209, 214, 218-19, 224, 228, 238
Montreal (Quebec), 43, 93, 169, 195, 201, 205, 213, 224
Morden, Albert Milton, 60, 106, 109-10, 189, 201, 209-10
Morleyville (Alberta), 109, 209
Mount Royal Rifles, 65th Battalion, 9, 135
Mountain Mills (Alberta), 217

Nanton (Alberta), 16, 58
Nataya, 55
Nez Perce, 209, 218-19
North Saskatchewan River, 9, 71, 136, 149, 153
North West Mounted Police (NWMP), 15-16, 20-25, 27, 32, 50, 53-54, 56, 58, 62-63, 68, 71-72, 74-76, 80, 84-85, 89-90, 92, 94-96, 100, 102-7, 113-15, 119, 121-23, 125, 127-29, 131-32, 134-36, 143, 145, 147, 49, 151, 153, 161, 165, 171, 176, 178, 180, 182-84, 188-91, 194, 199-200, 205, 207-8, 213-15, 217
Northwest Rebellion, 8, 10, 15, 130, 154
North-West Territories, 56, 63, 78, 82, 162, 223, 228

ACKNOWLEDGEMENTS

This book is based on an earlier work published in 1994. When I started investigating the Rocky Mountain Rangers in preparation for that work, I literally had no clue what I was doing. My research and writing of this book was exhilarating, sometimes frustrating, but an amazing learning experience. I learned the process of synthesizing multiple sources: local history compilations, archival documents, photographs and secondary source publications. It was a co-operative project, and I acknowledged those who assisted in the earlier publication.

In the intervening years, the growth of my writing as a craft and my personal education have inspired me to revisit the RMR. In addition, work as a historical interpreter and re-enactor has allowed me more grounding with the subject matter, and to learn the actual crafts of armaments, cavalry drills and tactics that would have been the order of the military of the day. It is an honour to see what was wrought from a tiny book, and this current rendition makes me grateful to the many people I have met because of it.

In particular, I acknowledge re-enacting enthusiasts Grant "Rattlesnake Jack" Rombough and his Single Action Shooting group, the Rocky Mountain Rangers, Number 4 Troop in Medicine Hat, and Jack "Major Stewart" Kunst and Heather Dagnault, who with other horsemen form the Rocky Mountain Rangers, Number 3 Troop, in Pincher Creek.

Distribution of the earlier book has also allowed more information to be uncovered. A trip to the Little Bighorn Battlefield National Monument at Crow Agency, Montana, unveiled to me that William Jackson, a survivor of that epic disaster, went on to service in the RMR. I also thank Spenser and Marilyn Anderson, who approached me with previously unknown material on their ancestor, Eugene "Paddy" Hasson, also a US Army veteran who found his way across the frontier border.

One of the most satisfying results of the 1994 RMR book was to see how often it was referenced as a legitimate source, and to meet authors and historians with whom I was able to discuss and share mutual interests. Among those are Major Chris Kilford, Dr. Robert Lampard, MD, Jock Carpenter, and Jack F. Dunn.

As in my 2007 publication, *Prairie Warships*, I would like to thank Don Gorman at Rocky Mountain Books and Rodger Touchie, Vivian Sinclair and the gang at Heritage House Publishing Company for their confidence in me; and my editor, Elizabeth McLachlan, for her meticulous work and endearing patience. Again I thank my good friends, Lori Porter and Doran Degenstein, for the proverbial kind words and kicks in the butt on which a writer feeds.

Lastly, I thank the two people in my life most affected by the time and energy my craft consumes—my wife Rose and daughter Robyn, who patiently tolerate life with someone buried in history and writing. This accomplishment is theirs as well as mine.

ABOUT THE AUTHOR

Raised on a family farm near Taber, Alberta, Gord Tolton is a historian, a re-enactor, an author and a raconteur. While working in the agricultural construction and service industries, he volunteered for several heritage-related societies and historic sites and became immersed in history while learning about writing, archiving and ongoing museum practices. Professionally, he has worked as the history co-ordinator for the United Farmers of Alberta (UFA), and for 20 years he has been associated with Fort Whoop-Up National Historic Site. Tolton's interests include the cross-border trade of the late 19th century, the 1885 Northwest Rebellion and the history of agriculture in Alberta.

Tolton is the author of *Rocky Mountain Rangers; The Buffalo Legacy; Prairie Warships: River Navigation in the Northwest Rebellion*; and *Deep Roots, Promising Future: The Centennial History of the UFA*.

Gord lives in Coaldale, Alberta, and is currently working on the biography of frontiersman John J. Healy.